NORTH CAROLINA'S CAPITAL, RALEIGH

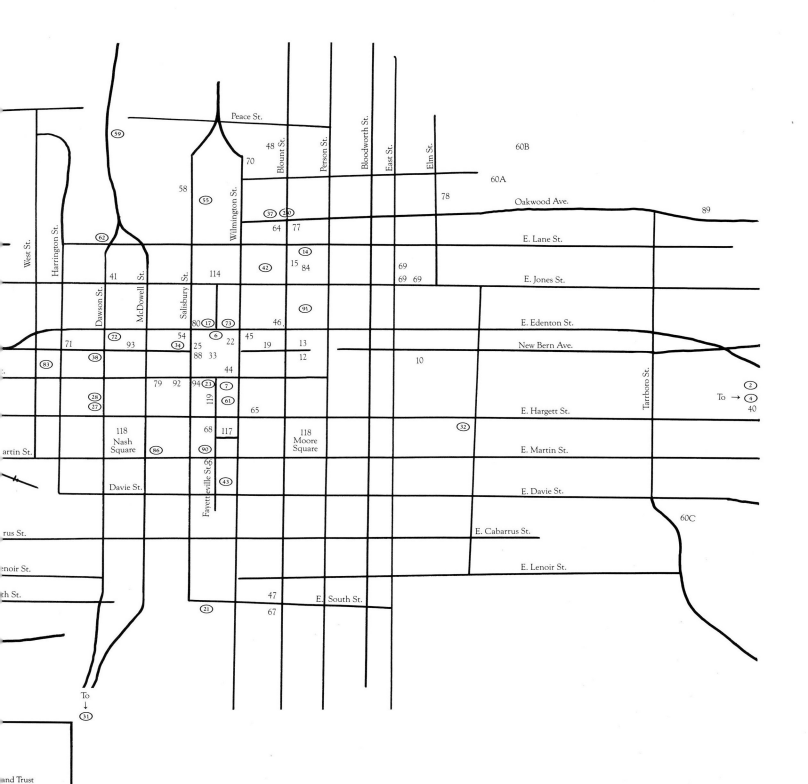

Raleigh
Historical Site Map

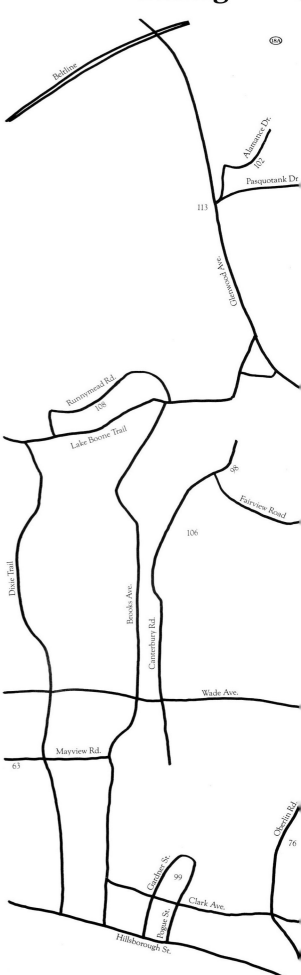

Key to North of Peace Street
Circled sites have been demolished.

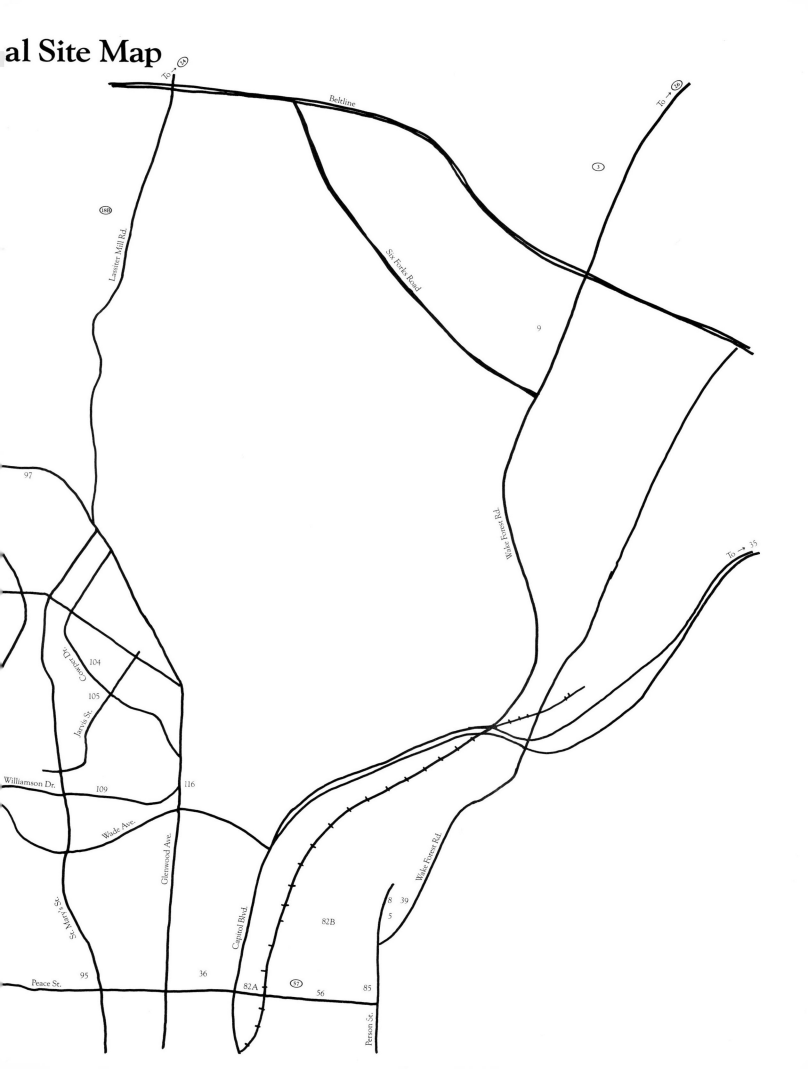

al Site Map

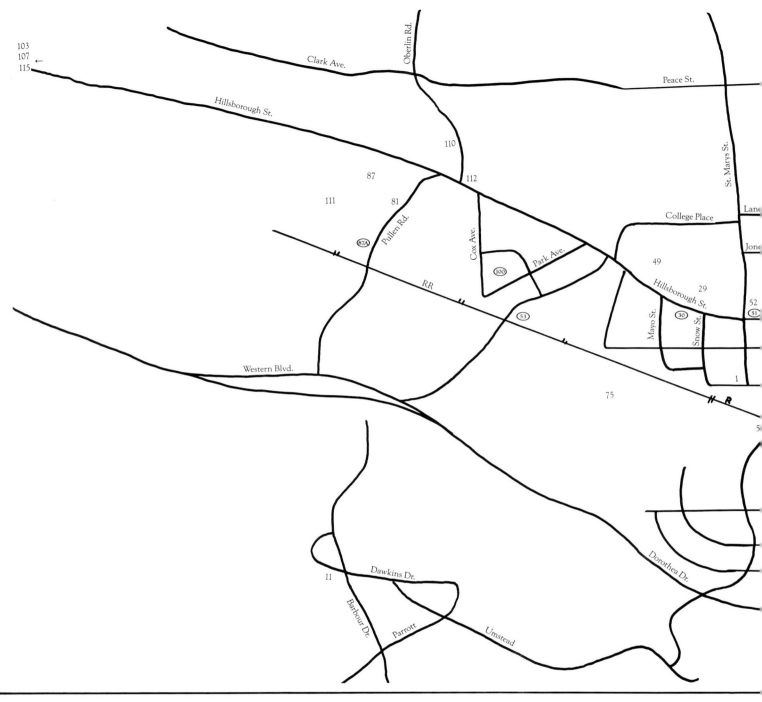

Key to South of Peace Street
Circled sites have been demolished.

North Carolina's Capital, Raleigh

by

Elizabeth Culbertson Waugh

and

Editorial Committee

Ben Forrest Williams, Chairman

Doris Procter Bason   Melissa Anne Peden
Beth Gilbert Crabtree   Elizabeth C. Waugh
William Henley Deitrick   Sarah Denny Williamson

Contemporary Photographs

Ralph Mills

Published by The Junior League of Raleigh, Incorporated, and The Raleigh Historic Sites Commission, Incorporated, with the cooperation of the staffs of the North Carolina Department of Archives and History and the North Carolina Museum of Art

Raleigh, North Carolina
1967

Bicentennial Editorial Committee 1992

Doris Procter Bason   Melissa Anne Peden
Margaret Story Haywood*   Ben Forrest Williams
Vivian Ernestine Irving*   Sarah Denny Williamson

Contemporary Photographs

Lewis Downey

* Representing the Raleigh Bicentennial Task Force

Copyright, Junior League of Raleigh, Incorporated, 1967

Manufactured in the United States of America

First published in 1967 by The Junior League of Raleigh, Inc.,
and The Raleigh Historic Sites Commission, Inc.

Second printing, September 1968, and third printing, November 1972,
by The University of North Carolina Press

Fourth printing, November 1983: Published by The Junior League of Raleigh, Inc.,
Printed by The Fisher-Harrison Corporation, Durham Division

Library of Congress Catalog Card Number 68-1288

ISBN 0-8078-1080-0

Bicentennial Edition, January, 1992: Published by The Junior League of Raleigh, Inc.

Printed by PBM Graphics, Inc., Research Triangle Park

Typesetting by Expedite Graphics, Durham

Library of Congress Catalog Card Number 91-77828

ISBN 0-9631710-1-1

Published by The Junior League of Raleigh, Inc.

© Copyright, The Junior League of Raleigh, 1991

PREFACE
1967

This volume, in its text, legends, and pictorial matter was designed as a chronological, brief, and readably lively account of Raleigh, 1760 to 1967, to be published coincident with the City's 175th anniversary. And though implicitly the book may teach and instruct, its initial purpose was to light new torches in imaginative and discriminatory preservation, a book to be owned for enjoyment, for delight.

One hardly needs to mention that in telescoping so many years into one volume, inclusion of subjects treated was determined on the basis of admitting aesthetically, or at least exemplary, representative buildings, pieces, and places within the book's chronological framework. Owners, architects, planners, and others closely associated with sites were not considered in selections.

The work on this book was a labor of joy and enthusiasm to all concerned — the author, book committee, photographer, and printer inasmuch as each was eager about the richness of material at hand and the imminent need for such a "preservation conscious" disclosure.

In this regard, there is relatively new North Carolina General Assembly preservation legislation which may now be invoked by Capital City officials and administrators, in order to insure continuance of worthy landmarks. And relative to the philosophy inherent in the work's illustrative choices — they were made not to be merely for the record but for current living enrichment and for future inspiration and comparisons. Obviously, many things are not worth saving and would be perpetuated only by the sentimentalists. But to avoid this, a progressive preservation program for a city or state should require continuous evaluation, planning, and sifting by an authorized body or agency.

For tighter and clearer time definition the book was divided into three parts. Part One covers the period 1760 to 1850 and begins with the wilderness that was Raleigh, ending with overtones of the impending great struggle. Part Two, 1850 to 1900, covers Civil War years and closes with the fluffy, turn-of-the- century time of innocence and fading leisure. Part Three, 1900 to the present, is concerned with the two World Wars, the machine's relatively rapid take-over which resulted in the City's metamorphosis. Each of these three textual accounts of what was happening in the City is then immediately followed by illustrations, either in period, or if extant, a recent photograph of the item treated. And accompanying the pictures are fairly generous legends describing each inclusion.

The author for this book was selected on the basis of her former published works in the field of Southern historical preservation and generally related knowledge; upon the clarity and lucidity of her writing style which seemed to be right for the broad audience at which the book was aimed; and upon her experience as first chairman of the Raleigh Historic Sites Commission, Incorporated.

The public seed of the work of preservation germinated under Raleigh Mayor William G. Enloe, at which time the Raleigh Historic Sites Commission, Incorporated, was established. It continued to grow with the abiding interest of Mayor James W. Reid and now thrives with the encouragement of Mayor Travis E. Tomlinson. Also, cooperating public agencies for the volume included the North Carolina Department of Archives and History and the North Carolina Museum of Art. Funds for the book's publication came by way of a generous loan from the Junior League of Raleigh, Incorporated.

Altogether, in perusing research material, the future of Raleigh seemed to be vouchsafed though its past appeared sometimes blurred by apathy and disregard for values other than commercial. But just here, and after reading in manuscript the evaluation of Raleigh's evolution, note should especially be made of the present, shiny edge of the coin. Since the City is the Capital of all of North Carolina, many institutions and agencies identify Raleigh as a more complete community than is usual. To mention a few of them — music associations and groups of many types; forty-two arts organizations; close higher education; City collaboration for the purpose of quality entertainment and activities; civic and patriotic groups; acting and dance companies; colleges; universities; sports centers; convention attractions; museums; the seasonal joy of parades and the beginnings of active preservation bodies and foundations. Relative to this latter, however, it must be mentioned that although this work progressed on a regular schedule for book publication, we were not able to beat the bulldozer — and at least six major Raleigh historic sites have been razed during the volume's preparation.

Apropos, it was John Ruskin, writing over a century ago, who said: "Architecture is to be regarded by us with the most serious thought. We may live without her, and worship without her, but we cannot remember without her. How many pages of doubtful record might we not often spare for a few stones left one upon the other."

North Carolina Museum of Art
Ben F. Williams
Raleigh, North Carolina
October 20, 1967

PREFATORY NOTE TO THE SECOND PRINTING

The first printing of this book was sold out within a month of its publication. With this success in mind it was decided by the Editorial Committee in agreement with The Junior League of Raleigh, Incorporated, and The Raleigh Historic Sites Commission, Incorporated, first publishers of the volume, that the second printing might well be taken over by The University of North Carolina Press at Chapel Hill. This was aimed at facilitating distribution and future handling. All concerned were deeply pleased that this Press, long notable for its publication of distinctive volumes, concurred in the matter of reprinting the book.

B.F.W. May, 1968

PREFATORY NOTE TO THE FOURTH PRINTING, DECEMBER 1982

The third printing of this book, published by The University of North Carolina Press with no prefatory note or change, was an extension of the second printing as an expedient measure to make copies available. At the request of the Junior League of Raleigh, Inc., the original committee with the exception of one member, William Henley Deitrick, now deceased, got together recently to consider another printing because no copies have been available for several years and a demand is still evident. The first three printings were done within 5 years, 1967-1972. Now, ten years later, the complexion of Raleigh has changed; new people have come to the area; a new generation is growing up; and there is renewed interest in knowing the atmosphere, the history, the ambience, and the evolution of Raleigh. The book is needed now more than ever to balance culture with commerce — and to indicate an audience broader than Raleigh — to show Raleigh as a governmental, educational, institutional and research center of North Carolina and the Southeast — to indicate Raleigh's leadership in preservation.

The "Raleigh book" has helped create an atmosphere which sparked the establishment of Mordecai Historic Park, the revitalization of the Oakwood Historic District nearby, and other programs and projects connected with the history and preservation of the city which appeal not only to residents but also to tourists, conventions, and visitors who see aesthetic and visual information on their visits.

In the preface to the original edition, the initial purpose of the book was "to light new torches in imaginative and discriminatory preservation — a book to be owned for enjoyment and delights." As Raleigh grows and expands, people are going to elect to live here for aesthetic and cultural reasons as well as economic ones. The above stated purpose will take on an added and an immediate meaning. The book may teach and instruct; it can also assist in attracting culturally oriented citizens and providing a balance — a quality of life.

As we stated in the original preface, the bulldozer would often arrive before anyone was aware of the impending demolition. Now the process of destruction has been slowed down considerably because of the interest and cooperation of civic leaders, organizations and various private groups, local and statewide.

One of the first was the Raleigh Historic Sites Commission, formed by the City Council in December, 1961. Elizabeth Culbertson Waugh, our writer, now deceased, was the first chairman and William Henley Deitrick the second; all the "Raleigh book" committee have served on this commission.

Until 1967 the commission operated under local resolution. Action in that year by the General Assembly of North Carolina further established it as an historic sites commission for Raleigh, defined its duties, and otherwise provided for acquisition, restoration and preservation of historic sites and buildings (1967 Session Laws, Chapter 1058). In 1971 there was statewide legislation for all cities to have historic properties commissions — Raleigh was the first — the model. In fact, the 1967 legislation for Raleigh became the established guide for the statewide legislation.

The 1961 commission, now known as the Raleigh Historic Properties Commission, has been joined by the Raleigh Historic Districts Commission, the Raleigh Appearance Commission and various neighborhood groups such as the Oakwood Preservation Society, the Cameron Park Association, Boylan Heights, Glenwood, University Park and others, for the common purpose of preserving the essence of their neighborhoods and to enhance the quality of life. Numerous private groups and societies have been active in supporting these activities by including them in their programs.

The stability of Raleigh is not only reflected in municipal and state government, public and private agencies, but also in private citizens as indicated by the number of original or longtime ownerships of worthy properties such as Midway Plantation, the Richard B. Haywood House, Briggs Hardware, Heilig-Levine, the Joel Whitaker House, the Mary Hunter Beavers House and Elmwood.

The tool of adaptive use has also come into play, providing economic advantage as well as preserving a flavor that could not be obtained otherwise. It is gratifying to note that the indiscriminate bisecting of the city with super highways and streets is coming to a halt and that those arbitrary changes made during the 1950s and '60s are being restudied, for we are beginning to learn that there is a saturation point, even for the almighty automobile. There is now consideration for the extension of the original city plan, which has worked well, and for balancing the scale relationship between streets, present buildings and future buildings, with focus on our Capitol.

With the present tools available, with knowledge gained, and with the added enthusiasm of new interest, we can look forward to North Carolina's capital, Raleigh, being a leader in the future.

Ben F. Williams December, 1982

Editor's Note: The changes in the printing in the headings of the various sites indicate those which have been lost, moved and/or restored since 1967 and in one case where significant information has been revealed.** We have made no change in the basic text.

PREFACE TO THE BICENTENNIAL EDITION
1992

The Bicentennial of the founding of our city provides us with a unique opportunity to reflect on the progress of Raleigh during the past two centuries. Those of us who got together to publish *North Carolina's Capital, Raleigh* over a quarter of a century ago realize now that we must make certain adjustments in the book if it is to be valid in the 1990s. An updated reprinting seemed to be appropriate as part of the 200th-year celebration. Three of the original editorial committee are no longer living: Elizabeth C. Waugh, Beth Crabtree and William H. Deitrick. We are fortunate to have two new members, Vivian Irving and Margie Haywood, join the committee. Longtime Raleigh residents, they both are well informed about its history and are appointees to the Raleigh Bicentennial Task Force.

As we reviewed the original book, we realized that the provenance of any vital object or site is never complete, never static, always changing. In the intervening years since the first publication, we have seen much progress illustrating the significance of wise historic preservation. Public awareness has been stimulated via the increasing number of preservation, architecture and art history course offerings in the curricula of North Carolina colleges and universities. Preservation groups have organized and citizens are speaking out.

When *North Carolina's Capital, Raleigh* was first published in 1967, its stated purpose was "to light new torches in imaginative and discriminatory preservation." Twenty-five years later that purpose still holds true, for history and preservation are ongoing, never ceasing to teach us, and constantly enhancing our lives — giving us roots, a foundation on which to build for future generations, and a "quality of life" that makes newcomers strangers but once.

Let us look back and see from whence we have come these past twenty-five years. The 1960s brought boundless growth and the idea that urban renewal meant leveling the landscape and building anew from the clean sweep. The "Raleigh Book" came out and people stopped to remember what had been, what Raleigh had lost, often needlessly.

In 1969, upon recommendation of the Raleigh Historic Properties Commission (then called the Raleigh Historic Sites Commission) the City Council designated the first group of Raleigh Historic Sites, and citizens began to see what Raleigh still did have. Today Raleigh has 90 designated Raleigh Historic Sites and three designated National Historic Landmarks. Wake County, including Raleigh, has 73 historic sites listed on the National Register of Historic Places.

Throughout the years the concept of the already recognized "large" house as "the" site to preserve has changed to include other structures which are representative of a way of life, to include neighborhoods which show a cohesiveness in the development of a town, and to include commercial buildings which speak of a city's economic life. Therefore, not only are individual structures important, but whole areas that can tell a story. Today, Raleigh has four locally designated historic districts and ten National Register Districts.

Buildings need a reason for being, a useful purpose to earn their keep, but not all historic buildings or houses can be museums nor would we want them to be. Adaptive use has come upon the scene as well as Federal tax credits for preserving certified historic structures for revenue-producing uses. This puts run-down properties back on the tax books, creates jobs and recycles our built environment. Preservation is good business. It attracts tourism to our Capital City. By the year 2000, tourism is predicted to be North Carolina's number one industry. But long past due are tax credits for restoring certified historic structures as private residences.

Preservation needs to be a part of the planning process, not a crisis-oriented movement. With a preservation element now a part of Raleigh's Comprehensive Plan, the pendulum could be swinging toward that goal. Raleigh is dealing with problems brought on by overdevelopment. It has already adopted a sign ordinance controlling the proliferation of billboards and the United States Court of Appeals has upheld its constitutionality.

But all has not been rosy. One has only to look at the

demolition dates since 1967, when the book was published, to see the multitude of historic sites which have been lost. The double tragedy is that not only has an important part of Raleigh's heritage been lost but, in many cases, parking lots will be the only land use for years to come. In 1992, plans for mass transit are being studied.

This Bicentennial updating will attempt to show what has been happening to these sites in the intervening twenty-five years, where there have been changes, where there have been gains and losses. One rejoices over the Raleigh and Gaston/Seaboard Coast Line Office Building which stood silent and vacant on a new site for over ten years before being restored and made productive again. The Tucker Carriage House speaks of imagination, perseverance, and just plain hard work to transform a stable into a dance/arts studio; although some of the most highly regarded architects said the disintegrating structure could not be saved. But the silent tears come with the demolition of the magnificent Tucker House which stood nearby and the loss of historically significant houses such as Broomfield, Travianna and the McPheeters House.

The purpose of this reissue has not been to begin anew, but to update to see what those lighted torches and new torches of imaginative preservation have brought forth in these twenty-five years, with the understanding that it was, perhaps, this original publication that helped spark the flame to light those torches. New text which has been added has been indicated in italics and, for the most part, placed at the end of the copy for that site. There has been no attempt to change the wording, the style, or the story of the original author.

In our work we have discovered that there are sites which speak of the wealth of Raleigh's black history which need representation. We have discovered that other historical structures were omitted. And what about those outstanding structures of "modern history" which have been built since 1967?

Raleigh's history is ongoing. As the new century approaches, our Capital City will continue its growing, changing character. Material is gathering for another time, another committee, another Raleigh book.

Ben F. Williams
and The 1992 Editorial Committee
December, 1991

Acknowledgments
1967

We gratefully acknowledge the assistance of Elizabeth D. Reid in the preparation of much of the textual material in this book and the full cooperation of the Photographic Staff of the Department of Archives and History and Gus Martin, official photographer of the North Carolina Museum of Art. Without this help and the generosity of those listed below, this publication would not have been possible.

Editorial Committee

Arthur Edwards
Lendon M. Lassiter
Mrs. Thomas B. Wood
William Powell
Mrs. William I. Procter
Mrs. Oliver Crawley
Madlin Futrell
Graham H. Andrews
Nancy Duckett
Mrs. Bruce Carter
Jane Hall
Mrs. William B. Little, Jr.
Lawrence Wodehouse
Mrs. Richard D. Smith
Sam Tarlton
Mrs. O. R. Browne
Dr. Justin Bier
Mrs. Polk Denmark
C. F. W. Coker
William M. Fleming
Mrs. Verne Caviness
Mrs. Godfrey Cheshire, Jr.
Landis Bennett
Mrs. James Denmark
Mrs. George Flint
Mrs. John S. Holloway
Betsy Marsh
Mrs. G. A. Moore, Jr.
Mrs. Ollen D. Mcleod
Mary Lou Pressly
A. C. Hall
J. R. Waitt
Angus Wilton Kelly
Mrs. Charles W. Styron
Joye Jordan
Mrs. Marcus L. Scruggs
Mrs. John C. Hanner

G. Milton Small
Charles Lee Smith, Jr.
Edith Johnson
Sara Wise
Betty Tyson
Lane Welles
Gus Martin
Robert B. Allen
Mrs. Robert J. Wyatt
James E. Briggs
Mrs. Hayes M. White
Mrs. John Cannon
Mrs. Paul Welles, Jr.
Helen Dortch
Mrs. Sprague Silver, Sr.
Herbert O'Keef
Mr. & Mrs. N. E. Edgerton
Dorothy Merritt
Mrs. William H. Bason
Mr. & Mrs. George E. London
Anna Riddick
Dr. & Mrs. Prezell Robinson
Mrs. George W. Paschal
Margaret Click Williams
Mr. & Mrs. W. N. H. Jones
Irene E. Yarbrough
Mr. & Mrs. Clifton W. Stoffregen, Jr.
Mary Rogers
Mrs. John M. Winfree
Mrs. William L. Steele
Mr. & Mrs. Charles H. Silver
Mrs. Joseph Umsted
Mr. & Mrs. Banks Talley
Mrs. Harry Lyons
Annie Smedes Vass
Mrs. Joseph A. Graef
Ferne Winborne

Mr. & Mrs. William A. Bason
Mrs. John Clayton Smith
Elizabeth Thompson
Mrs. Thomas B. Dameron
Julia Fisher Coke
George F. Bason
Mrs. Robert P. Holding
Mrs. Archie Henderson
Mrs. Walter Stearns
Mrs. James McKee
Mrs. W. L. McCanless
Elizabeth Dortch
Edward Seawell
Mary J. Hadley
Mrs. Marshall De Lancey Haywood, Sr.
Mrs. Sam Marshall
Mrs. William B. Wright
Mrs. Sam Beard
Mrs. H. V. Joslin
Ada Morris
D. Staton Inscoe
C. S. Tatum
Mrs. J. Russell Nipper
James Cheek
Sylbert Pendleton
Mrs. William T. Joyner, Jr.
Otha N. Lassiter
Mrs. Charles P. Green
Rufus Malloy
Thomas F. Joyner, Jr.
Elizabeth Tucker
Frank Manly
Annie S. Ramsey
John W. Lee
Douglas Stott
Isabelle Bowen Henderson
Mr. & Mrs. C. T. McClenaghan

Helen Harrison
Mrs. J. H. Doughton
Col. William T. Joyner
Baker Wynne
Arthur McKimmon
Dr. Ivan M. Procter
Mr. & Mrs. Earl Johnson, Sr.
Gavin Dortch
Mrs. Harry W. McGalliard
Mary Lindsay Smith

Mary V. Lassiter
Mrs. Henry N. Parker
Dr. & Mrs. W. C. Pressly
J. B. Pierce
Mrs. Robert E. Gaddy, Jr.
Mrs. Earl Wilborn
Mrs. Harvey W. Johnson
Flossie Brooks
Nan Hutchins
C. B. Mooney

Mrs. Thomas P. Inman
Mrs. Everett L. Smith
Mrs. Charles E. Johnson, Sr.
James Fitzgibbon
John Coffey
Mrs. Minnie Ransom Norris
James Beckwith
Albert Levine
Mrs. James H. Reeder

University of North Carolina Library, Chapel Hill
Visual Aids Department, North Carolina State University
Raleigh Woman's Club
Raleigh City Planning Office
News and Observer
Raleigh Times
School of Design, North Carolina State University
North Carolina State Library
D. H. Hill Library, North Carolina State University
Wake County Committee, Colonial Dames of America in the State of North Carolina
Olivia Raney Library
North Carolina Museum of Art Reference Library
Search Room, North Carolina Department of Archives and History
Historic Sites Division, North Carolina Department of Archives and History

Acknowledgments
1992

Raymond Lynn Beck
Dan Becker
Charlotte V. Brown
Marian Buis
Mabel J. Dorsey
Linda Harris Edmisten
Alice Eure
Mr. & Mrs. Spurgeon Fields

Barbara Freedman
Ernestine Hamlin
Al Honeycutt
J. Myrick Howard
Kaye Lasater
Walker Mabe
Elizabeth Reid Murray
Elizabeth Edmunds Norris

Delores O'Connor
Marge O'Rorke
Irene Roughton
James W. M. Smith
Sally Birdsong Smith
Anna Upchurch
JoAnn Warn

Chrysler Museum, Norfolk, Virginia
Executive Mansion Fine Arts Committee
Executive Mansion Fund, Incorporated
North Carolina Division of Archives and History
Raleigh Historic Properties Commission

"Cooperating Owner-Occupants of Included Sites"

1967

Mary Hunter Beavers House – Mr. & Mrs. Clifton W. Stoffregen, Jr.

Cameron House – Mr. & Mrs. Robert P. Holding

Colburn-Seawell House – Mr. Edward C. Seawell

Thomas Wright Cooper House – Mr. & Mrs. H. A. Underwood, III

Crabtree – Mr. & Mrs. W. N. H. Jones

Deitrick House – Mr. & Mrs. A. Gwynn Nowell

Dodd-Hinsdale House – Mr. John W. Hinsdale & Mrs. John M. Winfree

Elmwood – Mrs. William H. Bason & Mrs. Joseph A. Graef

Dr. Andrew Goodwin House – King's Business College

Haywood Hall – Mrs. Walter Stearns

Richard B. Haywood House – Mrs. Marshall
De Lancey Haywood, Sr.

Henderson Garden – Isabelle Bowen Henderson

503 East Jones Street (James W. Lee House) – Mr. L.G. Bullard

Lewis-Smith House – Mrs. Charles Lee Smith, Sr.

George Matsumoto House – Mr. & Mrs. Banks C. Talley, Jr.

Midway Plantation – Mr. & Mrs. Charles H. Silver

McPheeters House – Miss Susan McPheeters

Paschal House – Mr. & Mrs. George W. Paschal

Pine Hall Farm – Mr. & Mrs. Sherman Crites

L. L. Polk House – Mr. & Mrs. Pretlow Winborne

Anna Riddick House – Miss Anna Riddick

Philip Rothstein House – Mr. & Mrs. Philip L. Rothstein

Tatton Hall – Mr. & Mrs. N. E. Edgerton

Elizabeth Thompson House – Miss Elizabeth Thompson

Travianna – Mr. & Mrs. William A. Bason

W. W. Vass House – Miss Eleanor Vass

White-Holman – Mr. & Mrs. W. L. McCanless

Baker Wynne House – Mr. Baker Wynne

Wynne Tower – Mr. & Mrs. Ben F. Williams

1992

Graves-Fields House – Mr. and Mrs. Spurgeon Fields

Rogers-Bagley-Daniels-Pegues House – Mrs. Ernestine Pegues Hamlin

CONTENTS

LIST OF SITES

Part I
1760 -1850

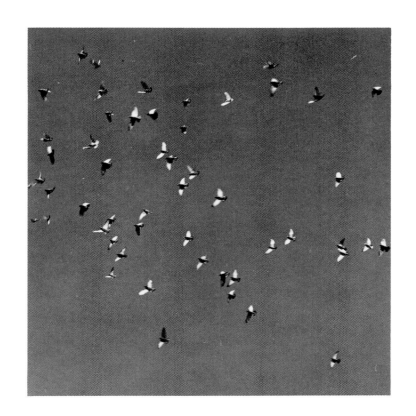

Raleigh Sky

Part I
1760-1850

IN A GROVE OF OAKS

In the year 1671 an itinerant British preacher, who came to America via Jamaica, Florida, and the Chesapeake, noted in his journal: "Afterwards, it being upon me, I travelled into *Carolina* and two Friends accompanied me, it being all Wildernesses, and no *English* Inhabitants or Path-ways, but some marked Trees to guide People. The first Day's Journey we did pretty well, and lay that Night in the woods as we often used to in those Parts." *Those Parts*, though they remained a wilderness for another sixty years or so, were to become the environs of North Carolina's Capital City.

Raleigh's location, however, was not born, like Athena, whole-made without adversity. By 1744 nearly every promising community in North Carolina was contending for the honor of the site. Among them were Edenton, Halifax, New Bern; and not even a regional coalition could sway the majority in the Assemblies between 1744 and 1790.

When Wake Cross Roads or Wake Court House, as the place was often called, was considered, its detractors argued that the capital should not be "situate" in a lonely grove of oaks, inland from any port, a place without populace, amid thorn and briar with nothing to recommend it but a courthouse, an inn, two or three scattered residences, the best of which having only a plain gambrel roof. Further, it made no difference that this inn was on the stage road connecting Petersburg to Charleston. The highroad also went through other competing localities, Fayetteville for one; and as for Wake Cross Roads being a "sentrical" location in the State, so, give or take a few miles, was Smithfield.

The fight continued as the General Assembly carried its records from town to town by oxcart, wagon, coach when a session was called. And when records did arrive, it was often found that when the appointed day came for the meeting, there was not a quorum of solons for processing legislation. Nor had all documents arrived intact. Exasperated at this point, the Convention of 1788 decided, when it met in Hillsborough, that a permanent seat of government must be settled upon. And on January 5, 1792, sitting in New Bern, the General Assembly acted upon the earlier decision. That resolution had not specified the capital's exact location except to admonish that " . . . it shall be left to the discretion of the General Assembly to ascertain the exact spot, provided always that it shall be within ten miles of the plantation whereon Isaac Hunter now resides, in the county of Wake."

Accordingly, nine Commissioners, eight representing the State's judicial districts and Willie Jones, member-at-large, were chosen to remove to Wake County and select the exact site from at least seventeen land tracts which had been offered for sale. And on March 20, 1792, five of the Commissioners met at Hunter's Tavern where they did no work. Instead, as usual under the circumstances, they adjourned to Wakefield, the home of Colonel Joel Lane. Here they were met later by the at-large representative, Willie Jones of Halifax.

The solons enjoyed Lane's hospitality for more than a fortnight. And it is to be assumed that the host's house was more commodious than anything else in the vicinity since the Assembly had also met there in June of 1781, albeit, paying 15,000 pounds in Revolution-depressed currency for bed, board, and horse pasturage – a figure far more than Colonel Lane received for the thousand acres

3

which later became Raleigh. It is not surprising that some time later Lane added a "guest" house to his properties at Wakefield.

During eight days of their stay at Wakefield the Commissioners journeyed, not stopping for Sunday it was said, in the business of cruising those various parcels of land which were for sale. And upon their return, they still were not in accord, but had to ballot thrice for agreement. Finally a thousand acres, the number stipulated by the Assembly, were bought from their host for 1,378 pounds.

Forthwith, William Christmas, senator from Franklin County, whose map is reproduced in the front of this book, was hired as surveyor of the purchased property. *The Commissioners helped with the survey as directed by the General Assembly.* Christmas' compensation for six copies of the new plan for Raleigh was four shillings for each lot which he surveyed. His work used up the better part of four days and the name "Raleigh," which was said to have been first suggested by post-Revolution Governor Alexander Martin, was duly affixed to the tiny, new "citie."

ONE SQUARE MILE

At least Raleigh was uniquely favored in one aspect of its long-awaited siting in that it did not just grow happenstance from a likely curve in the course of a stage road, nor from existing city lanes or plantation paths – it was planned.

Following injunctions from the 1791 Assembly, the Commissioners-planners originally envisioned that part of the designated one square mile would be divided into 276 one-acre lots. It would be bounded peripherally by the patently evident names, North, South, East, and West streets. The grand, axial center should be six acres called Union Square, the site of the future State House, as it was to be known. And flanking its corners at some distance were to be four four-acre squares named Caswell, Nash, Burke, honoring the State's first three Governors after Independence, and Moore, respecting Attorney General Alfred E. Moore. Titles to these city lungs should be vested in the State and the land forever inviolable except for "publick" use – a mandate which admittedly against great pressures has, through *200* years, been stretched in meaning. In the nineteenth century the Governor's Mansion, the third in a succession of governors' residences in Raleigh, was built on Burke Square – a site which had originally been designated on William Christmas' map as "a proper situation for the Governor's House." A school for deaf mutes was erected on Caswell in 1848. And except for a few citizens' stubborn staunchness, Moore Square, in the 'fifties of this century, would have become a parking lot.

The Commissioners named the important first streets for the eight judicial districts and in deference to some of those towns which lost out in the Capital's location, axially radiated four of these streets out from Union Square – pointing them toward the directions of said cities, Fayetteville to the south, Halifax pointing north, New Bern to the east, and Hillsborough to the west. These thoroughfares, too, were to be ninety-nine feet wide, thirty-three feet wider than any of the rest. Other street names, bounding but not radiating from Union Square, respected other districts, Edenton, Salisbury, Morgan, Wilmington.

For the rest, the Commissioners used well-deserved prerogatives, naming the streets for themselves and for Speaker of the Senate William Lenoir, for House Speaker Stephen Cabarrus, for Colonel Joel Lane and for General William R. Davie – both distinguished and late of the Revolutionary Militia.

With future building in mind, the planners wisely reserved lots numbered 138 and 154 of the west edge of town for brick-making. And since in 1790 almost a fourth of the State's population were slaves, a figure not including 4,975 free Negroes, it is to be assumed that here was the labor force which cleared the new streets of those oaks and hickories which were also mentioned on the William Christmas map.

The felled timber went by wagon to the brickyards where it was used to fire the kilns which baked the local-clay brick to be used in the first State House. And, as originally proposed, returns from the sale of lots within the City's square mile were earmarked both to pay labor costs thus far and to be put in the treasury against the day in 1792 when the cornerstone of the first State House would actually be laid. Though the building was not entirely finished, it was in November of 1794 that architect Rhodham Adkins terminated his work on the new structure. It faced, according to the vogue of the day, toward Jerusalem – proper "Orientalization," they called it. Branded ugly and "misshapen," it was not an architecturally imposing "edifice" by any standards and would have to be glamorized with a new dome, false porticos, and a layer of stucco by 1821.

Finally, a town cemetery was sited just outside the eastern city limits beyond East Street between New Bern and East Hargett. It would be divided into quarters, the northern two reserved for Raleigh citizens and their friends, the southwestern quarter for strangers and the southeastern for Negroes. And by 1803 the Commissioners would appoint a committee for the "repairs of the Grave Yard."

A VOTELESS TOWN

It did not seem meet for the ladies of such well-established and sophisticated cities as New Bern and Wilmington to come to the "proposed only" town, out from nowhere. But now that the seat of government was assured, or so it was thought, a few families did gravitate to the Capital and stayed to buy lots. And though Raleighites would have a municipal charter in 1795, they could not yet be classed as vocal citizens inasmuch as they would not be allowed to vote until 1803. Even then they would, before enfranchisement, have to own a lot, or a portion thereof, within the City's corporate limits or to have been an actual resident for three months prior to election day. He should also have to be a "free male of full age." Nor was the Governor, himself, too well off at the time with an $1,800 annual salary and a house in Raleigh "not fit for the family of a decent tradesman."

Meantime, on February 7, 1795, a system of seven commissioners, to hold office indefinitely, was appointed by the General Assembly for the purpose of making decisions for the new town. And only in cases of a commissioner's default by death or otherwise were citizens allowed to fill their representative's vacancy, by vote. Firstly appointed by this body was an intendant of police, the chief officer of the City, namely, John Haywood. The commissioners themselves, however, reserved the right to press citizens into nightly patrol duty, especially on occasions of suspected slave uprisings.

An act of the General Assembly in 1794 decreed that the Governor should live in Raleigh six months in the year. In 1798 the Assembly further decreed that the Governor should live all year in Raleigh. As well, if he should have to be absent from the City for more than ten days, this intelligence should be advertised in state-covering newspapers which should report His Honor's reasons for absence, where he was going. More, his private secretary should remain in the State House during his sojourn.

Voteless, the City did need a public mouthpiece and it is a singular fact that before the end of 1799 both the *Raleigh Register*, which for the next fifty years was to become the leading newspaper, and the *North Carolina Minerva and Raleigh Advertiser* had brought their hand presses to Raleigh. The two newspapers, one Federalist, the other anti-Federalist, used up much of their space politically snarling at one another. Still, though neither paper published its circulation figures, it was the *Register* which had the news edge on the opposition since Joseph Gales, its self-made, British-born editor, had come from Philadelphia and had retained connections in the Federal Capital even after it was moved to Washington in 1800. In truth, the North Carolina delegation in Congress had in the first place invited Gales to bring his establishment to Raleigh. Abraham Hodge and his nephew, William Boylan, on the other hand, had come to Raleigh via New Jersey and Fayetteville. And though the Hodge press had been used officially by Washington at Valley Forge, the *Minerva's* friends on the national horizon were not so formidable.

Front-page quarreling between the two newspapers reached a climax in 1804. Though both Gales and Boylan loudly disfavored dueling, neither was above fisticuffs. Gales was severely beaten by Boylan in a famous Raleigh fistfight. And when Gales sued Boylan for assault at the Superior Court session in Hillsborough the following year, he was awarded a punitive hundred pounds sterling which, after deducting attorney's fees, he promptly donated to the now-forming Raleigh Academy.

Apparently the donation was a helpful gesture for in 1804 the Raleigh Academy opened on Burke Square its building with its "brick Chimney at one end, two Doors and eight Windows below. . . and 10 Windows in the second story. . . ceiled with Plank throughout, painted Inside and Outside. . . finished in a workmanly manner." With such beginnings the private Academy was to become one of the most important in the State and remain so until 1829 at which time the headmaster, the Reverend William McPheeters, left the school. The Academy was started none too soon since the Journal of the Assembly of 1802 indicates that a bill to establish public schools was rejected after the first reading. And as late as February 4, 1830, the *Register* would say of the State's public education, "It is a melancholy fact, that many of our farmers of wealth and character, nay, even many of our instructors and clergy are seriously deficient in Orthography, and Reading and Writing, and the commonest rules of vulgar Arithmetick."

PIOUSLY SWINGING

The population of Raleigh at the beginning of the nineteenth century was 669, which included eighty-five families and about that many bachelors. The City could now boast three or more hostelries, all with acceptable accommodations. One of them, built during the War of 1812 and called the Eagle Hotel, advertised in leading Southern newspapers that "this tavern is now open for the reception of travellers and boarders in the new three story building north of the State House and fronting Union Square. . . spacious. . . completely finished. . . stables equal to any. . . well supplied table served from a neat and cleanly kitchen. . . luxuries, beds. . . attendance. . . this tavern shall excel any in the Southern States."

A fire engine, which could expel water at eighty gallons a minute up to 132 feet, had been bought by public subscription and several boarding houses had opened, one of which advanced its prices so substantially when the General Assembly members met that the old cry was once again raised. It happened when the Cumberland County representative, who could not afford the boarding house tariff, moved that the "Assembly adjourn from this place and meet at the town of Fayetteville." The move was defeated.

The State Bank of North Carolina would be incorporated in 1810 and Raleigh's branch built in 1813-1814, a sturdy brick building on the east side of Union Square. Indeed, from the beginning, Union Square and the State House, not the County Courthouse, had been the vortex of the City's activities. Besides government processes, all a part of the building's scene were club meetings, orations, special Sunday school classes, Fourth of July celebrations, church activities of various sects, dancing lessons, and theatricals. In fact, the funeral service of Presbyterian Joseph Caldwell, first president of the University of North

Carolina, was conducted in this building. And tradition has it that while Hannah Casso, daughter of an early Raleigh innkeeper, was celebrating her pre-nuptial ball in the State House, an urgent call came for her to return to her father's inn where, in one of the tavern's dependencies, she was asked to name a new baby. The child was the son of the Johnsons, Jacob and Polly, who worked as hosteler and weaver for Hannah's father. She named the boy Andrew, the same who became the seventeenth President of the United States.

During the first decade of the nineteenth century the "Subscription Assembly" or public ball continued in the State House though now, at these affairs, the grand minuet was going out of fashion and the timbre of the whole place was changing. Replacing the slow dances were jigs, reels, contradances, cotillions. Going out, too, for the smart coterie were Colonial knee breeches for the men and the side peplums for the women. Lively music was played by Negro fiddlers and whiskey cascaded.

The legislators had always enjoyed entertainment when in session and Raleigh had risen to the challenge. *Treasurer John Haywood's home on New Bern Avenue was the site of many dinner parties and breakfasts.* In 1815 the New Theatre, Raleigh's own, advertised the five-act *Castle Spectre* and the two-act *Love Laughs At Locksmiths*, both to be performed the same evening by the Raleigh Thespian Society which had been organized back in 1807 for the Capital's entertainment and for continuing support to the Raleigh Academy.

FLAT OF ITS BACK

The General Assembly back in 1802, when Eli Whitney had demonstrated his cotton "saw-gin" in Raleigh, had bought the patent rights and imposed a five-year tax of two shillings and sixpence on all machines used. After that, agricultural industrialization looked up in the State. But except for the few land-cotton wealthy, Raleigh citizens, between 1800 and 1825, were not destined to prosper. The City would have a difficult time all the way between swaddling clothes and knee pants.

Living in the Capital City, too, was extremely dear, especially the price of small creature comforts and pleasantries. According to the account books of W. and J. Peace, Raleigh merchants of the period, a silk handkerchief cost $1.25, twelve needles, 25¢, a pound of tea, $2.50, and a yard of broadcloth, $7.00. Loaf sugar for "sweeting one's julip" was 45¢ a pound while whiskey was far cheaper at $1.60 a gallon.

Travel was also expensive. The stagecoaches left Petersburg, Virginia, at three in the morning on Monday, Wednesday, and Friday, arriving in Warrenton at eight o'clock, after seventeen hours on the road. They left Warrenton at three o'clock the next morning and were due in Raleigh the same day at six in the evening – fifty-five miles in fifteen hours at a cost of about $3.50 to $4.00.

Though travel was not cheap or comfortable, the sweet, wild sound of the stage-horns sounding "clear in the evening air" must have joyed the hearts of wayfarers and Raleigh citizens who not only met friends and relatives at the stage stop but came, just to see, visit, get mail and first news, even before the newspapers.

Raleigh now reflected the lower rung of a State which had sometimes been called the "Rip Van Winkle," "Ireland of America," "Good State to be from." And it had finally become clear that inasmuch as the Neuse and its tributaries would never be navigable as far inland as Raleigh, as previously held, the Capital was not to become a port, nor even a wharf city. People lived here whose money was invested elsewhere – on the coast, in Virginia, in Charleston. As one historian looking back on the period said, "Raleigh had to be looking up all the time because, flat of its back, it could not look anywhere else." The City would have only 2,244 citizens by 1840. And its original one square mile boundary would not have to be pushed out to four square miles until 1857.

Still, a few things were happening. It had become increasingly important that the Governor should be domiciled in a more imposing Raleigh structure than the current "plain residence of wood," at the corner of

Fayetteville and Hargett streets. Hence in 1813 eight more acres, lots retained by the State after the original sale, were sold to build "The Palace." Such work as this plus other attendant building generated money for artisans and thereby aided the local economy.

When finished, the new brick residence faced north some distance from the State House, blocking Fayetteville Street. And although "outwardly plain and inwardly uncomfortable, it was considered *grand* on account of the magnitude of its halls and chambers, and was therefore, in imitation of Tryon's residence in New Bern, styled '*The Palace*'."

Altogether, things could not have been too depressing. One objective observer, for example, a British officer traveling through the State in 1818 said: "Raleigh. . . seems a clean, little country town. At one end of the. . . only street stands the Governor's brickhouse, and at the other the senate. . . . The houses are small. . . built of scantling. . . . The stage stops half a day at Raleigh, which enabled me to have a morning's quail shooting. . . . Society at Raleigh is by no means in a pitiable condition."

PARALLEL COLUMNS OF FLAME

The tails side of the coin did, however, seem to come up for Raleigh in many ways. In 1816 a disastrous fire destroyed two blocks, fifty-one of the City's buildings. Of this fire no one's rhetoric could be more sadly eloquent than that of editor Joseph Gales in the *Raleigh Register* for June 14, 1816. "Oft did the threatening volume bend its insatiate flame westwardly, as if looking with wanton rapacity for further prey."

And though the City had just organized a real fire company and bought a new steam fire engine which could now throw a vertical stream 126 feet, six hundred gallons per minute, demon fire struck again in 1821. This time "the flames rushed to Hargett street, sweeping all in their path. Here they leaped across to the opposite corner and levelled to the earth all the buildings on both sides of Hargett, two dreadful parallel columns of fire, to Wilmington street. They likewise hurried north with unchecked fury, until stopped by the unconquerable energy and pluck of a woman."

It seems historically proper and fitting that this "plucky" woman was old Raleigh innkeeper Peter Casso's daughter, Hannah Casso Stewart, who had married Raleigh merchant John Stewart. She was most certainly the heroine

of the 1821 catastrophe as she "heeded not the advancing columns of flame. . . the crashing timbers. . . forgot the natural timidity of her sex. Armed with wet blankets and hastily filled buckets, she stood in the very jams of the terrible heat until others, shamed into action by the recklessness of her daring, rushed to her aid."

As if that were not enough, just ten years later the cherished State House of 1794 which, as earlier mentioned, had been vastly improved by money from further sale of City lots in 1818-1821, burned to its foundations. That was on a morning in June, 1831. Most of the town gathered and as the burning timbers crashed into the rotunda, the prized Carrara marble statue of George Washington, commissioned of the Italian sculptor Antonio Canova, shipped to Boston, thence up Cape Fear to Fayetteville and brought to Raleigh by oxcart, lay crushed in incandescent pieces. Witnesses remembered, "Like its great original, serene and unmoved among the fires of Monmouth or of Trenton, the statue stood. . . untouched . . . majestic, every lineament and feature and graceful drapery white-hot of supernatural brilliance and beauty. Then suddenly the burning timbers fell. . . ."

Some State records, the speaker's chair and a Thomas

Sully copy of Gilbert Stuart's Lansdowne portrait of General Washington, which had been commissioned in a generous moment by the 1816 Assembly, were about all that was saved from the fire. Again then, the air stirred with proposals to move the seat of government "to anywhere else." This time a motion to move the Capital to the confluence of Cape Fear and the Haw rivers was defeated only by a single vote.

Apparently the General Assembly had grown accustomed to the little City's visage and a new, more elegant State House was planned immediately for Union Square. Its final cost would be the shocking figure of more than a half million dollars but the money expended would be justified in the building's gentle beauty.

To haul stone for the building, an "Experimental Railroad" leading to the Rock Quarry southeast of town was suggested by Sarah Hawkins Polk, wife of Colonel William Polk. Becoming a principal stockholder in the venture, Mrs. Polk invested wisely inasmuch as she was to realize more than three hundred percent on her money.

The "Railroad" was a modest affair costing, to lay the bed, the "sleepers" and iron rails which were fastened to them, about $22.50 a mile. Its cars were pulled by an old horse "guaranteed not to run away." Its mile-and-a-quarter track and rolling stock were finished January 1, 1833.

The populace loved it and a special car was put on for gentlemen and ladies "as desired to take the exercise of a railroad." They came from miles around, often interfering with the stone hauling. The train's scenic route started from the east portico of the burned-down State House. It turned "right at Hutchings House, until it reached the middle of the ridge a hundred yards south of New Bern avenue; thence down said ridge to within fifty yards of Camp Russell; thence bending to the right, running under the site of Lambright's Beer Garden and so on to the Quarry." It hadn't been much. But it had been North Carolina's first railroad. And it had hauled the stone for what was to become known as "the most elegant State House in the Nation."

THE TORNADO, THE BAKER,
THE WAGON-BED MAKER

Meantime, a real steam railroad, the Raleigh and Gaston, was coming into the City. Its eighty-six miles of roadbed lay between Weldon and the Capital and its iron-stripped, wooden rails served well, at least for a while, to carry the company's first locomotive, the Tornado, so named for its "fiery speed."

The *Register* for March 24, 1840, announced to the City—"Magnificent enterprises! We have now ocular demonstration of that, which no man would have believed thirty years ago. . . . The Raleigh and Gaston railroad is 86 miles in length and has been constructed altogether by individual stockholders, the State having uniformly declined embarking in the enterprize. . . . The whole line is now finished, is said to be admirably built. . . . We hail the rumbling of the first locomotive. . . ." The Tornado's

maiden run puffed into Raleigh about the same time the new State House was completed and a double celebration was surely in order.

People came, the curious, the holiday seekers, and celebrants from as far away as Virginia and for three days beginning June 10, 1840, all Raleigh doors were thrown wide, in the manner of a family reunion. Ruffin's Richmond Band played. A magnificent "procession under the marshalling of General Beverly Daniel, marched from the Courthouse to the depot." Judge William Gaston, a stockholder, delivered an address and on the occasion was called one of the finest orators of the century.

And again it is seemly that for the feasting, Hannah Casso Stewart would cater the occasion with five loaded banquet tables, each ninety feet long. The odor of

9

"scorched pig" pervaded the whole square mile that was Raleigh. Presiding as toastmaster was Weston Gales, Joseph's son. The Governor was there as well as every other notable and not so notable in the City. Thirteen formal toasts were delivered and as spirits warmed spirits, seventy-six more extempore ones were given.

In the evening Union Square and Fayetteville Street were hung with colored lamps, and transparencies of the new State House and the Tornado shone everywhere. In the senate chamber those who weren't dancing talked of the "great wonders of the iron horse and the splendid architecture" of the building. None prophesied that the Raleigh and Gaston, financed by private capital at the staggering cost of $1,343,380.44, would one day have to be taken over by the State.

The population of Raleigh was now, in the 'forties, 2,240 but things seemed to be moving toward big-town stature. One traveler into the South about this time, Frederick L. Olmsted who was a landscape architect, wrote in one of three volumes he later published, "Raleigh. . . is a pleasing town. . . streets wide. . . lined with trees. . . white wooden mansions. . . courtyards of flowers and shrubbery around them. The State-House. . . a noble building. . . stands in a square field. . . which remains in a rude state of undressed nature and is used as a hog-pasture

. . . country about Raleigh is little cultivated. . . it is a mystery how inhabitants can obtain sufficient supplies from it to exist."

Perhaps he did not tarry long enough to see other sights, attractions, changes. A New Englander had just come to Raleigh and had inaugurated, along with his bookstore activities, a system of conveying his volumes by an especially designed wagon, to all parts of the State. Among his books was *Turner's North Carolina Almanac*. Several dry goods merchants had opened new establishments and a few of the artisans and stonemasons had stayed in the Capital after working on the State House, to buy the goods. A successful new confectionery shop had located on the corner of Morgan and Salisbury streets. There were coach makers. And for the carriage trade a jewelry store, a millinery, a boots and shoes shop, and a tailor had hung out their signs and advertised in the *Star*, the *Standard*, or the *Register*. Too, and though in the woods, Raleigh had become less insular. *Niles' National Register* for June 13, 1840, indicates, "A convention of those interested in the manufacturing business in North Carolina, is to meet in Raleigh on the 13th instant for the purpose of arranging the domestic market of cotton yarns. . . ." The City was at last showing on the national canvas.

AH, VANISHING WILDERNESS

Earlier in the century Raleigh's log cabins had slowly given way when certain regional architectural idioms merged into what has been called the Federal or Regency style. Supplanting these building traditions came next the American neo-classical period, generally ascribed to the years 1820-1860. It had come to Raleigh relatively early and its best illustration was, of course, the 1840 capitol building.

This Greek Revival was almost paralleled by a Gothic Revival which its protagonists fostered in the belief that Gothic forms, symbols, and inspiration had sprung from Christian rather than pagan sources. Raleigh, however, was sufficiently affluent and catholic enough in taste at the time to commission, for home-town structures, buildings from the pencils of Gothic proponent Richard

Upjohn, classicist Ithiel Town, and his partner, the innovator, Alexander J. Davis – all nationally known.

Neo-Gothic architecture did not lend itself so readily to residential uses but neo-classicism would prevail in Raleigh until after mid-century. It would then freeze, immobilize in mid-stream as all things did when the metronome of war ticked off approaching minutes foretelling the conflict. It would not reappear until the crushing devastation of war and "Reconstruction" had partly run their vindictive courses, until Raleigh could again struggle to its knees.

And so, if the City's first fifty-eight years had been innocently, pleasantly turbulent, its next fifty would be a time to test the whole storehouse of its mettle.

Raleigh Grove

Wakefield

Circa 1760
Raleigh Historic Site 1972, National Register Property 1970
Restored 1976

The builder of this house, Colonel Joel Lane, was ambiguously enough, both a good Tory under Governor Tryon and a sturdy American patriot after the Revolution. He may surely be called the father of the Capital City inasmuch as practically nothing transpired in Raleigh's early history which was not directly concerned with this pioneer.

He had settled here before Wake County was sliced out of Orange, Cumberland, and Johnston counties and this house preceded

the City's founding by thirty-two or more years. As he and his family lived here, he became, at various times, a committeeman for the building of a Wake County courthouse, prison, and stocks and Judge of the Court of Pleas and Quarter Sessions, 1771. He was Lieutenant Colonel of the Wake Regiment of 1772 and a member of the North Carolina Provisional Congress at Halifax in April of 1776. He represented Wake County in eleven sessions of the State Senate and was a member of the first Board of Trustees of the University of

North Carolina, serving from 1789 until the time of his death in 1795.

Wakefield originally faced east and was located about 150 feet in that direction from its present site, 728 West Hargett Street. The residence was so named for Margaret, Governor Tryon's wife, nee Wake. It has not come down to us where the siding of the house was cut, where the hardware was forged, nor where the chimney bricks were fired. And it can only be presumed that all the fabrication was done by slave labor on the place. It is known, however, that on the original grounds, there were orchards, extensive slave quarters, an ice house, and later in Lane's life, the guest house has been described as a miniature of Wakefield.

The house's ownership went through successive hands – Lane's son, Thomas, Lane's son-in-law, Dr. Allen Gilchrist, to lawyer Peter Browne; and from 1818 to 1909 title was vested in some of the Boylan family. It was during the Boylans' ownership that a wing and a latticed porch were added, since removed from the west side of the house, with the restoration, and added to the rear.

The gambrel roof of this house probably came to the South's Tidewater and Piedmont regions in the late seventeenth century via the Netherlands, thence to England, and to North Carolina. It was an inexpensive design since we know that it lived well as a two-story building but was more economical to build as a "story and a half." Structurally it is put together with wooden pegs. Its first doors were hung with H and L hinges. And though care was taken with Wakefield's relocation, its eighteenth-century chimneys were damaged. Perhaps on some future day the present owners, the Wake County Committee of the Colonial Dames of America in the State of North Carolina, who began the restoration, will restore, with historical accuracy, this original brickwork.

As seen in this interior, Wakefield's quiet, practical, simple, ultimately beautiful paneling and detailing are as contemporary as tomorrow.

The house has been restored to its 1790s appearance with the 1840 wing removed to the rear of the property for rental. The damaged chimneys have been replaced and the house restored with period furnishings. Joel Lane House, Inc., an arm of the Colonial Dames, has added an eighteenth century Wake County kitchen and both a period garden and an herb garden. This house museum is open by appointment.

Down through the years, it had always been understood that the Lane family's unmarked cemetery was on the east side of Boylan Avenue, across from the original site of the house. In 1969, when the site thought to be the unmarked graveyard was scheduled to be paved for a parking lot, the Raleigh Historic Sites Commission, through the Archaeology Section of the Division of Archives and History, conducted an archaeological dig. Nine graves were discovered. The remains from those graves were reinterred in a single coffin in the City Cemetery and appropriately marked.

Clay-Hill-on-the-Neuse

South side of Highway 64 East, just across the Neuse River

Clay-Hill-on-the-Neuse
Built 1765 - Burned 1923

On this Neuse River plantation, a hunting ground for the Tuscaroras, Colonel John Hinton, Sr., who had distinguished himself in February of 1776 by fighting to save the southern states from the British at Moore's Creek Bridge, built his log cabin. The place was entered from the second story, by a movable ladder, the better to deter Indians and animals. Later, on the same land which had been taken up by grant from the Earl of Granville, the Colonel and his wife, Grizelle Kimbrough, built a more "capacious clapboard house with a square-brick foundation," called the River Place.

John Hinton, Jr., eldest of the senior Hinton's eight surviving children, however, had been born in the log cabin. Wealthy through his parents by 1776, he also served as First Major with his father, the Colonel, in the conflict of Moore's Creek.

On June 17, 1765, when he was seventeen years old, John Jr. had married Pherebee Smith, aged sixteen, for whose family Smithfield, North Carolina, had been named. The young man apparently considered his marriage more seriously than later generations since just before the wedding he had built Clay-Hill-on-the-Neuse for his bride. Surrounded by a neat paling fence, the house was made of heart pine and was put together with wrought iron nails. The slanting porch cover, supported by fluted columns, had a sky-blue plastered ceiling, the plaster being two inches thick.

The front door led directly into a large, wainscoted parlor replete with ornamental woodwork, solid mahogany and walnut furniture. From the parlor's right, a door led into the dining room and thence to a butler's pantry. From here all food was conveyed over a stone-paved walk from the outside kitchen. Also on the first floor was a bedroom with contiguous dressing rooms and closets, but without a fireplace which Major Hinton considered unhealthy in a sleeping room. On the second floor were the great common hall and three bedrooms.

This house, built a few miles north of Wake Cross Roads, was obviously designed for gentle living. Family papers of Major John, Jr. and Pherebee's descendants speak of Clay Hill's scented lavender bed linen, its thinnest china, the silver which was impressed with a simple "H," its piano. There were flower gardens of hyacinth, roses, lilac and herb gardens of tansy, rue, sage, and thyme. And to be counted among feasts, balls and the like which went on in the "great house," was the wedding of Joel Lane's son, Henry, to his first cousin, Mary Hinton, daughter of Major John, Jr.

The uncle of Andrew Johnson supervised the spinning on the plantation. Among others who supported the gracious living at Clay Hill were "Uncle Brisco" who had been Colonel John Hinton, Sr.'s, body servant during the Revolution and who ever after loved to tell about the War. There was "Gunny," a Negro from Guinea who drove the carriage, the second vehicle of this kind to come into Raleigh. And there was an aristocrat named "Mingo" who had been a tribal chief in his native Africa and was, for this reason, never required by the Hintons to do manual work. Mingo Creek, which parallels the Norfolk and Southern Railroad in Raleigh, before it enters the Neuse, is named for him. "Mammy Kizzy," or "Kitty," the dairy maid at Clay Hill, always wore fresh flowers in the large holes in her ear lobes, a fashion she had brought from Africa.

Betsy Hinton, an elderly descendant, died shortly after the Thirtieth Ohio Volunteers of Sherman's Army, camping at Clay Hill, ransacked the place in the spring of 1865. The property then passed to out-of-town relatives who sold it to strangers. Its trajectory from then on was always downward.

All that is left of Clay Hill is the family graveyard. The house burned in 1923.

Entry in Wake County Records

Isaac Hunter's Tavern
Built Before 1770 - Destruction Date Unknown

It is not precisely known why the Hillsborough Convention of 1788 ordained that North Carolina's permanent Capital should be located within a ten-mile radius of Isaac Hunter's Tavern. It may have been that the keeper of the Inn was a particularly respected hosteler or perhaps he was a friend of some Assemblyman. Again it is possible that his Tavern on the old Petersburg-Fayetteville stage road, four miles north of the site which was later selected for the State House, was the only sufficiently well-known place which was strategically located in the middle of the State – a factor the solons were considering in site selection.

In any case, the 1791 General Assembly carried out the Convention's ordinance and specified further that there should, within that ten-mile specification, "be built and erected a State House sufficiently large to accommodate with convenience both houses of the General Assembly, at an expense not to exceed ten thousand pounds."

It was some time before 1770 that Isaac Hunter had acquired his original plantation lands, about 600 acres, from the Earl of Granville. And subsequent acquisitions, transferred to him by the State between 1779 and 1792, brought the total to 7,137 acres.

To date no description of the Inn itself has been found but on this surely magnificent property it must be surmised that for both travelers and family-living alike, it was one of life's pleasanter adventures to pause there.

Isaac Hunter was a lover of the hunt and of horses. He maintained his own race track on the plantation and according to tradition, "chased deer from Crabtree to Walnut Creek" – part of that deer run now being the Fayetteville Street of 1992.

The Inn was still operating in 1825 when the Marquis de LaFayette stopped there. And as late as 1942 remnants of what was thought to have been the kitchen dependency of the old Tavern could be seen on the original site. Its outside chimney was intact and its three rooms were plank sided, the siding held together with wooden pegs. Also, these planks, attesting to the quality of even the Inn's kitchen, were covered with beaded clapboard.

Isaac Hunter died an old man on March 18, 1823. He lies buried somewhere on the plantation but his grave is not now marked.

Shotwell Community

Walnut Hill
Circa 1775
Burned 1973

Located near Shotwell Community, wandering, old Walnut Hill has the distinction of physically documenting, with its additions and subtractions, the needs and tastes of six generations of one family. Their descendants continue its ownership in 1967.

Inasmuch as there are no records as to when the first, small part of this house was built it is important to know that the land was deeded by Malachi Hinton to Thomas Mial, a captain in the Wake County Militia, on June 7, 1775. And from that date plus certain construction characteristics, it may be assumed that the place was started not too long afterward.

Over the years the Mial-Williamson family added more land to the plantation and turned it into an organic, self-sufficient compound for living. Still standing, in fact, are the cobbler's workshop, Frog Pond Academy where members of the family and others were schooled, barns, and a large gin house which rests on great piers of rough-cut stone.

The house today is T-shaped, the leg of the T forming one of the earliest floor plans seen in America. That segment is comprised of the two-room, hall-parlor design, with a stairway concealed in the partition wall. Attached to this back portion is a box-corniced dependency, circa 1800. The cross of the T is dated post Civil War and is typical of the period, with its wide, upper and lower-floor halls and four big rooms. Dormer windows were added in the early part of the twentieth century.

Alonza Thomas Mial, 1823-1897, grandson of the original builder, had already fired the brick preparatory to building a fine house up the road from the old place. He had previously planted the elms for its approach. But then a Michigan regiment of the Union Army came, and using the place as headquarters, cracked up the brick and the new residence was never built. The elm-bordered avenue leading up to the ghost house that never was, remains majestically there. During that War, also, the great wax seal attached to the land grant from the Earl of Granville, for some of the Mial-Williamson acres, was melted down to be used otherwise, wax being extremely scarce at the time.

The present homestead with its twelve rooms is decorated with simplified, neo-classical trim, a treatment which was used after the Civil War when the house was renovated and enlarged. It is good that Walnut Hill continues as a clock, recording and mirroring time's vicissitudes, the attitudes, likes, and dislikes of whomever it protects.

In 1973 the family rented the main house to Drug Action of Wake County, Inc., to use as a rehabilitation center for heroin addicts – a secluded place where broken lives could mend and grow again. However, in the early morning hours of June 24, 1973, before the center opened, the house burned. Only its six chimneys rose above the ashes in bleak silence. Arson was confirmed, but the culprits have never been found.

Gin House, Walnut Hill

National Register Property 1986

Mordecai House
Circa 1785 and 1826
Raleigh Historic Site 1972, National Register Property 1970
Restored 1972

Known throughout most of the nineteenth century as the Mordecai House, this Greek revival mansion with its unusual mixture of Doric and Ionic capitals, might more properly be called the Lane-Mordecai residence. The original or north section was built circa 1785 and was given in that year to Henry Lane by his father, Joel Lane. And tradition indicates that the property had originally been a grant from King George II and later was acquired by Joel Lane.

A lawyer and Raleigh member of the 1805 Court of Conference, Moses Mordecai, twice married into Henry Lane's family – first to Margaret Lane and after her death, to her sister, Ann Willis Lane. Thus the name of Mordecai was attached and it is known that before his death in 1824, Moses Mordecai, for the purpose of enlarging this house, engaged the services of Architect William Nichols – the same who remodeled the 1794 State House. Four rooms facing south and a porch on the east were added at this time.

The siding for the place was cut from heart pine, put together with wooden pegs and hand-wrought nails, and has remained structurally solid as many generations of the family have come, lived, and parted from its shelter. The interior throughout is elegant in its simplicity with a delicately modeled staircase, quiet wainscoting, and carefully crafted mantelpieces.

In its palmy days, the house was the focal core of a large plantation and counted among its dependencies were stables, barns, smokehouse which stored a year's supply of bacon, a cotton press, blacksmith shop, and a gin house. Slave quarters were in the usual long row and each had its own backyard vegetable garden.

Shoes from the skins of animals killed on the plantation were made in the smithy's shop and flax for sewing them together was grown in the fields. In the carriage house were kept a four-seated buggy, a barouche, a large carriage, and a sulky for the children. Wild flowers abounded about the place but planted formally in the gardens were lilies, poppies, old-fashioned roses, white violets, and flowering herbs.

Surviving accounts indicate that seasonally, after the cotton and several hundred bushels of sweet potatoes were harvested, corn shucking began. Slaves attached to the plantation sang "husking" songs as they worked; and given apple brandy at harvest time, they often came to the "great house" to serenade the family. Some of these servants' names have been recorded as Aunt Cely, Harry White who was the steer driver, Nanny, the flax spinner, and Davey, the cobbler.

If one could ride his time machine back into the eighteenth and early nineteenth centuries, this house would surely reveal the most sumptuous living that Wake County afforded between the Revolutionary War and antebellum days.

Although the house remains on its original site on Mimosa Street, the plantation acres have long since been sold in smaller parcels, some of which extended as far as the Raleigh section now known as Hayes Barton.

Further research showed that when Moses Mordecai died in 1824, his will specified a sum of money for a fit house for his family and it was his widow, Ann Willis "Nancy" Lane Mordecai, who in 1826 engaged the services of Mr. Nichols to enlarge the house, as shown at the right. This neoclassical style of architecture had been used earlier on two government buildings in Raleigh – the 1816 Governor's Palace and the 1821 remodeled State House. When William Nichols employed this style on the south portion of Mordecai House in 1826, a local newspaper referred to it as the "earliest specimen of that order among us" for residences.

In 1967 the City of Raleigh purchased the property and turned it over to the Raleigh Historic Sites Commission to develop as an historic park. Preserved to mirror the tastes and times of five generations of the same family – the Lanes, Mordecais, Turks, and Littles – Mordecai House contains much of its original furnishings.

Today Mordecai Historic Park includes not only the manor house and two of its original dependencies, but also is the location of five other historic buildings that have been moved to the park – an 1842 kitchen, the Andrew Johnson Birthplace, an early Raleigh Office Building circa 1847, the Badger-Iredell Law Office circa 1810, and an 1847 plantation chapel. An 1830s style garden has also been recreated. Mordecai Historic Park is operated by Capital Area Preservation, Inc., by contract with the City of Raleigh.

Mordecai House

Old State House
Painting by Jacob Marling
Oil on canvas, 20" x 26"
North Carolina Museum of History

Union Square

Old State House
Built 1794 - Burned 1831

Reproduced here is Jacob Marling's oil on canvas painting of North Carolina's first State House. As described in Part I of this book, the building housed its first legislative session in 1794, was remodeled by 1821, and burned to its foundations in 1831.

Marling came to Raleigh sometime before 1813, suffered financial losses and shortly became the first director of a reading room and museum known as the North Carolina Museum or Marling's Museum as it was often called. The establishment, on Fayetteville Street, advertised curiosities, drawings, paintings, rare coins, and books. Later the painter settled into John F. Goneke's "Concert Hall" and again he let it be known through the *Raleigh Register* that "Ladies and gentlemen who may wish their portrait or miniature taken shall have them well executed, on moderate terms." Here he painted portraits in watercolor and oil and was assisted by his wife, Louisa, who taught art at the old Raleigh Academy. Apparently Marling lived and worked comfortably at Mr. Goneke's place inasmuch as it is known to have offered "conveniences. . . entertainment . . . and twenty-seven different kinds of liquor."

The artist's most productive years were between 1825 and 1831 during which time he painted numerous portraits of General Assembly members. These and the "First North Carolina State House" are clean, crisp and are in the best tradition of early nineteenth century American painting.

The State House canvas is small, only twenty by twenty-six inches, but its historical importance is undisputed. It was obviously painted after Architect William Nichols remodeled the building, which would place its date between 1821 and 1831. The picture, with its delicate and primitively honest style, finds Raleigh locals in the foreground who may well have been members of the legislative body. Two young Negroes are seen romping in the Square and a woman balancing a bundle on her head goes about her errand. The trees to the left, with their heavy foliage, are credited by some with saving the State House fire of 1831 from spreading out of the Square.

The well, dug circa 1794 on the southeast side of the State House, supplied the water to fight the flames. It was the oldest known surviving well in downtown Raleigh and was used until 1912 when it was condemned. Today a small water fountain, near the southeast corner of the Capitol, stands in the middle of the relocated original curbing of that eighteenth century well, which is now dry and covered and a few feet from the fountain.

The renovated building, as Marling saw it, was brick overlaid with yellow stucco. The four pilasters of the east facade stood upon a massive foundation covered by stucco which was scored to resemble stone blocks.

Jacob Marling died in 1833 and is buried in the old City Cemetery. This canvas is in the possession of the North Carolina Museum of History.

In 1831 when the old State House burned, perhaps Marling realized that his painting remained the best documentary evidence of the remodeled State House. However, two other Marling paintings give clues as to the earlier likeness of the first State House.

Marling's portrait of William Miller, Governor of North Carolina from 1815-1817, shows in its background the State House before the remodeling was begun in 1818. Perhaps it was painted during Miller's term as governor. The State House in the background shows either the northern or southern portico and a tall cupola with a weathervane on it, rising high above the roof, rather than a dome with an ornamentation as seen in the later Marling painting, shown here.

The 30 1/4" X 25 l/2" portrait of Governor Miller is owned by the Philanthropic Society of the University of North Carolina, Chapel Hill.

The same tall cupola is shown rising above the trees in Marling's painting called "The Crowning of Flora," which depicts the elaborate May Day exercises of the Raleigh Academy on Burke Square in 1816. This 30 1/8" X 39 1/8" oil on canvas painting is in the collection of the Chrysler Museum, Norfolk, Virginia.

Corner of East Morgan and Fayetteville streets

Peter Casso's

1795 - Burned 1833
The above sketch is of the Hogg-Mordecai Building which replaced Casso's.
*This building was demolished in 1938 for the Justice Building.***

Among those who are history-minded it has become an exciting theme to speculate upon just how and when Peter Casso's Inn, Raleigh's most romantic old landmark, disappeared. As mentioned before, the Inn was the Capital's original stage stop, town bell site, social center, and an alter meeting place for legislators.

Its beginnings are familiarly cherished and well-documented as revealed in many contemporary sources. As, for example, first it is known that Casso bought the land for $292 and in 1795 established the Inn plus its dependencies, innyard, and stables on the north half of the block bounded by Wilmington, Morgan, and Fayetteville streets. The Innkeeper himself advertised the place in the *Raleigh Register* of 1799. "The houses consist of one dwelling house... three stories high with a shade on one side and a bar room on the other, with five fire places...." He describes other structures on the site and adds: "A stable sufficient to contain 40 horses, a saddlery, grain-houses and smokehouses, a good garden, well, plank-fenced and a horse yard paved. The furniture consists of 20 to 25 excellent beds with every other suitable article."

Site of Peter Casso's

Another description comes from an April 17, 1804, *Raleigh Register* piece. "The subscriber takes this method to inform his friends and the public that he still keeps a Public House of entertainment for decent travelers and others. . . . He has always plenty of fodder, oats, and corn, with a stable equal to. . . any in the State and the best liquor that the County can afford. . . . He is respectfully the public's most obedient and humble servant. . . Peter Casso."

There is some speculation that the place burned in one of the several Fayetteville Street fires of the first half of the nineteenth century. But if a subsequent building had taken its place, why was it thereafter always called Casso's Inn? Why did one historian, writing in 1932, state unequivocally that, "An original inn now remains, built by Peter Casso who was a soldier in the War of the Revolution?"

In 1922 another Raleigh author, who made the sketch of the building as it appears here, insisted in her text that, "Casso's still stands on the corner of Morgan and Fayetteville Streets. . . and were the fire escapes and such modern additions taken away, would remain much as it used to be when the stages rolled to the door."

Again, why was Casso's daughter, Hannah, still running a boarding house on the old site long after her father died in 1807 and well after the building was supposed to have burned, if she were not using the family building? Too, how, if Casso's burned, was the Jacob Johnson house which stood in the innyard, saved and only moved from the site after the Civil War?

Apropos, reproduced here is a Raleigh circus parade showing elephants walking west on Morgan and turning south into Fayetteville. In the 1898 photograph is seen part of a typically eighteenth-century building. Was it Casso's? And why, even in 1967, are some of the Fayetteville Street rooftops contiguous to the Casso site earlier in character, the rest being false fronts of a later period and farther away from the Casso corner.

Perhaps part of the entire one-half block was saved from the fires. Maybe it was truly Casso's Inn which was razed in 1938 to make land for the Justice Building. Or was the building which was then demolished not Casso's?

Later research has shown that by 1793 Warren Alford had built a tavern with stables and other necessary buildings on a one-acre lot on the southeast corner of Morgan and Fayetteville streets which Peter Casso acquired in 1795. Further research has also shown that Casso's main building, which faced Morgan Street, burned in the 1833 Fayetteville Street fire. The sketch to the left is that of the Hogg-Mordecai structure built in 1835 on the same site. In 1938 the building, which by then was called the Dortch Building, was demolished to make way for a new Justice Building.

Hogg and Mordecai also constructed several adjacent brick buildings in the 1830s. And sadly, in 1972 the adjacent building, which had been designated a Raleigh Historic Site in 1969, was razed. Its roofline can be seen in the sketch.

Mordecai Historic Park   *1 Mimosa Street*

Andrew Johnson House
Circa 1795
Raleigh Historic Site 1972
Moved to Mordecai Historic Park 1975
Restored 1977

This tiny house, twelve by eighteen feet, was the birthplace of President Andrew Johnson. In part, it was constructed of used lumber inasmuch as old nail holes were found when some of its heart pine timbers were removed to be replaced by cyprus. The walls and upstairs floorboards are original but the downstairs flooring has been renewed.

Authorities disagree as to the construction year of the little residence. Presumably, however, it was built about the time Peter Casso established his Inn, 1795, since it first stood as a dependency in the courtyard of that Inn at the corner of Morgan and Fayetteville. It is known that here the Johnson family lived as employees of innkeeper Casso.

Jacob Johnson, the father of Andrew, died in 1812 and in 1824 young Andrew, aged sixteen and having been earlier apprenticed to a tailor, left Raleigh for Carthage, North Carolina. From there he went to Laurens, South Carolina, but returned to Raleigh and together with his brother, William, his mother, his stepfather, Turner Daugherty, and all their furniture, journeyed by wagon to Greeneville, Tennessee.

After that Raleigh saw little else of Andrew Johnson except on occasions such as in 1845 when he returned here to investigate insinuating reports regarding his paternity and again in 1867 for the dedication of a City Cemetery monument to his father.

The little place obviously escaped the three disastrous Fayetteville Street fires and was moved to 118 East Cabarrus Street shortly after the Civil War. It was here occupied by local families until in 1904 it was bought for $100 by the Wake County Committee of the Colonial Dames of America in the State of North Carolina and given to the City.

From that site its remains traveled to Pullen Park where, being near a railroad, it became the shelter of passing hobos and winos. Finally, in 1938, with the help of Federal money, it was moved to a new Pullen Park site away from the tracks, and restored.

In 1975 the house was moved to Mordecai Historic Park where, under the guidance of restoration specialists from the North Carolina Division of Archives and History, it was restored to its earlier appearance, that of an eighteenth century kitchen with an upstairs plastered room where the Jacob Johnson family lived.

3015 Wake Forest Road

"Crabtree" Jones House

Circa 1795
Raleigh Historic Site 1969, National Register Property 1973

"Crabtree" Jones House

Nathaniel Jones, whose family came from the Eastern Shore of Virginia in the seventeen forties, patented the land for this estate and built the home reproduced here. The tract was originally bought, as were so many eighteenth-century plantations near Raleigh, from the Earl of Granville. Apparently Nathaniel built his first residence only a few hundred yards from Crabtree Creek and found, unfortunately, that during the Creek's flood stage the dwelling became an inaccessible island in the middle of what was normally a mild rivulet.

Doubtlessly, this is the reason for the high-land siting of this, his second plantation house, built about 1795 on the old Wake Forest Road and just north of the City. Its timbers were cut from primeval growth on the owner's property and the hand-dressed, beaded weatherboarding was put together with nails, made on the place, by the farm's slave blacksmiths.

The building is T shaped, the T's shaft being as deep as the house's front wing is wide. The original dining room occupied the basement beneath this rear portion and at various times the porches have been altered. Otherwise, the original plan mainly prevails. The interior finish reflects the hearty, no-nonsense simplicity of pre-Revolution taste. There are nine mantels throughout, all finished differently and the doors are fabricated in the old Bible-and-Cross design.

"Crabtree" Jones House has always been the appellate designation for this property, perhaps because in this way it became distinguishable from the other Jones families of Morrisville, Cary, and other parts of the State.

"Crabtree," used as a parade and drill ground for Confederate Colonel Harry K. Burgwyn during the Civil War, has remained in this Jones family more than two hundred years. Its present owners are descendants of the original Nathaniel.

A commercial realty company purchased the house in 1973 from descendants of Nathaniel Jones. With the house vacant, vandals struck; however, since 1974 it has been used as a residence. But with commercial development coming ever closer, the future of this eighteenth century house is uncertain.

28

100 block South East Street

City Cemetery
1798

In Raleigh's early years, this, the City Cemetery, was accounted for and was located off East Street just beyond the little town's original eastern boundary. Its narrow, cobblestone carriage ways are today as they were when laid in the late 1890s. The iron fence which encloses the five acres on three sides once served to keep domestic animals out of Union Square. It was removed to the cemetery just before the nineteenth century ended, as explained in the Board of Aldermen Minutes of February 4, 1898. "It is with much pleasure that we are able to report that an agreement has been reached between the State and the City authorities by the terms of which the old iron fence is to be taken from around Capitol Square. This iron fence will be used by the City in enclosing the old City Cemetery."

In June of 1810 Raleigh had a "Pastor of the City," among whose services, at a salary of $500 a year, was the handling of burial ceremonies in this graveyard. His name was the Reverend William McPheeters and he himself was buried here, 1842.

Other names, now familiar to readers of this book, lie here including Joseph Gales, editor of the City's first newspaper and for nineteen years Raleigh's Mayor; his son, Weston Raleigh Gales; Jacob Marling, portrait and landscape painter; Jacob Johnson, father of the Country's seventeenth President; two of Joel Lane's daughters, Martha and Grizelle; John Rex who, before his death in 1839, bought for $481 fifteen and a half acres in southwest Raleigh and gave it to the municipality as a hospital site to be used for the "sick and afflicted poor of the City of Raleigh;" and merchant William

Peace, donor of $10,000 plus the land for Peace College.

Various local organizations including the Raleigh Historic Sites Commission have contributed to restoration and preservation of this landmark which, over the years, had been much neglected.

In more recent years, the Wake County Historical Society, Inc., has sponsored walking tours of the cemetery. At the main entrance to the cemetery on South East Street is a large granite "plan" showing the location of the graves of many of the city's early prominent citizens.

When the cemetery was originally laid out, two of the four quadrants were for residents, one was for strangers, and one for blacks, both slave and free, many of whose graves were unmarked. Now in the northwest corner of that section stands a granite marker which reads: DEDICATED IN MEMORY AND TO MARK THE RESTING PLACE OF RALEIGH'S AFRICAN-AMERICAN CITIZENS CIRCA 1798-1872.

Barbour Drive on the Dorothea Dix Campus

Spring Hill

Rear Portion, After 1771 - Before 1798, Date Destroyed Unknown
Front Portion, Circa 1815, Raleigh Historic Site 1979, National Register Property 1983

Colonel Theophilus Hunter, Sr., like his brother Isaac, also owned and operated a public house near Raleigh. The place, on the old Fayetteville road and four miles south of the City, was one of the earliest houses built in Wake County. It was here that Hunter lived until the place was destroyed by fire some time after 1771, the year Governor Tryon stayed there, and before 1798, the date of the innkeeper's death.

After the Lodge burned, Theophilus Hunter, Sr., built the original or smaller part of Spring Hill as his residence. In this house he must have presided affluently since he had been, at one time and another, a member of the General Assembly, a major in the Colonial Militia, presiding justice of the first Court of Pleas and Quarter Sessions, a Lieutenant Colonel in the North Carolina Militia, and County Surveyor. His substantial plantation with its house on the most shamelessly beautiful knoll, stretched from Raleigh's Walnut Creek almost to Cary.

Inheriting the place upon his father's death, Theophilus Hunter, Jr., added the larger section to Spring Hill. And it was he who was credited with having the notion that children had no business sitting around the fireplace with adults, hence the two chimneys. There were flues, a door separating them, for the two "great room" fireplaces.

Timber for Spring Hill came from the plantation's own sawmill and it is said that only the perfectly cut pieces were laid aside and then used in construction of the house. This is easily believable as the place was found to be in such excellent structural condition when the State acquired the site early in this century for the Dorothea Dix Hospital that it was decided to use rather than demolish the old residence.

The house was kept in the Hunter family until after 1865, when part of Sherman's army was quartered on the grounds. Then the property passed out of the family to various other owners. Theophilus Hunter, Jr., died in 1840 and is buried on the property in an unmarked grave. *The grave of his father is one of the earlier marked graves in Wake County, 1798.*

The towering chimneys, the small twin house built by Hunter the elder, and all of the original dependencies of Spring Hill have been demolished but the altered house remains in *1992* on its powerful vantage point overlooking the City.

Spring Hill is now a House Museum which functions as headquarters for the Dorothea Dix Hospital Volunteer Services and the Volunteer Service Guild as well as the location of memorabilia and exhibits of the hospital, which is the first State Hospital for the Mentally Ill in North Carolina.

31

209 East Morgan Street, 1798-1985

White-Holman House
Circa 1798
Raleigh Historic Site 1969, National Register Property 1971
Moved to New Bern Place 1985

Still standing on its original site at 209 East Morgan and complete with its own peg-legged ghost, is the White-Holman house, pictured here. William White, North Carolina Secretary of State between 1798 and 1810, and son-in-law of Governor Richard Caswell, had ten children and apparently built this residence about 1798 to accommodate all of his progeny. He died, according to the *Raleigh Register*, November 8, 1811. And it is to be recalled that one of his daughters, Eleanor, married Governor David L. Swain (1832-1835) on January 12, 1826. Eleanor then, and White's other daughters, Susan, Emma, and Sophronia, were believed to have been their father's heirs to the property.

The Federal style house was spacious throughout, its woodwork handcarved, and its surrounding land accommodated improvements for townhouse living. As the City encroached, portions of the land were sold and in 1896 the house was enlarged and much of the original architecture character covered over. One wing was removed later to be used in a residence next door.

William Calvin Holman, born in 1848 in Lancaster, Massachusetts, came to North Carolina in his 'teens. In 1885 he moved to Raleigh and bought this residence from the White estate for $2,422.25. Holman married a Salem, North Carolina, woman, Anna Belo, and one of their daughters presently owns the property.

The ghost's peg-leg tapping bothers neither family, guests, nor neighbors in that he never moans, drags a chain, or otherwise disturbs, but simply climbs and descends a concealed stairway in the original part of the house. It has been suggested that he may be one of William White's particularly gifted woodcarvers who was not content, upon death, to leave his work behind.

It is hoped by the Raleigh Historic Sites Commission that this residence, one of Raleigh's earliest "town dwellings," may be preserved and maintained as an eighteenth-century landmark.

"Whitehall," as the house was often called, was purchased by the city from descendants of the Holmans in 1968. The Morgan Street/New Bern Avenue connector sliced off the side yard. In 1985, to preserve it prop-erly, the city and Capital Area Preservation, Inc., (formerly called Mordecai Square Historical Society) turned the house around to face New Bern Place and Haywood Hall, then sold it with restrictive covenants to Whitehall Associates who have rehabilitated it with its 1880s additions for adaptive use as offices. The interior still includes the magnificently handcarved mantels and overmantels.

206 New Bern Place

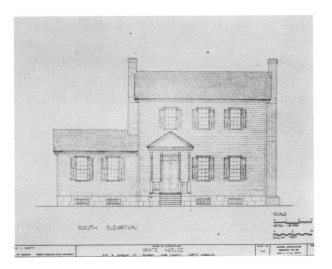

211 New Bern Place

Haywood Hall

Circa 1799

Raleigh Historic Site 1969, National Register Property 1970

As compared with other existing residences of the period, Haywood Hall has been little changed since construction of its commodious halls and rooms was begun about 1799 by its builder-owner, John Haywood, for his second wife, Elizabeth "Eliza" Eagles Asaph Williams. The 211 New Bern Avenue house still stands on foundations of locally quarried stone.

The place was sited on land which, according to a July 1, 1797, map of the City and a 1799 tax valuation, was owned by Joseph Tagert and had no improvements. The lot was large enough to accommodate all the necessary "fixments" for gracious nineteenth-century city living. Bordering on Blount Street were stables and

barns for horses, a pony, and a cow. The carriage house was about midway on the Blount Street side of the property. Slave quarters for domestic servants stood at the Edenton and Blount intersection. The enclosed yard north of the house was given over to ornamental walkways, to growing flowers for all family occasions, and the remaining free ground was planted in fruit trees and vegetables for household consumption. A family cemetery, surrounded by japonica and boxwood, lay beyond the garden.

The classically Federal exterior of the house with its bilateral symmetry, its fluted, Doric columns, simple fenestration, and beaded siding speaks for itself. Structurally it is typical in that some of its upright heart pine members measure fourteen by fourteen inches square. The interior, as shown in this detail, probably reflects some of the personal characteristics of the original owner in that the wood-carved pineapple and apple seen in this house were symbols of hospitality.

Usually, when the Assembly was in session, John Haywood entertained with a sumptuous breakfast each of the members. These occasions took place in the large room just to the left of the main entrance. Here, also, transpired political meetings and grand balls inasmuch as the room, now divided into two, was originally perhaps the largest room among the City's private dwellings.

The master of Haywood Hall had been unanimously elected in 1787 to the office of State Treasurer, which post he held for forty years. He was a founder and vestryman of Christ Church and was Raleigh's first Intendant of Police, or Mayor. He helped in selecting the site and in the founding of the University of North Carolina and was on its Board of Trustees for as long as he lived. He died November 18, 1827, at seventy-two.

The present owner, Mrs. Walter Stearns, is John Haywood's direct descendant.

From the 1830s until the 1880s, John Haywood's daughters conducted a girls' school on the property. Four generations of Haywoods lived in this house for 178 years. This unique property, with its outbuildings and gardens, is the oldest house within the original city limits still on its original site.

Mary Haywood Fowle Stearns died in 1977, bequeathing the entire property to the National Society of the Colonial Dames of America in the State of North Carolina to maintain as a house museum "for people to learn of the history of this area." Operated by the Haywood Hall Committee of the Dames and by Friends of Haywood Hall, it is open to the public on a limited basis and by appointment.

"The Crowning of Flora"*
by Jacob Marling
1816

The Reverend William McPheeters came to Raleigh in 1810 to be both Pastor of the City and Principal of the Raleigh Academy. Under his tutelage courses were available in Latin and Greek, mathematics, philosophy, astronomy, rhetoric, logic and chemistry; drawing, painting and embroidery were offered for $15 additional tuition. Louisa Marling, wife of Jacob Marling, was the teacher of drawing and painting in 1815 and was accordingly singled out for praise in the Raleigh *Star* on November 17, 1815:

"The trustees had the peculiar gratification of being able, for the last half year, to afford to the female department, a teacher every way qualified to give instructions in drawing and painting – Mrs. Marling, who was occasionally assisted by Mr. Marling, of whose abilities it would be unnecessary to speak here."

And Mr. Marling's "abilities" have produced a rare piece of history in this painting, "The Crowning of Flora." Here Marling has captured the elaborate setting and decorations for the May Day exercises of the Raleigh Academy on Burke Square. According to an account in Lynchburg's *Echo* of July 10, 1816, and recorded in the Summer, 1988, newsletter of MESDA, "The Luminary:"

"On the first day of May, the young ladies belonging to the Raleigh female academy assembled under the wide spreading trees which embosom their building, and proceeded to the election of a queen. Miss Mary DuBose of Georgia, was the successful candidate. She was conducted to the rural throne. . . [and] crowned with a chaplet of flowers. . . . [An] address to the queen was read, by Miss Anne W. Clark, of Georgia. . . . The echoes of the grove were awakened by the melody of music, and the mirthful scene impressed all so happily, that the students will long believe *this day was not lost.* Mr. Marling, so well known for his skill and taste in painting, was present, and sketched a likeness of the May queen, as she appeared in her ensigns of royalty; and the lovers of the fine arts, may expect to be gratified with a sight of the picture, at his exhibition gallery, when it shall have received the finishing touches of his pencil."

Perhaps the gentleman in the middle on the right is the Reverend William McPheeters, the man on his left the Academy's music instructor, and could it be possible that the tall man at the far right is the artist himself?

What is even more intriguing is that through the trees on the right can be seen the cupola and weathervane of the first State House before it was remodeled by William Nichols, beginning around 1818. And to the left, Marling has painted the recently completed Raleigh branch of the State Bank of North Carolina with its classical double portico of Doric columns, which in 1816 was so vividly seen from the southwest corner of Burke Square.

Jacob Marling died in 1833. Several of the portraits, which were in his possession at the time of his death, were sold by the Administrator of his estate in 1835. Among them were the portraits of Governor William Miller and Dr. William McPheeters. The painting, referred to then as "The May Queen," was found in the effects of Mrs. Marling upon her death. Its whereabouts was not known for many years afterward. According to "The Luminary," it was illustrated in 1943 in The Old Print Shop *Portfolio*, a sales catalogue, as a "Young Ladies Seminary in Virginia. *Artist Unknown.*"

A gift of Edgar William and Bernice Chrysler Garbisch to the Chrysler Museum, Norfolk, Virginia, the painting has now been identified as Jacob Marling's "The Crowning of Flora," depicting the May Day activities, not at a Virginia Ladies Seminary, but at the Raleigh Academy on Burke Square in Raleigh, North Carolina.

*Added for 1992 edition

The Crowning of Flora
Jacob Marling
Oil on canvas, 30 1/8" x 39 1/8"
Courtesy of the Chrysler Museum, Norfolk, Virginia, Gift of Edgar William and Bernice Chrysler Garbisch

Burke Square - 200 North Blount Street

The Raleigh Academy
Built 1804 - Destroyed Before 1889

Shortly after Raleigh was laid out, education began to concern most citizens inasmuch as prior to establishment of the Raleigh Academy, shown here, students were either sent away for "learnin," remained unlearned, or attended the one existing school which was run by German Guthrie and a Mrs. Langley.

In November of 1801, forty local people asked for State aid in starting the Academy and at the same time petitioned the Legislature for the use of Burke Square or Burke's Garden, as it was sometimes called, as a likely place to site the proposed institution. They got both. And on March 27, 1802, the General Assembly appointed as the School's Trustees: William White, Sherwood Haywood, John Craven, Nathaniel Jones, Matthew McCullers, William Hinton, Joseph Gales, William Boylan, Henry Seawell, Samuel High, Theophilus Hunter, Jr., John Ingles, Simon Turner, and John Marshall.

Raising the money for a building, however, was more complicated. For that goal, the efforts of practically the whole town were enlisted. Subscriptions were undertaken, the ladies gave "Academy" teas, the Thespians performed for the cause, donations were solic-

ited, and lotteries were held. Finally, on July 2, 1804, the two-story frame building was opened for the education of both sexes.

Fees for matriculation included three dollars per quarter for reading and writing, four dollars for advanced English, and five for classics. Other courses taught were Bible, Latin, Greek, geography, and mathematics. Such a curriculum would seem heavy, indeed, for the teaching staff of two, Miss Charlotte Bodie and a French Hugenot refugee named the Reverend Martin Detargny.

At the time, the Academy's building, fifty by twenty-five feet, was considered extremely commodious though in 1807 another building, "The Female Department," was erected. The School served well then for the next quarter century as the Piedmont's educational Mecca and only declined about 1829 when other institutions were established and competition became too keen.

In 1830 the buildings and equipment were sold to William Peace who was then treasurer of the Academy's Trustees. And, here it must be mentioned that the famous Lovejoy Academy was on this site as of January, 1842, and continued there until 1877.

16 North Boylan Avenue

Elmwood

Circa 1810

Raleigh Historic Site 1969, National Register Property 1975

Named for the trees which originally bordered its circular carriage way, Elmwood was built by North Carolina's first Chief Justice of the Supreme Court, John Louis Taylor, on a sixty-five acre tract which he bought from State Treasurer John Haywood in 1810.

Though the address of the house is now sixteen North Boylan Avenue, its original five-acre residential lawns swept to Hillsborough on the south, St. Mary's on the west, Glenwood on the east, and to "Devereux Grounds" on the north. Later, continuation of Boylan Avenue to the north was jogged westward in order not to disturb this dwelling.

Toward the rear of the mansion every potential need and creature comfort of the period was anticipated. There were, among other structures, an ice house which was filled when Raleigh ponds froze, a carriage house, kitchen dependency, wood house, smokehouse, brick ash house for storing ashes later to be made into soap, stables, a barn, and a sweet-water well. Flower and vegetable gardens, fruit trees of all kinds, and shrubs abounded on the site.

The original asymmetrical house, as measured drawings indicate, was built with only seven beautifully proportioned rooms but with later additions on the west and with an added north wing – made by attaching the outside kitchen to the house, its rooms now number as many as fifteen.

The bannister of the stairway, which inclines to the three floors, is mahogany and much of the woodwork inside is classically hand-carved. The heavy wainscoting also appears on the three floors.

Early occupants of the place were four judges, Taylor, the builder, Judge William Gaston who wrote *The Old North State*, Chief Justice Thomas Ruffin, and Judge Romulus M. Saunders, Minister to Spain. The house was bought by W. H. Willard in 1872 and was later passed to North Carolina historian Samuel A. Ashe, the former's son-in-law. Two of Caption Ashe's daughters, Mrs. William H. Bason and Mrs. Joseph A. Graef, own and live in Elmwood today.

Judge John Louis Taylor was born in London in 1769, of Irish ancestry. He came to America at the age of twelve, was educated at William and Mary College, settled in Fayetteville to read the law, and was admitted to the bar at twenty-two. He was married to Julia Rowan for whose family Rowan County is named, and after her death, married Judge Gaston's sister. He died in 1829 and was buried under one of the elms of Elmwood. His body was later moved to Oakwood Cemetery.

In 1981 Federal tax credits for the rehabilitation of certified historic structures for income-producing uses were enacted. The location of Elmwood and these credits enhanced the value of the house as office space. The family sold the property in 1983 to a partnership to develop commercially, and in doing so, to preserve and protect it. Office space was created and occupied for several years; but since early 1990, tenancy had decreased and in mid-1991 the house was virtually empty and in need of repairs.

Elmwood derives its importance both from its outstanding architecture and from the many distinguished North Carolinians who have owned and occupied it. Known as the "House of Judges," it is one of the most distinguished homes in Raleigh, as well as in North Carolina. It is devoutly hoped that it will soon be restored again to its rightful place in history.

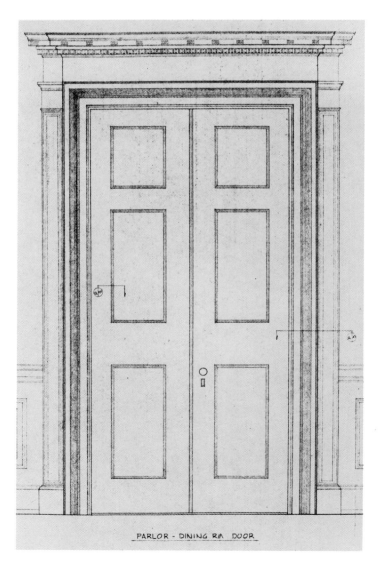

PARLOR - DINING RM DOOR

Yates Mill Wheel, 1960s photograph

Lake Wheeler Road at Penny Road

Grist Mills

Edwards' Circa 1766, Lassiter's Circa 1776, Whitaker's Circa 1777
All Destroyed in This Century
Yates Mill – Early Nineteenth Century
Raleigh Historic Site 1990, National Register Property 1970

About two miles apart and located on Crabtree Creek, Whitaker's, Lassiter's, and Edwards' mills have been swallowed by northward expansion of the City. They are known by the names of their late nineteenth and early twentieth century owners, but at least two of these original dams and buildings were sited on Issac Hunter land in the last part of the eighteenth century and pre-date the founding of Raleigh by fifteen or more years.

Whitaker's Mill was built by Issac Hunter in 1777 and for a number of years it was operated as a paper mill by one Elihu Sater. During the Civil War it became a Confederate powder mill. Profiting by word of explosions in other powder-converted mills, the owners of that time, House and Bose, built six or seven separate buildings, connecting them only with plank walkways. In an effort to diminish explosion danger, copper nails were used in their con-

Lassiter's Mill, 1910

Lassiter Mill Road at Crabtree Creek

struction and workers, before going in, shed their footwear in fear of sparks from shoe tacks against metal. And yet in April, 1865, one of General Sherman's inexperienced sergeants and three Yankee soldiers were sent to blow up the mill and powder houses. They did so, but unfortunately, also blew up themselves in the act.

For four years after destruction, the mill site lay idle and was then bought, in 1869, by J. D. Whitaker and his brother, Willis, from A. B. Ward. At this time the earth and wood of the dam were replaced by stone and around 1918 the place was sold to J. W. Dixon. That mill was known to be humming in the early 'twenties of this century but was later destroyed.

Lassiter's Mill, above, or "Great Falls on the Crabtree" as it was originally called, was the six-acre tract of land which Isaac Hunter reserved for siting his first grist mill. Little is known of the man named Pink Warren but it is said that he and his father built most of the early Crabtree Creek mills, and the father was quoted as saying that "Great Falls" was the oldest of them all. This mill burned in 1804 and was rebuilt sometime later.

After the Civil War John C. Drewry and Wiley Webb formed a company to start a 5,000-spindle cotton mill on the site but plans were abandoned and the luscious area, when street car tracks were extended north, became Raleigh's popular picnic and boating resort, Bloomsbury Park.

By 1908 only a few stones of the original dam were left and it was at this time that Cornelius Jesse Lassiter, who had operated a lumber mill since 1891 on a tract seven miles north of this site, bought the place. Cornelius Lassiter's descendants say that when he was a boy during flour shortages of the Civil War, he could only have one hot biscuit a week. For this reason he told his mother, Margaret, that one day he would build himself a flour mill so he could have all the biscuits he wanted. So he did.

Lassiter, with eight other men, used up the better part of two days clearing the forest to make a road for hauling in building supplies to rebuild the dam and mill house. That woodland road stretched from the present Lassiter's to a path now known as Glenwood Avenue. Two forty-horse turbine wheels were installed to generate the plant's

power and, aside from the milling and recreation businesses, the Lassiters shortly added a lumber mill – seen far right in this circa 1910 photograph. Cornelius Lassiter died in 1949 and his heirs continued operating the place until it burned in 1959. Their milling, however, continues on another site.

Edwards' Mill, upstream about two miles from Lassiter's, was bought around 1866 by J. Thomas Edwards and his son, Demetrious M. Edwards, from the estate of Scott Tucker who had bought it from Hines Whitaker. The title, at that time, was searched back a hundred years, dating the original dam about 1766, and seeming to place it, strangely enough, ten years earlier than the other two.

Apropos of Edwards' Mill and writing about it in 1928, a Raleigh *News and Observer* correspondent said that even these wild and secluded spots are "Threatened by encroaching civilization. A new road is to be cut through the woods . . . from the new site of Meredith College west of the City . . . coming into Leesville Road a few hundred yards below Edwards' Mill." And the old place has long since been claimed by the Raleigh-Durham highway.

The snowy detail of Yates Mill and the building, right, located on Yates Pond south of Raleigh, were taken relatively recently. This mill is the only one of the four treated here which is still standing and was formerly one of the most diversified since, at various times, it generated power for lumber manufacturing, corn and wheat milling, and wool carding.

The mill was bought before 1861 from William Boylan by four men, most of them familiar names to earlier parts of this book – James Dodd, Thomas Briggs, James Penny, and William Primrose. The other three owners then sold their shares to Mr. Penny and it was during the Civil War that Phares Yates bought the property and 600 acres surrounding it from Penny. Subsequently it was acquired by A. E. Finley and later given to North Carolina State University.

Yates Mill can definitely be dated to around 1810-1820, but some parts of the structure could date back as early as the mid-1750s. A mill site was originally surveyed for Samuel Pearson in 1756 and granted to him by the Earl of Granville in 1761. Pearson's son inherited the mill in 1800, but in 1820 was forced to sell the property in a sheriff's sale.

William Boylan was the purchaser.

In 1989, Yates Mill Associates, a non-profit group, was organized to preserve Yates Mill and to work with North Carolina State University in a joint effort to preserve the structure and the site as a visual, yet educational, reminder of Wake County's rich agricultural heritage. As work begins, the site becomes even more intriguing. A breached stone dam and other stones which appear to be foundation stones have been uncovered on the south side of Penny Road. Could this be the remains of the mid-1750s mill, or is Yates Mill an eighteenth century mill rather than early nineteenth century? Hopefully research, time and adequate funding will make answers to these questions possible.

Yates Mill, 1960s photograph

Lake Wheeler Road at Penny Road

2 West Edenton Street

The Eagle Hotel
Built 1812 - Demolished 1922

The architectural purity and the subtle "Southerness" of the Eagle Hotel, opened at the corner of Halifax and Edenton by proprietor Charles Parish, charmed the City for a hundred years. As documented by this 1890 photograph, which reveals the State House fence with its adorning gas lamps in the foreground, the Eagle enjoyed a choice location and was considered "Raleigh's finest."

When finished, on July 1, 1812, it was advertised as having, among other niceties, the "luxuries of rooms, beds, attendance, etc." and promised that "an ice house and bathing rooms will be constructed next season." It must be said here, however, that apropos these proposals, Honorable David L. Swain, who was Governor between 1832 and 1835, recalled in his *Early Times in Raleigh*, "I hope he performed all the promised, though I found no bathing rooms at the Eagle, ten years thereafter."

The place was, except for the original State House and perhaps Casso's Inn, the Capital's first brick building, certainly its most

aesthetically satisfying. And though the structure would seem to be almost square in the accompanying photograph, it was actually L-shaped. This fact is faithfully recorded on an 1872 aerial map prepared by C. N. Drie who drew his *Bird's Eye View of the City of Raleigh*, from actual balloon ascensions.

The Eagle, altered under different managers in the nineteenth century, was variously re-named. It was first changed to the Guion, later the National Hotel. It was used as a school and during the Civil War, according to the contemporaneous ledgers of Vitruvius Royster, it was used as headquarters for Confederate conscription. Finally, in 1881, Governor Thomas J. Jarvis influenced the General Assembly to buy the property, proposing that it be used for State office space. The early, monumentally historical place was torn down in 1922 to make room for the State Department of Agriculture Building.

123 New Bern Avenue

State Bank

Cornerstone Laid 1813
Raleigh Historic Site 1969, National Register Property 1970
Moved Approximately 75 Feet East and 25 Feet South 1968
Restored 1969

This building, the Raleigh branch of the State Bank of North Carolina, remains where it was erected, on the historic property at eleven New Bern Avenue. The State Bank was chartered in 1810 because until then, there was no State banking institution. As well, dissatisfaction prevailed at that time between the State and the two existing private banks, those of New Bern and Cape Fear. And especially, the new arrangements were to "equalize the relation between currency and specie."

Plans were shortly made to situate the State Bank's central branch in Raleigh, with others at Edenton, Wilmington, Fayetteville, New Bern, Tarboro, and Salisbury. The capital stock was not to exceed $1,600,000 and of that, $250,000 was to be reserved for the State.

During the War of 1812 there was justifiable fear that the British Navy would attack North Carolina's coast and all specie money was quickly transferred from those coastal towns to the inland State Banks at Raleigh and Tarboro. The main bank at Raleigh was thereby strengthened sufficiently in 1813 to afford this brick structure. Its original entrance was on the New Bern Avenue side; its bricks were hand-fabricated; its first president was Colonel William Polk of Revolutionary War fame who also made his home in the bank building.

In 1832 another bank succeeded the first as the building's owner and successfully operated its banking affairs until the Civil War intervened to send it into bankruptcy. After the War, on January 13, 1873, the United States District Court, acting upon its insolvency decision, ordered all of the bank's "vaults, effects, building, and lands" to be turned over to Christ Church, which stood on contiguous property, for their purchase price of $9,925.

The building has since been kept in repair and used for various purposes by the Church. And it is hoped that nothing will mar, change, or replace the old Bank on its original site since it has been declared by the United States Department of the Interior's Historic American Buildings Survey to be "worthy of the most careful preservation for the benefit of future generations. . . ."

After being used by the church for its Rectory, for its Sunday School, and as Raleigh's first Cerebral Palsy Center, the State Bank was purchased in 1968 by North Carolina National Bank which moved it approximately 75 feet east and 25 feet south. It was then meticulously restored by NCNB to its original use, having completed the entire adaptive use cycle. This building, which is the oldest commercial building in Raleigh, and said to be the oldest brick building in Wake County, is now owned by the State Employees Credit Union.

Colonel William Polk House

Circa 1815

Burned 1975

Colonel Thomas Polk, a well educated patriot, saw action in the American Revolution and won fame when, under almost impossible circumstances, he procured supplies for the Revolutionary Army. He had helped in establishing the city of Charlotte and had been surveyor for the North and South Carolina border.

His son, Colonel William Polk, like his father, fought in the Revolution. Enlisting as little more than a child, he served at Brandywine, was twice wounded, seriously at the battle of Germantown, and spent that disastrous winter with General Washington at Valley Forge. *He lived to be North Carolina's last surviving member of the Continental line.*

In 1799, after the death of his wife, Grizelle Gilchrist, Polk moved from Mecklenburg County to Raleigh and a year later purchased a tract of land just outside the north boundary of the city, east of Halifax Street and extending to Grassy Branch which is now inside Oakwood Cemetery. On this land he built a plantation, complete with outbuildings, stables, granaries, cotton gin, and quarters for his Negroes.

In 1801 Polk married Sarah Hawkins of Warren County. He served as the first president of the Raleigh branch of the State Bank of North Carolina, without compensation, and he and his family lived in the bank building when it was completed. Then, in 1815, he began construction of his residence on his plantation at the head of Blount Street. It was said to be the finest house in Raleigh. His old friend, General LaFayette, dined there when he visited Raleigh in 1825. Polk was also a trustee of the University of North Carolina for 42 years and was active in the civic and social life of Raleigh.

After William Polk's death in 1834, his son-in-law, Kenneth Rayner, acquired the property and by the 1840s began selling off parcels. In 1871 the residence itself was bought by R. Stanhope Pullen. In Drie's *Bird's Eye View of Raleigh*, 1872, this house still stood at the head of Blount Street. It was then moved to midway between North and Polk streets for the extension of Blount Street. The Polk homestead land was then bought, in 1872, by Colonel A. B. Andrews.

On its new site the building was used as a Baptist school for girls and later a boarding house. In 1903 the place was sold to William H. Williamson, some of it torn down and again it was moved, this time to the Pilot Mills area where it has since been occupied variously by another school, the Junior Order Hall, a community center, and various commercial purposes.

It was during one of these moves that Colonel Polk's favorite item of decor, and one which was characteristic of the man's personality, was lost. The piece hung over the family's parlor mantel and was a spread-eagle scroll bearing Commodore Perry's words, "We have met the enemy and they are ours." The carving, made of plaster, was thrown out into the rain, by the workmen. Also, as may be seen in the photograph, the builder somehow ordered one too many mantels and being a thrifty Scotsman (the name was originally Pollok) he could not simply dispose of the expensive fixture. Instead, he placed it as a sort of bas-relief in the pediment of the two-story, front portico.

By the time the Polk House burned in March of 1975, it was beyond recognition as one of Raleigh's handsomest mansions.

Head of North Blount Street

*1 East South Street**

Governor's Palace
Built 1816 - Destroyed 1885

After it became law (1794) for North Carolina governors to live in the Capital, a residence and small, separate office were provided for them at the corner of Fayetteville and Hargett streets. These buildings were anything but pretentious, according to contemporary reports, and in 1813 a commission including the State Treasurer, Comptroller, Secretary of State, and six private citizens was authorized to sell a sufficient number of State-owned, Raleigh lots to raise $10,000 for a brick "Palace."

Property values were depressed because of the War of 1812 and it became necessary to sell 184 acres of public land in order to raise the necessary amount. Reserved for the building was an eight-acre tract, the site of the present Memorial Auditorium, and on July 15, 1814, the *Raleigh Register* advertised for construction bids. James Calder of Washington, North Carolina, was given the contract for preparing plans for the structure. Finished in 1816, it was first occupied by incumbent Governor William Miller of Warren County.

The exterior dimensions were seventy by fifty feet, the foundation was of hewn rock, and an iron rail served the stone steps. The fanlighted main entrance, leading from the Ionic portico, was paneled; and directly opposite this door a spiral staircase ascended from the central hallway through the second floor to the attic. The attic and upper floor were pierced by a skylight which illuminated the building's central spaces.

After the State House fire of 1831 the residence was temporarily used to house the General Assembly but its livability as a private residence was never particularly recommended by any of the governors who lived in it between 1816 and 1865. In fact, at various times appropriations had to be made for alterations, renovations, and eventually, gaslighting.

Finally, the building was declared unfit for the governors' residence after General Sherman, using it as his Raleigh headquarters, moved out of the place after the Civil War. Hence in 1876 the building was used for the Centennial Graded School until it was razed for a new school structure in 1885.

The photograph reproduced here was made just prior to demolition.

*Site of the Memorial Auditorium.

Washington at the Passage of the Delaware
Thomas Sully
Oil on canvas, 12 1/2' x 17'
Boston Museum of Fine Arts

Thomas Sully Paintings
Authorized in 1800 - Commissioned in 1816

In 1800, fired by post-Revolution enthusiasm, the General Assembly authorized Governor Benjamin Williams to buy two portraits of George Washington and designated that they were to hang in the yet unfinished first State House. The portraits were not commissioned, however, for many years because of the seeming expense involved. And it was not until 1816 that the matter was reopened and American painter Thomas Sully was invited to do the proposed Washington likenesses.

It is unfortunate that because of a "slight" oversight the original painting, "Washington at the Passage of the Delaware," shown above and costing $600, never arrived in Raleigh. It came about when someone failed to give the painter specific dimensions of the wall upon which it was to be hung. And when Sully was well along with the work, it was discovered that the picture, twelve and a half feet by seventeen, was far too large for the allocated wall space.

Generously enough, Sully then released the State of its obligation and the painting was sold to a Boston frame maker, later to be hung, 1892, in the Boston Museum of Fine Arts.

The standing "Portrait of Washington" is a copy, an endorsed practice at the time, of the "Lansdowne" portrait of Washington by Gilbert Stuart who was a famous contemporary of the General. This canvas, commissioned for $400 plus $100 for the frame, arrived in Raleigh November 26, 1818. And it is known from correspondence between Governor William Miller and the artist that the picture's transit from Philadelphia to Raleigh cost, for storage, drayage, and freight, $6.80. This painting was one of the scarce items which survived the State House fire of June, 1831, and it hangs now in the central position within the Capitol's House Chamber.

Thomas Sully was born in Lincolnshire, England, in June of 1783, as the youngest son of Matthew and Sarah Sully who were actors. They and their nine children migrated to the old theatrical town of Charleston, South Carolina, in 1792 where young Sully began to study painting. In 1805 he moved north, having in the meantime married his brother's widow. Through such friends as Gilbert Stuart he settled in Philadelphia and became an American citizen in 1809. There, in 1810, he hung out his shingle which read "History and Portrait Painter." He died in 1872.

Marinus W. Pike of Philadelphia, who prepared canvases and frames for Rembrandt Peale and Thomas Sully, prepared this original frame which retains his label, for the "Portrait of Washington."

The Conservation Staff of the North Carolina Museum of Art restored this painting in 1980-81 with funds provided by the North Carolina Council of State, the Raleigh Fine Arts Society and the North Carolina Society of the Cincinnati. During this restoration work the conservators discovered that in the lower left-hand corner, the artist had signed the canvas with an interlocking TS and the date 1818.

"Lansdowne" Portrait of Washington
Thomas Sully copy of Gilbert Stuart
Oil on canvas, 8' x 4' 11 3/4"
North Carolina State Capitol

Dr. Fabius Haywood House
Built 1818 - Destroyed 1911

The son of State Treasurer John Haywood, Dr. Fabius Julius Haywood was born in Haywood Hall on October 26, 1803. He was graduated from the University of North Carolina in 1822 and from the University of Pennsylvania Medical School in 1827. Returning to Raleigh, he was one of the City's most respected physicians and is thought to have been the first medical man in the State to use the "new" anesthesia, chloroform, in operative procedures. He married beautiful, wealthy Martha Helen Whitaker, granddaughter of a Colonial surveyor for the British Crown, Joseph Whitaker of Virginia. Grandfather Whitaker had surveyed the line between North Carolina and Virginia and, for his work, had been paid in plantation land rather than in pounds sterling. Martha was one of his heirs.

Living in a large house farther south on Fayetteville Street, Martha Whitaker must have known and fallen in love with Fabius Haywood, as a neighbor in the little town. In any case, their marriage, it is said by descendants, was a good match and five children were born of it – Fabius, the younger, Sallie, who died when only six years old, Mary, Joseph, and John. The tasteful and straightforward Georgian style house was their home. Earlier the building had been used by a Raleigh branch of the Bank of New Bern.

Located on the southwest corner of Morgan and Fayetteville streets, its grounds spanned the lot numbered 163 on an 1847 Raleigh map, through to Salisbury, the residence facing Fayetteville, Dr. Haywood's office, West Morgan Street. The office was a separate, small building. And about the office, it is well documented that near by were planted mulberry trees because on the third floor of this house, the Haywoods cultured silkworms which they had earlier fattened on the mulberries.

Union officers, 1865, were quartered in this residence and about 1880, after Dr. Haywood became ill and moved to live with his daughter, Mary, in the old Fowle house, the property was used variously as a club and as housing for commercial firms. It was destroyed by the State in 1911 for the erection of a building to house the Supreme Court, the State Library, and the Historical Commission.

As a rather unusual postscript, it must be added that the house, tall and eloquent, was painted into the background of Jacob Marling's canvas of the first State House. And Haywood family tradition says that Dr. Haywood's father appears in this painting as the man in the foreground, with his hand over his ear.

Figure in doorway of Dr. Fabius Haywood house –
showing Fayetteville Street

Dr. Fabius Haywood House

Corner of Fayetteville and West Morgan streets

4700 Six Forks Road until 1978

Mary Hunter Beavers House
Circa 1819
Moved to 10809 Honeycutt Road 1978

Mary Hunter, granddaughter of Isaac Hunter, of Raleigh's original siting fame, was the daughter of Sarah Rogers and Jacob Hunter, Isaac's eldest son. Jacob died in 1798 and Mary married Almond Beavers in 1819, the same year this place is thought to have been built. According to custom then, the house might well have been a wedding gift from Mary's mother, Sarah.

Almond Beavers died in 1828 and Mary, the mother of five children, married Robert Perry, father of two sons, in 1831. Suc-

cessively, several generations of the Hunter family were heirs to the property and in 1933, the aging place, its crumbling dependencies, and thirty and a half acres surrounding it were bought for $3,500 by Clifton W. Stoffregen. The Stoffregens wired it for electricity, turned the back wing of the original L-shaped house into bedrooms and bath, added a kitchen wing, left, a porch, right. They enclosed the rear-wing porch and built other rooms to adjoin it, making the place, rather than the traditional L, almost square. The owners also

removed the slave quarters and, taking boxwood cuttings from early planting in the front, produced a small, formal garden in the rear.

In the restoration, care was taken to preserve the six- inch, mellowed pine flooring, the remaining hand-made glass panes, height of the eleven and a half foot ceilings, the beaded, eleven-inch baseboards, wooden pegs of the house's frame, and the original, enclosed chimneys. And the natural stones of the foundation, gathered from the property, were cemented together at the time of the renovation.

Mr. and Mrs. Stoffregen, Jr., who inherited the place and currently live there, continue with the house's revitalization. As a professional forester, Stoffregen is particularly concerned with preserving the 200-year-old white oaks which surround the property – trees which pre-date the house by many seasons.

This residence is located at 4700 Six Forks Road.

"If I ever left, I'd take the house with me," stated Bill Stoffregen in 1973. This he did in 1978 when he moved it to 10809 Honeycutt Road to escape encroaching commercial development. The early nineteenth century structure is now incorporated into a much larger house.

State Capitol Rotunda

George Washington by Antonio Canova

Unveiled 1821 - Burned 1831

Recarved and Replaced on Original Foundation 1970

It was Thomas Jefferson, writing from Monticello to our General Assembly on January 22, 1816, who suggested that such a work as the Legislature had described and wished to commission should come from the chisel of Antonio Canova, eminent Italian sculptor of the day. In his correspondence, Jefferson also forewarned his inquirers that, in all probability, Canova would do the piece in the neo-classical manner, complete with the subject in ancient Roman dress. The Jefferson warning, however, did not keep Raleigh citizens from being surprised when they actually saw the Romanized Washington at its State House unveiling on December 24, 1821. The figure remained the most famous art work in America for many years and was the envy of other capital cities throughout the Country.

The piece, larger than life, was cracked to pieces, as is already known, by falling timbers in the State House fire of 1831, only ten years after it had arrived in the City. It was hoped, in any case, that the sculpture might be repaired and the rotunda of the new 1840 State House was designed with this in mind. But these hopes were soon dashed when Robert Ball Hughes, who had been hired for the restoration job, absconded with his fee plus important pieces of the marble figure itself. And so it was never repaired. In 1911, however, the Italian Government presented the State with a plaster cast of the working model, which at present may be seen in the North Carolina Museum of History in Raleigh.

Earlier in this century, attempts to have the figure recarved from the same pointing-up model which is still preserved in the Canova Museum in Possagno, had failed. A more immediate proposal toward this aim was rejected by the 1967 Legislature only to be reversed in the same session by a patriotic Fourth of July appeal through Representative Mrs. John Chase of Wayne County. The statue will be reproduced and will be restored to its original site in the Capitol's rotunda.

It is fitting to note that it was exactly 152 years earlier, on July 4, 1815, that the original idea of acquiring a statue of Washington for North Carolina was first implanted in the minds of the citizens and legislators in Raleigh, by A. G. Glynn.

Antonio Canova was born in Possagno in 1757. His more important work includes statues of Princess Borghese, Hercules and Lichas, Clement XIII, tomb bas-reliefs, and neo- classical pieces of all kinds. He died in 1821 and though his body was interred in Possagno, his hands were buried in Venice.

On October 10, 1970, a recarved Canova statue of George Washington, from the original pointing-up model, was dedicated in the rotunda of the State Capitol. While preparing the site for the statue, which weighed 4,500 pounds with a base weighing 17,100 pounds, workmen discovered the original brickwork foundation filled with debris from the 1831 fire, under the stone floor of the rotunda. This original foundation was reinforced and filled with concrete, the debris having been removed. The stone floor was then replaced and the statue installed. Antonio Canova's George Washington had come home again.

2100 Spring Forest Road

Travianna
Circa 1825
Demolished 1982

Travianna, near Raleigh on Spring Forest Road, was built early in the nineteenth century, perhaps on the Isaac Hunter tract.

The place, having been used as a tenant house, was seriously deteriorating before its reclamation in the 1930's. Now, two rooms on either end of the structure have been added and the original, outside dining room and kitchen have been restored as guest quarters. Otherwise it has remained essentially the same as it was when built. Its interior detailing is surprisingly sophisticated what with the heavily plastered walls, matching baseboard and chair rail, solid brass hardware, and its finely moulded woodwork.

Except for the three front doors which are quite unusual, the plan is typical of the early nineteenth century lean-to farm house seen so often in this part of the South. And although the pitched-roof, rectangle design with its two bilateral chimneys was common in all of the Colonies, the outswept porch of this house is of Southern origin. The innovation probably came first to North Carolina coastal towns enjoying commerce with the West Indies where this type of post treatment existed. Obviously the innovation was a welcome adaptation since it afforded sheltered outdoor living space and read rather as another room, one which reached out to invite, for a time, the passing traveler or guest.

The 1930 reclamation was the work of Ivan Clendenin; in the 1940s, Mr. and Mrs. Tom Grier added an additional wing to the rear. The name Travianna was given to the place by the present owners.

In 1978 Travianna and 24.77 acres surrounding it were purchased for development. Although the house was sound and of the size and scale of the houses in the new neighborhood, it was demolished. A street placed near the site of the old dwelling is named in its memory.

Northwest Corner South Dawson and West Hargett streets

Cosby-Heartt House
Built In Two Parts
Early 1800s - Circa 1830 - Demolished 1954

Cosby-Heartt House

Torn down in 1954 to be replaced by a filling station, this two-period residence was the creation as well as the home of Dabney Cosby, local architect, and an earlier, unknown builder. The original, Federal-style section, seen in the above photograph, was a heavy, serenely plain, brick structure built at the corner of Dawson and Hargett streets.

At the time Architect Cosby bought the place he joined the

existing building to his own new addition, the balconied, Tuscan Villa house, a mid-century vogue which was thought to have been regenerated by New York's popular architect, Alexander Jackson Davis. The fireplaces particularly distinguish the older house from the later, some of the newer having ornate, Americana supporting consoles for the mantels while the earlier ones were simple, utilitarian planes.

Dabney Cosby came originally from Augusta County, Virginia, and practiced his profession both there and in North Carolina. In Raleigh he operated his own Hargett Street brickyard in which he trained his one hundred slaves to mold plaster and fire brick for his designs. And, as seen in this Greek-motif moulding of the front house's drawing room, Cosby was apparently a sensitive practitioner and a successful teacher to his artisans.

Walls of the older part were eighteen inches thick, those of the new about twelve, and were covered with stucco while the rear wall, perhaps with expansion in mind, was finished with wooden siding. The ceilings were fifteen feet high, fenestration was generously wide, and plaster mouldings around the fireplaces were curved to enclose the chimney stacks. The floors were made of wide oak flooring and joined with expert care.

Concerning the floors, it is said that when Dabney Cosby's daughter heard that the Yankees were nearing Raleigh she had Uncle Billy, an elderly slave, cut through the oak floorboards in the front hallway, and there install a trapdoor. The carpet-covered opening became a repository for all family valuables.

Cosby died during the Civil War and it was his daughter, married to Leo D. Heartt, a Raleigh merchant, who inherited the property. Thus, the name Heartt was thereafter associated with the place. It remained in the builder's family until it was demolished.

114 South Dawson Street

McPheeters House
Circa 1830
Demolished 1973

The McPheeters house at 114 South Dawson is the only remaining residence in its block and seems to be a contained microcosm of Raleigh's past and present. The place was designed about 1830 by a neighbor of the owner, local architect, Dabney Cosby. Architect Cosby had the bricks fired by slave labor at a plant on Hargett Street and though covered with white stucco, they were so carefully laid that they might well remain, like Roman brickwork, indefinitely – if not swallowed by the bulldozer. Examination of the masonry also reveals double-brick bearing walls which continue into the earth to form the house's foundation. For insulation, a dead air space was left between these two wall components.

The interior of the residence remains spacious and unchopped, unlike so many of the period which have been axed into smaller living units. On the first floor the drawing room, library, parlor, and dining room may all be thrown together by opening two-panel doors and the hardware of these sliding doors operates them as it did in the beginning.

The Reverend William McPheeters, who was born in Scotland in 1778, came to Raleigh with his wife, nee Margaret Ann McDaniel, in 1810. Immediately upon arrival he assumed the duties of "Pastor of the City," a position previously held by W. L. Turner.

Also, McPheeters had come here to take Turner's post as head-master to the Raleigh Academy. This he did and remained that school's "excellent educator" until 1826 when he resigned to establish a girls' boarding school.

In the meantime, the Academy's trustees had bought land on Jones Street and built a residence for the Reverend and his family. But when McPheeters left the school it was local merchant William Peace, who, having earlier advanced money to the Academy, bought back the Jones Street property. And McPheeters was free to build his Dawson Street home.

From this house, and among his other activities, William McPheeters officiated as Minister of the First Presbyterian Church, a body which he had organized on January 21, 1816. It was during his pastorate here that a church was built at the corner of Morgan and Salisbury, one which became, for a time, the meeting place of many Raleigh Christians. The Reverend McPheeters died in Raleigh, 1842.

The Dawson Street property has remained in the McPheeters family throughout its long life and at present its chatelaine is Miss Susan McPheeters, granddaughter of the builder.

After the death of Miss McPheeters, her heirs sold the property for commercial development. The house was demolished in 1973 and the land is still utilized as a parking lot.

59

Main Building, now called Smedes Hall   *Saint Mary's Campus, 900 Hillsborough Street*

Saint Mary's School
1834 and 1835
National Register District 1978
East Rock, West Rock, Smedes Hall, Raleigh Historic Sites 1969

The General Assembly of 1833 granted a charter to the trustees of Raleigh's Episcopal boy's school, and the North Carolina Diocese of the denomination promptly bought 159 1/2 acres west of the City for the school's location. The land was purchased from Colonel William Polk at a cost of $1,619.37. But construction of the school's first two buildings, East Rock, 1834, and West Rock, 1835, could not have been too costly inasmuch as the stones used in them were discards from those quarried for the second State House. Actually, it seems that any citizen who could haul away the unsuitable rock was welcome to do so. Perhaps the institution was not too successful

since it lasted only four years and was suspended by action of the trustees in July of 1837. The property was then bought by Duncan Cameron in payment for debts equal to $8,886.66 which the budding school had incurred.

In 1842, a northerner, the Reverend Aldert Smedes, advertised by means of newspapers and circulars in New York City that he desired "to open a school for Young Ladies in the City of Raleigh, N. C., on the 12th day of May next. . . the School Buildings, situated in a beautiful and elevated Oak Grove, furnish the most spacious accommodation. . . . Terms for Board (including washing and incidental expenses), with tuition in English, Latin, etc., $100 per Session, payable in advance. . . extra charges. . . for French, Music, Drawing. . . Needlework."

Saint Mary's then began to prosper, witnessed by the fact that it remained open during the Civil War, both for schooling and as a sanctuary for such people as Mildred Lee, daughter of Robert E. Lee, Mrs. Jefferson Davis, three Davis children, and others. It is known, too, that school kept after the War, when Confederate money was worthless, since in 1865, Dr. Smedes let it be known that the fifty-dollar board fee might be payable in provisions: "$8 per barrel of flour; $6 for corn; 16 2/3 cents per pound for lard, poultry, molasses and sorghum allowance in like proportion." More food came from the campus garden, books from homes, and heat from the brick kiln in the Main building's basement.

Today, as when the stagecoach brought day students "out from Raleigh," East Rock, West Rock, the little chapel, Smedes Hall, and "the grove" speak of the original beauty of Hillsborough Street.

Further research has determined that the boys' school actually closed in December, 1838.

As Saint Mary's celebrates its sesquicentennial in 1992, its campus is a haven of history. The campus is listed on the National Register of Historic Places. Five buildings are individually designated as Raleigh Historic Sites – East Rock, West Rock, Smedes Hall, the college chapel, and the Eliza Battle Pittman Auditorium. The 1903 Bishop's House, often called Ravenscroft, has now been restored under lease arrangement by the Historic Preservation Foundation of North Carolina, Inc., for use as its headquarters.

And setting apart "the grove" from traffic laden Hillsborough Street is a magnificent brick and wrought iron wall. Saint Mary's, 150 years later, is still building on its past while looking innovatively toward tomorrow.

East Rock

East side of Snow Avenue facing Hillsborough Street across from Saint Mary's Campus

The Cameron House
Circa 1835 - Dismantled 1938

Duncan Cameron, the son of an Episcopal minister, was born in Mecklenburg County, Virginia, in 1777. Coming to Martinsville, North Carolina, as a young lawyer in 1797, he later transferred to Hillsborough and was admitted to the State Bar at the age of twenty-one.

In 1804, there in Orange County, he built a family seat called Fairntosh with a 30,000-acre greenbelt surrounding it and used some thousand slaves to work the land. That plantation became and remained a second home for several Cameron generations.

As president of the State Bank of North Carolina in 1829 and committee chairman for building the 1840 State House, Judge Cameron had become so involved in the new Capital's affairs that he was constrained to move to Raleigh where, about 1835, he built the mansion pictured here. Designed by Architect Thomas Wiatt, it was located across from St. Mary's School on Hillsborough Street and faced north.

Obviously the place became one of Raleigh's most select social and political rendezvous and it is a well-founded tradition that the house was the author's backdrop for *The Clansman*, a book by North Carolina's Thomas Dixon on which the silent film, *Birth of a Nation*, was based.

The residence can hardly be called Greek revival though its portico is Ionic because the adaptation is so distinctly Americanese. It was dismantled in 1938, the land to be used for multiple dwelling units, but portions of its materials and interior detailing were salvaged by Mr. and Mrs. Robert J. Wyatt and the pieces reused rewardingly in a house now at 911 Williamson Drive.

Duncan Cameron's son, Paul Carrington Cameron, who was born in 1808 and grew up at Fairntosh, became North Carolina's wealthiest man. He lived to rebuild his fortune after the Civil War.

And it was Paul's son, Colonel Bennehan Cameron, born in 1854 at Fairntosh, who with his wife Sally Mayo Cameron of Richmond, Virginia, in 1902 made changes in the Hillsborough Street place.

It is also useful to know that, though the transactions were never legally recorded, Judge Duncan Cameron gave many of his slaves a parcel of the Raleigh homesite land along what is presently known as Oberlin Road. Descendants of those families yet remain on the plots; and the contiguous property, now called Cameron Village, was so named because it was part of Duncan Cameron's original family estate and the developer wished to honor him. Judge Cameron died in 1853.

Highway 401 South near 70 East

Broomfield
Circa 1838
Demolished 1979

On the old stage road between Raleigh and Fayetteville, now the intersection of highways U. S. 70 and U. S. 401 south, the land on which the house reproduced here stands has been the campsite for soldiers of three conflicts: British General Charles Cornwallis encamped his men here while enroute to defeat General Nathanael Greene during the Revolutionary War's Battle of Guilford Court House, 1781. On this plantation, too, and before the place was built, English Governor William Tryon paused to recruit soldiers for subduing the Regulators' insurrection in Hillsborough. He stayed to cut through the wilderness and build old Rhamkatte Road on which he hoped to march his men west. In April of 1865, General William T. Sherman commandeered the land and this house, constructed about 1838, for quartering some of his army during the surrender of Raleigh. After the soldiers' withdrawal, Mrs. Laurens Hinton who was living in the residence during the Civil War and who became a refugee into Raleigh during the occupation recalled: "The Yankees had nearly destroyed the house. . . front porch had been taken down, floors. . . windows taken out. . . shutters down. . . a Yankee general sent a wagon and carried off all the furniture. . . ." The house was redeemed after the War and renovated.

Called Broomfield, the plain, clapboard place, illustrative of so many of the time and region, was probably built by slave labor for Joseph T. Hunter. He was the grandson of early innkeeper Theophilus Hunter, Sr., whose lodge (partly or wholly burned be-

fore 1798), stood originally not too many yards from this building. *One building of the Hunter Lodge complex was still standing in 1925.*

Joseph Hunter, in 1852, sold the place to his cousin, Laurens Hinton and the old house remained in the Hunter- Hinton descendants' families until recently. It is hoped that historically important Broomfield may be saved from the commercialism which threatens it, and preserved.

Descendants of Theophilus Hunter firmly believe the construction date was circa 1820. No matter – Broomfield was destroyed for commercial development in 1979. The site is now a mobile home sales lot. Only the brick steps remain as a clue to its vivid past.

566 East Hargett Street

Colburn-Seawell House
Circa 1838
Demolished 1969

Eleazer Reed Colburn, original owner of this 566 East Hargett Street house, was a successful builder of stone bridges and is said to have owned extensive granite quarries in his native Massachusetts.

As an expert on the quality of granite, he was invited to Raleigh, about 1832, by the builders of the second State House. Here, as consultant, it became his duty to pass judgment on every piece of stone which was to be used in that building.

Apparently he was pleased with the City and stayed on, after his work was finished, to settle here permanently, to marry Mary Hopkins Moody, and to acquire a local rock quarry at what is now East Martin and Swain streets. Further, believing in States' rights, he soon became an ardent Southerner. He subscribed to stock in the North Carolina Railroad when it was offered, then in turn, invested his gold reserves in Confederate bonds. And among his business contracts, it is known that he furnished granite for the original Dorothea Dix Hospital foundations.

Upon his death the Hargett Street property passed to his only surviving child, Mary Ellen Colburn, who was born in Raleigh in 1834. And it was her husband, Richard B. Seawell, who planted maple trees on both sides of Hargett from Swain Street almost to Fayetteville Street so that Mary Ellen might walk uptown to church,

in the shade. The place is still owned and lived in by a direct descendant, Edward C. Seawell.

Basically the residence has been little changed in 129 years of service to its family. It was built on land which extended east to Tarboro Road, south to Davie Street, and included several hundred feet more land to the west, on Hargett. The classical, double portico remains as it was built and one of the dependencies, a two-room smoke house, still stands. The siding is heart pine lightwood which, even now, stubbornly resists a nail. The foundation, chimney bases, and main walkway are stone.

Inside, the mantels, of various designs, are high and beautiful. The door locks are iron with brass knobs. The floors and wainscoting are of broad and perfectly matched pine, now aged to the color of amber. The two closets retain their wooden pegs for hanging garments. Finally, attesting to the original owner's business interests, the hearthstones in each room are single blocks of granite.

The lower portico columns, supporting the second floor porch, of the Colburn-Seawell House are said to have been the columns of Main Building, now Smedes Hall, at Saint Mary's School. This property was bulldozed to make way for the Hargett Street YWCA.

65

Colburn-Seawell House "Past and Present"

The State Capitol
The Second State House
Completed In 1840
Raleigh Historic Site 1990, National Register Property 1970
National Historic Landmark 1975

Having so narrowly escaped losing much of the documented record of their historical being in the State House fire of 1831, the General Assemblymen were determined to replace the building with one as nearly indestructible as possible. It should be of granite.

Accordingly, a Building Committee prepared plans, somewhat reminiscent of the first State House, and the cornerstone was laid on June 4, 1833, by Governor David L. Swain. This Committee, however, whose aim had been to build "an object of just pride. . . and the admiration of every enlightened stranger," vastly underestimated the cost of their fireproof structure since the foundation alone used up the original $50,000 appropriation. Building went ahead anyway.

The selected architects, Ithiel Town and Alexander Jackson Davis of New York and David Paton from Scotland, made changes in the Committee's original proposals and artisans were imported from out of State, even as far away as Scotland, to complete the work. Contract for the foundation had been given to William

Stronach; the ironwork of the fence enclosing Union Square, to Silas Burns; drafting and supervision to David Paton. And when the construction was complete, at a cost of $530,684.15, that figure amounted to more than six times the 1840 revenue of the whole State.

At least it was finished and the City prepared, by announcement, to mark the grand occasion. "Raleigh, May 1st, 1840. The pleasure of your company is respectfully requested at an ENTERTAIN-MENT, to be given in this City, commencing on the 10th of June next, in celebration of the completion of the STATE CAPITOL AND THE RALEIGH AND GASTON RAIL ROAD." And, as recounted earlier in this book, that happening was, indeed, a splendid affair.

Now, at last, unlike the 1794 State House, it was again possible for all State business to be transacted in one building – the executive, judicial, and legislative. The officials concerned must have been delighted because many of them were mentioned in material

Philadelphia Nov.ᵗʰ 4ᵗʰ 1836.

To/ David Paton Esqᵣ
    Dear sir,

            Your communication of the 21ˢᵗ
ultimo enclosing plans of the several Stories of
the State Capitol at Raleigh was received a
few days ago, but owing to pressure of business
I have not been able to give any thought to
the subject contained therein until yesterday, &
I hasten to assure you of my decided appro-
bation of the plan which you suggest of removing
the stairways entirely from the Rotunda.

            A stairway at best is not a handsome ob-
ject;— for public buildings, they take up a great
deal of room and if brought so prominently
into view as first contemplated in the rotunda
it would be to impair the effect of the room
even if the utmost expense and workmanship
were devoted to its construction, besides the in-
jury which the Statue would sustain from its
connection with steps, and hand rails. —

            The Statue of Washington should stand
alone, as a work of art, unconnected with the
coarser objects of the chisel and plane; and

by removing the supreme court and Library
to the third or attic Story the difficulty is
at an end: There is abundant room for
the stair ways in the lobby entrances as you
have drawn them and I recommend the com=
missioners to this mode of avoiding any in=
terference with the harmony and proportions
of these prominent objects of their State Cap=
=itol.   With great respect sir,
        Your obdt. servt—
            William Strickland

P. S. I enclose your letter & plans by this days
mail, agreeably to your request—.

Reproduced here is a letter to the building's architect from William Strickland, consultant, which documents the fact that original plans for stairways in the State House, designed for the rotunda, were changed to their present position in the east-west wings in order to leave the prime rotunda space for the restored statue of George Washington.

The State Capitol

Capitol Square

buried in the leaden box of the cornerstone. Among other items deposited there was a copy of the Mecklenburg Declaration of Independence, the United States Constitution, a Bible, rules of order of the House and Senate, coins, a copy of all State newspapers, the Building Commissioners' names, State officers, and names of speakers of both houses of the General Assembly.

The new building, more often referred to as the State Capitol, had taken its architectural inspiration from a sacred building designed in the Athens of 438 B.C., for the Greek goddess, Pallas Athena Parthenos. Her colossal, Phideas-sculptured figure stood in the inner court of her temple, a sanctuary which had been named for her, the Parthenon.

Obviously, when finished, the new Capitol had little in common with the Parthenon. And with so imposing a model as its builders had in mind, one may wonder why the building did not turn out to be a pale and ridiculous recall of a world masterpiece. Yet it did not.

Rather, it was born out of successful adaptation of myriad classical forms and motifs, to be used at a later point in time and by a far-removed culture, right down to the fireplaces which originally heated it. At once highly disciplined and freely romantic, it moulded all of its neo-classical eclecticism into its very own kind of masterpiece.

In the 1970s, work was done on the State Capitol to bring it back to its 1840-60s appearance – a new copper roof, paint, carpet and refurbished furniture. Even with air-conditioning added and an updated heating system, the "neo-classical eclecticism" still casts its spell as is reflected in the designation of the State Capitol in 1975 as a National Historic Landmark.

The Governor retains his ceremonial office in this magnificent building. In 1976 the State Capitol Foundation was created to assist with on-going restoration and research.

120 Hillsborough Street

Charles Earl Johnson House
Circa 1840
Demolished 1970

Charles E. Johnson, the first of six so named, owned Bandon Plantation near Edenton and it was his son, Dr. Charles E. Johnson, who came to Raleigh in the late eighteen forties and bought the house pictured here, at 120 Hillsborough Street, in 1850. The following four generations of Charles E. Johnsons grew up in this residence.

Dr. Johnson was a student at the University of Virginia, a graduate, at twenty, of the Pennsylvania Medical College, and was married to the daughter of Governor James Iredell. It was about the time of this marriage, his second, that he added four front rooms to this house, two upper and two lower. He also built the neo-classic portico with its Corinthian pilasters and columns. A detail of them is shown.

Originally the physician's office was constructed just east of the residence and a latticed breezeway connecting it to the house became the repository for the Doctor's strings of "healing" leeches. The little professional building was later moved to the Edenton Street side of the lot where it remained until moved again, this time closer to the big house. Here it served as outside kitchen and servants' quarters until 1930.

While living in the house Dr. Johnson became the first chairman of the Board of Directors of Dorothea Dix Hospital and Surgeon General for the Confederate troops of North Carolina. He lost two sons at Gettysburg. He died in 1876.

Another of the Doctor's sons, Charles E. Johnson, Jr., joined the Confederate forces when fourteen years old, survived, and became a director of the Seaboard Airline Railroad, president of two Raleigh banks, and the first president of Carolina Power and Light Company. He died in 1923.

As one may see by the photograph, on the previous page, of the Johnson house and two of its neighbors, the three houses represent use of the three classical orders, Corinthian, Doric, and Ionic, in one block of Hillsborough Street.

The Johnson property is presently owned by the First Baptist Church.

The three houses, shown on the previous page, were demolished to make way for additions to the church and additional parking.

Charles Earl Johnson House

5300 Castlebrook Drive

Pine Hall Farm
Circa 1840

Located off New Hope Road in St. Matthew's Township, Pine Hall Farm, shown here as it remains today, is one of the Raleigh environs best preserved country houses. Its original central portion was built around 1840 and its early, perhaps its earliest, owner was Nathan Ira Myatt who was married to Mary Elizabeth Bridgers.

The residence was one of three Greek revival plantation houses in the vicinity but the two others no longer stand. This one, in the beginning, was the dominating structure for 5,000 acres of farm land and was obviously designed and constructed for maximum, hearty living. The lower portico is Doric, the upper, Ionic, and the columns appear to be solid tree trunks, hand planed into form. In them, configuration of the wood's grain, through the paint, may still be

identified. The original facade is altogether bilaterally symmetrical, even to chimney details.

The central part's interior was typically neo-classical with the usual, wide dividing hallway, two twenty by twenty bedrooms upstairs, parlor and one bedroom of the same size on the first floor. The flooring and trim were heart pine and a seventeen member cornice decorated the parlor. The dining room and later the kitchen were below grade.

The two flanking wings were added by J. M. Gregory who also did Pine Hall's fine restoration work in the nineteen forties, about a hundred years after the house was built.

North side of Peace Street opposite West Street

Will's Forest or The Devereux House
Circa 1840 - Demolished Circa 1900

Will's Forest, a late nineteenth-century picture of the mansion reproduced here, came by its name in a strange but well documented way. It appears that a slave ship bringing a cargo of human beings west from Africa, about 1760, was wrecked off the Carolina coast. Six known, half-starved survivors were picked up by huntsmen and brought to Raleigh where, although later clothed and well fed, four of the six died. The remaining two, Will and Mark, were not claimed as slaves and were cared for by Colonel Joel Lane, the "Father of Raleigh." Lane supplied their needs and built them a cabin on the corner of his property, demanding nothing in return, and the two lived there contentedly, it is said, until they died. In the meantime, perhaps because of old Will's charm, that section of what was to become Raleigh had acquired the name of "Will's Forest."

This house, built by Joel Lane's granddaughter, Nancy Lane Mordecai, was sited not far from Will and Mark's ancient cabin. About this same time, Nancy Mordecai's daughter, Margaret, married Confederate Major John Devereux, thus the place was often called the Devereux House. The Greek revival residence, in all its classical grandeur, became a Mecca for most of Raleigh's gentry and for the City's important visitors.

Major Devereux was born in Raleigh in 1819 and it was because of his work as Assistant Quartermaster of State Troops that North Carolina soldiers were said to have been better fed and clothed than any others in the Army of Northern Virginia. He died in April of 1893 and it was not long before the mansion was destroyed for inevitable reasons, to divide its land into lots. Its memory is perpetuated by Devereux Street, Will's Forest Street, and Devereux Meadow.

North Street side of 407 North Blount Street

Henry Clay Oak*

Circa 1400
Raleigh Historic Site 1984

Throughout this century some one or another variously misguided interest has tried to ax this tree, probably the most ancient white oak in the Municipality. It is not only venerable but historically meaningful to all of North Carolina since it is reasonably certain that it was under these limbs that Henry Clay wrote his "Texas Question" letter, a missive which most likely lost him the presidency.

It happened on the seventeenth, an April bright morning in 1844. The presidential campaign of that year was in full lather and Clay was a Whig candidate against the Democrat James K. Polk. Clay, however, was by far the most popular figure in the Country as witnessed here by the fact that hundreds of citizens came from throughout the State, in wagons, camping for four days in the City, just to see the "Great Pacificator" and to join the sumptuous cel-

MR. CLAY ON THE TEXAS QUESTION.

The following Letter from Mr. CLAY to the Editors was forwarded from Raleigh on the day of its date, but did not reach our hands in time for publication earlier than to-day.

TO THE EDITORS OF THE NATIONAL INTELLIGENCER.

RALEIGH, APRIL 17, 1844.

GENTLEMEN: Subsequent to my departure from Ashland, in December last, I received various communications from popular assemblages and private individuals, requesting an expression of my opinion upon the question of the Annexation of Texas to the United States. I have forborne to reply to them, because it was not very convenient, during the progress of my journey, to do so, and for other reasons. I did not think it proper, unnecessarily, to introduce at present a new element among the other exciting subjects which agitate and engross the public mind. The rejection of the overture of Texas, some years ago, to become annexed to the United States, had met with general acquiescence. Nothing had since occurred materially to vary the question. I had seen no evidence of a desire being entertained, on the part of any considerable portion of the American people, that Texas should become an integral part of the United States. During my sojourn in New Orleans, I had, indeed, been greatly surprised, by information which I received from Texas, that, in the course of last fall, a voluntary overture had proceeded from the Executive of the United States to the Authorities of Texas to conclude a treaty of Annexation; and that, in order to overcome the repugnance felt by any of them to a negotiation upon the subject, strong and, as I believed, erroneous representations had been made to them of a state of opinion in the Senate of the United States favorable to the ratification of such a treaty. According to these representations, it had been ascertained that a number of Senators, varying from thirty-five to forty-two, were ready to sanction such a treaty. I was aware, too, that holders of Texas lands and Texas scrip, and speculators in them, were actively engaged in promoting the object of annexation. Still, I did not believe that any Executive of the United States would venture upon so grave and momentous a proceeding, not only without any general manifestation of public opinion in favor of it, but in direct opposition to strong and decided expressions of public disapprobation. But it appears that I was

. . . .

In the future progress of events, it is probable that there will be a voluntary or forcible separation of the British North American possessions from the parent country. I am strongly inclined to think that it will be best for the happiness of all parties that, in that event, they should be erected into a separate and independent Republic. With the Canadian Republic on one side, that of Texas on the other, and the United States, the friend of both, between them, each could advance its own happiness by such constitutions, laws, and measures, as were best adapted to its peculiar condition. They would be natural allies, ready, by co-operation, to repel any European or foreign attack upon either. Each would afford a secure refuge to the persecuted and oppressed driven into exile by either of the others. They would emulate each other in improvements, in free institutions, and in the science of self-government. Whilst Texas has adopted our Constitution as the model of hers, she has, in several important particulars, greatly improved upon it.

Although I have felt compelled, from the nature of the inquiries addressed to me, to extend this communication to a much greater length than I could have wished, I could not do justice to the subject, and fairly and fully expose my own opinions in a shorter space. In conclusion, they may be stated in a few words to be, that I consider the annexation of Texas, at this time, without the assent of Mexico, as a measure compromising the national character, involving us certainly in war with Mexico, probably with other foreign Powers, dangerous to the integrity of the Union, inexpedient in the present financial condition of the country, and not called for by any general expression of public opinion.

I am, respectfully, your obedient servant.

H. CLAY.

---

ebrations honoring his visit.

For the preceding week Clay had been a guest of his Congressional colleague, the Honorable Kenneth Rayner. This Congressman, as son-in-law to Revolutionary War hero Colonel William Polk, had inherited the Polk home off the corner of Blount and North streets where now the tree, but not the house, remains.

Here, on that warm day, according to a contemporary account, the presidential contender had a small table and chair brought out of the Rayner home, placed under the tree's enfoliating branches and sat down to write that annexing Texas without Mexico's consent would be: "compromising the character of the nation, involving us certainly in war with Mexico and probably with foreign powers, dangerous to the integrity of the Union, inexpedient to the financial condition of the country and not called for by any general expression of public opinion."

The letter, written to the *National Intelligencer* and excerpts reproduced here, was passed to a number of Whigs who were in the office of United States Senator George E. Badger, at the corner of Halifax and East Edenton streets. And when Clay was asked to defend his position, he replied, "Right or wrong, I am standing by the doctrines of the Whig Party. I had rather be right than be President."

Obviously Clay had been right and war with Mexico did follow. But at the same time he had alienated all political factions, including slave and anti-slave segments in the Congress and James K. Polk became the eleventh President of the United States.

This magnificent oak, which some believe dates from 1700, is endangered by disease and stress on the root system, caused by encroaching pavement and thereby limited water. Only its demise will truly determine its age. May that exact figure remain debatable for many years to come.

* Sadly, the oak was felled October 9, 1991.

305 Hillsborough Street

Lawrence O'Bryan Branch House
Built 1845 - Demolished 1955

Lawrence O'Bryan Branch was born November 28, 1820, in Enfield, North Carolina. He was early orphaned and subsequently reared by his uncle, John Branch, who was Governor of the State between 1817 and 1820. In 1838, at the age of eighteen, Lawrence Branch was scholastically the head of the largest class to be graduated up until that time from Princeton University.

He married Nancy Blount in 1844 and came to Raleigh in September of 1848 where he became president of the Raleigh and Gaston Railroad, 1852. He was also elected to Congress in 1855.

The mansion, shown on this page, had been built by a member of the Blount family in 1845 and Nancy Blount Branch had inherited it. Both she and her husband were strong Democrats and Confederate sympathizers; and during the War, while Branch, a Con-

federate brigadier general, was at one front or another, this residence became rather a headquarters for Raleigh women's war work, knitting and sewing for soldiers, as well as a depot for storing gifts and donations for the fighting men. But General Branch did not return to the place. He was killed in 1862 at the Battle of Antietam and brought back to Raleigh to lie in state at the Capitol Building. He was buried in the old City Cemetery.

Upon the death of Nancy Blount Branch, at the age of eighty-six, the mansion was sold to E. C. Hillyer who remodeled the originally Doric house into the more flamboyant Corinthian order, as it is seen here.

The property was razed in 1955 to be replaced by a building to accommodate the Baptist State Convention.

Mordecai Historic Park, 1 Mimosa Street

An Early Raleigh Office Building or Post Office

Circa 1847
Raleigh Historic Site 1969
Moved to Mordecai Historic Park 1972, Restored 1976

The evolution of mail distribution in the City was relatively slow. First it had come, beginning in October of 1794, both via Federal post riders and by private horsemen who were paid by their patrons. And beginning on January 1, 1795, the original Deputy Post Master, William Shaw, was appointed. Later, in 1803, a tri-weekly service brought in mail by stagecoach, depositing it at the inns – Casso's and the Indian Queen. By 1840, the Raleigh and Gaston and later other railroads apparently gained a postal franchise.

During the first half of the nineteenth century, however, being Raleigh "postmaster" was an avocation and mail was disbursed from his home or from any available building. This miniature, wooden, neo-classical "temple" at 208 West South Street may have been one of such used for the purpose. At least some older Raleigh citizens state unequivocally that it was "the first post office" and as well, it is in the tradition of one type of public and private office buildings seen in the period. Conclusive documentation, however, as to its early use has not yet been established.

A local physician, Dr. Fabius Haywood, is said to have bought the building in 1873, hauling it through the mud of Fayetteville Street to its present location.

The original structure, held together with square nails, included one room with the portico. Its heart pine flooring is still intact as well as the fireplace and mantel. The feathered siding is beautifully beaded.

In 1950 two rooms and new roofing were added for the purpose of better using the place as rental property. It is owned, at present, by Mrs. Walter Stearns, a descendant of Dr. Fabius Haywood.

In the late 1960s and early '70s, urban renewal came to "Southside," and this rare surviving example of Raleigh's antebellum Greek Revival commercial architecture faced possible demolition. In 1972 the Raleigh Historic Properties Commission purchased the structure from the Raleigh Housing Authority for one dollar and in a cooperative effort between the Commission, the City of Raleigh, and the United States Department of Housing and Urban Development, moved it to Mordecai Historic Park where it was restored four years later. Furnishings were collected, refurbished and donated by the Raleigh Postal Service.

For five days, July 1-5, 1976, as part of our country's Bicentennial celebration, this little building was manned by volunteers from the Raleigh Postal Service as a working post office with its own special cancellation.

Midway Plantation

1848

National Register Property 1970

One of the best preserved of the antebellum plantation houses near Raleigh is Midway, located about seven miles east of the City on Highway sixty-four. It was built in 1848 for Major David Hinton II, by his father, Charles Lewis Hinton, who was twice Treasurer of North Carolina. Major Hinton married Mary Carr, sister of Governor Elias Carr, and today the place is owned, lived in, and handsomely preserved by their descendants, Mr. and Mrs. Charles Hinton Silver. The Plantation was so named because it lay midway between two other Hinton family properties, The Oaks and Beaver Dam.

It is unusual that many of Midway's original dependencies, including an outside kitchen, coach house, barn, commissary, chapel, doll house, school, and overseer's house, still stand in good repair around the great house. Time has taken the wash house, slave quarters, and smoke house.

Spring of 1865 found the place in the sadly dramatic position of being, after the Battle of Bentonville, directly in the path of Union General John A. Logan's command as it marched toward Raleigh. The soldiers, drunk from looting Midway's wine cellar, broke window-panes, locks, doorknobs, burned the gin house, the cotton press containing 150 bales, and confiscated all of the Plantation's livestock. And only by command of a superior officer were the house and remaining buildings saved from the destroyers.

It was just before this siege and while Major Hinton was away with the Confederate Army that Mary Carr Hinton buried the family silver, threw a tin box of gold pieces into Hinton's Pond, and fled to Raleigh. The silver was later retrieved and the pond was successfully drained to recover the gold. Also at this time, a portrait of Mrs. Hinton was ripped from the wall and used as a saddle blanket. It was recognized by a kindly Negro in Raleigh who saw it being whirled by a Yankee soldier, on the end of his saber. Somehow the Negro reclaimed the tattered canvas and returned it to the family.

The Doric Greek revival building is masterfully proportioned as seen from any elevation and its modernization was effected so that the original floor plan was preserved. A wide hall running the fifty-foot depth of the house divides two bedrooms with baths and the library on the right from the dining room and parlor on the left. Upstairs there are two large bedrooms and a storage closet, now converted into a bath. The house is plastered throughout and part of the 1848 wallpaper still covers one side of the great room. The roof line, chimneys, the fluted trim of the exterior, interior, and fireplaces – all coalesce with such direct simplicity that the place would seem to be aesthetically ageless.

Time, though, has taken the barn, commissary, and chapel; and ownership has passed to another generation.

Midway Plantation   *Highway 64 East*

Northeast corner West Jones and North Dawson streets

State School for the Blind and Deaf

Established 1848 - Dormitory 1898
Raleigh Historic Site 1978, National Register Property 1976

The General Assembly of 1844, from its Literary Fund, appropriated $5,000 for the establishment of a school for deaf mutes. This original institution, opened in May of 1845, was housed in a residence on Hillsborough Street and its enrollment numbered seven.

In 1848 a special building for the students was constructed on Caswell Square, a plot which had been dedicated, in the first plan of Raleigh, to public use only. The Lossing-Barritt engraving, shown on the page following, is that building. In 1851 the blind were also admitted to the institution. The following year it was actually incorporated as the North Carolina Institution for the Education of the Deaf, Dumb, and Blind and remained such until 1895 when deaf children were moved to Morganton.

Over the course of the years, additions and renovations were made as needed to the original building and other structures were added to the square. These facilities were used until the present plant, the Governor Morehead School located off Ashe Avenue, was opened in 1923. With that change, the facilities were again renovated, 1927-1928, at a cost of $85,000 and converted into offices for the State Board of Health. In 1953 when the new Health Building was erected, portions of the earlier structures were dismantled. However, in 1955 the lone remaining building of the original compound was again renovated at a cost of $6,100, to be used for State offices and remains standing at the corner of Jones and Dawson streets.

The 1927 decision to use the former school for State offices marked the first time the State had departed from the traditional practice of keeping all of its offices exclusively within the immediate vicinity of Capitol Square.

The Chateausque style building, shown above, was constructed in 1898. Designed by Frank P. Milburn as a dormitory with an auditorium, it is the only building remaining of the first state supported school for the blind and deaf in North Carolina. Still used by the State, it was renovated in 1989 and painted a red brick color to make it look more like its original appearance.

By 1869 a school for the Negro deaf and blind had opened in Raleigh. Said to be the first of its kind in the United States, the school's first campus was on South Bloodworth Street, and one of the original buildings still stands in the 600 block.

State School for the Blind and Deaf

Corner of McDowell and Jones streets, looking northwest

In Capitol Square

Part II
1850 - 1900

Prison-Labor Built Sidewalk
Governor's Mansion

Part II
1850-1900

NIGHTINGALE, SWAN, AND ROSE

At mid-century industrialization was making Raleigh's already affluent rich, while the poor who worked for them became poorer. Generally, however, citizens were ambivalently reaching out to identify with a new and pervasive Romanticism on the one hand while hoping that the prosperity-making and ever-growing machinery evolution with its fourteen-hour work day would go away. Instead, it multiplied.

So perhaps subconsciously counterpointing the rhythm of change, this rare Romanticism, alongside Raleigh's factory smoke, filled the air. Women swooned more delicately, speeches had become more prolix, cursive writing in correspondence and ledgers more flourishingly beautiful than ever. Odes to the swan, the rose, the butterfly, and the nightingale in book, song, and dance made bosoms heave, men silent.

Raleigh had become increasingly aware of being part of something big, the U.S.A. And this realization had changed from a post-Revolution chauvinism into a crystalized regional personality. There was no Palladio here to dominate taste and lay down architectural rules. People could now, without restraint or self-consciousness, work into their building designs anything their hearts dictated. They could borrow any form, any inspiration or a mixture from Egypt, Rome, Greece. This they did indeed, adding creative spice of their own—cupolas, turrets, lace woodwork, medallions, new forms in cast and wrought iron, and brickwork which had never been seen before and possibly never would be seen again.

The result was a unique architecture Americana, perhaps mis-labeled "Victorian." And surely, nowhere in the South were there better examples of this Romantic and long-castigated eclecticism than in Raleigh. And though most of these buildings have gone the way of the ball hammer and bulldozer in the twentieth century, a tiny few do remain, but precariously. This design vogue would prevail, along with neo-classicism and some institutional neo-Gothic, exclusive of the War years, until the end of the century.

CENSUS SLOWPOKE

With certainty of the Capital's being fixed in Raleigh, the City's population had doubled during the 'forties. In the 'fifties, however, and in spite of its industrial beginnings, citizen numbers would remain almost static at 4,518. The California gold fever had taken some people. The cholera epidemic of August, 1849, had taken others. And one cannot open any Raleigh paper of this period without seeing a boxed notice of reward for apprehension of runaway slaves. Freed slaves, too, were migrating north.

Nonetheless, Raleigh had become an important railroad center when in 1855, with proper speeches and ceremonies, the line between the Capital and Weldon was extended to connect with Norfolk, Portsmouth, and Baltimore. The North Carolina Railroad also stopped here during these years on its "speeding course" between Salisbury and New Bern.

Shortly, "ladies and gents" began to partake of these seemly innovations by following the European social pattern of "taking the waters" at various spas which, enterprisingly enough, had sprung up in at least ten rail-approachable places in the State. Raleigh even had its own spa on East Street. Season tickets were three dollars and for your money, cessation of all ails was assured.

Even so, the spa treatment was perhaps safer for the afflicted than local doctors' prescriptions which in mid-century still favored leeching for wounds. Bleeding, blistering, emetics, and purgatives were considered stock remedies for most other problems. The germ and microbe theories had not caught on in the City and only two Raleigh medical men had tried the new chloroform in surgical procedures. Up until the time of those physicians' brave experiments, operative patients had been strapped to the table, given a drink of brandy or laudanum "to quiet the nerves" and a drummer boy hired to drown out any disturbing outcry which might be heard on Fayetteville Street. Local houses still had no screens so as land opened in the Piedmont, Raleigh began to have its share of "miasma" fevers, hitherto common only in the low country.

If not medicine, at least hygiene was moving along, as suggested in an 1850 Raleigh *Star* editorial. "All should bathe. . .step into a tub of cold water, eight or ten inches deep. . .give yourself a most agreeable and refreshing bath . . .you will not need to be urged afterward." Too, it is satisfying to know that an asylum for the mentally handicapped had been built. The need had been voiced to the General Assembly by Dorothea Dix when she visited here and found the mentally ill in jails, barns, sometimes chained in cellars. And the General Assembly of 1855 disallowed by law the whipping and branding of women by their husbands.

Raleigh had added a music store and, as well, a much needed planing mill since until this time all wood construction materials had been manually cut and dressed. The community boasted grist mills and paper factories, too, whose employees were paid an annual $163. But Raleigh had not yet become anything of a market center for cotton.

On November 19, 1850, old favorite, the *Raleigh Register*, became the State's first daily newspaper. As earlier recalled, the paper's founder, intellect, shorthand expert, and deist, Joseph Gales, had retired to Washington, D. C., to be with others of his family back in the 'thirties. And in 1839 Weston Raleigh Gales, so named by father Joseph for the son's birthplace, became sole owner of the paper. When Weston died unexpectedly in 1848, it seemed that the *Register's* family dynasty might fail but Weston's son, Seaton Gales, age twenty-one and a student from Chapel Hill, took over, though it was said, with great trepidation. Young Seaton was helped and advised by shop foreman Thomas Covington, who had worked on the paper with the earlier two generations of the Gales family. And with Covington's guidance, Seaton shortly added something else—a telegraph service, the first in the State to be used by a newspaper. Raleigh could now send and receive instant news.

Although residential log cabins yet remained at the corner of Edenton and Salisbury and on the northeast corner of Jones and McDowell in 1850, Raleigh's splendid, up-to-date Yarborough Hotel was opened on Fayetteville Street the same year. Edward Yarbrough, former proprietor of the old Guion, became its first administrator. Here the politically important and fashionable of the City would gather for the next seventy-five years.

On July 4, 1857, a bronze copy, cast by W. J. Hubard, of Jean Antoine Houdon's Richmond statue of General George Washington, was unveiled in Union Square. Purportedly, the sculptor had taken the General's exact measurements for the original of the piece when Washington visited "Foggy Bottom" on the Potomac in 1785. At this celebration it is known that the populace still slaked its thirst with water from the Square's 1794 well.

HOURS OF TERROR

"The Yanks are Coming" now had a far different meaning from that which it would have in 1918. To save the City, Governor Vance quickly determined that the only course which might be effective was to treat with Sherman directly. A commission, formed for that purpose, was dispatched. They returned with the General's verbal assurance that providing no hostile acts were committed against his troops, Raleigh would be spared.

Then followed a pathetic little tableau. At sunrise of a cloudy day, April 13, 1865, a "cortege" for the City rode out south of Raleigh to meet Sherman. Its mission was to formally surrender the Capital. In the carriage were Raleigh's Mayor and a few other leading citizens. One of them, riding in the seat with the driver, carried a stick with a white cloth tied to its tip. He planted the surrender symbol above the empty Raleigh fortifications and the group waited in the rain until eight o'clock that morning when, through field glasses, Sherman's advance cavalry came in sight.

Keys to the Capitol were stoically turned over to the strangers and Sherman set up headquarters in the Governor's "Palace" at the end of Fayetteville Street. That night rumors were rampant. Of all Raleigh's populace only the children slept. They bolted doors, hid everything they could and prayed. Their terror was justified since Lincoln was murdered the following night.

According to Sherman's memoirs, word of the assassination was relayed to Raleigh by telegraph and received by Sherman at Raleigh's Union Depot just as he was boarding the train for Durham. Though for a time Sherman tried to keep the news secret, it was soon out and the local situation at once became explosive. Spoiling for spoils of war as well as for reprisals for their fallen idol, some of the hundred thousand Yankee soldiers bivouacked in and around Raleigh prepared to sack and burn the City. Especially volatile was a segment of Union General John Alexander Logan's command, encamped on Dorothea Dix Hill. They were already an armed and torchlighted mob.

Raleigh was saved only when General Logan, who had come into the City via Morrisville earlier that day, intervened with threats which he hastily backed up by gun emplacements—pointing the firing pieces directly at his own men. The soldier-mob was stopped just at Rocky Branch bridge.

During the War, Raleigh citizens had already been reduced to surviving on a little cornbread, greens, and sorghum; to making their own shoes; using curtains, bedspreads, and tablecloths for clothing. Now it was said that after the occupation not a chicken was left in town except the weathercock atop Christ Church. And although Raleigh had seen no actual combat, a half century would have to elapse before many of the War's uncounted wounds would begin to disappear.

Yet on the alter page of the ledger some monumental achievements resulted from those fearsome four years. For example, local political and social domination by the oligarchical families would be modified into a more democratic City and State representation. An inadequate school system, jarred into re-appraising itself by the necessity of founding new educational establishments for Negroes, brought in a more universal approach to the Capital's schooling. Wake County's hitherto agrarian economy would diversity into all kinds of industries; a whole intellectual awakening would be generated; and an indelible, post-War pencil would mark the time for Negroes to participate in the body politic, signaling their climb toward Constitutional guarantees. Slavery had ended and the City and State would do their parts to re-cement the Union.

Altogether, however, even so short an account of Raleigh's record would be incomplete if the "Reconstruction" reasons for what happened to delay those affirmatives for that fifty years, were not cited.

"CARPETBAGGERS," "SCALLOWAGERS," AND "SHERMAN'S BUMMERS"

In April of 1865, wrote Governor Vance, "A Saturnalia began." Free speech was suspended. Surviving Raleigh newspapers, on pain of having their presses demolished, were not allowed to criticize the invaders for seizing property without recompense to the local owner. The ancient right of *habeas corpus* was vacated. Schools were closed. For many years Raleigh was to stand outside its shoes and look on silently, having no word in its own destiny. Military rule was the order and citizens were disenfranchised. In their places, Northern radicals installed Negroes, who obviously in the past had had no widespread chance at education, into all strategic offices having to do with the responsibilities of government.

In the General Assembly they, along with their supporters and instructors, the "Carpetbaggers," "Scallowagers," and "Sherman's Bummers," soon demanded ten percent of any appropriations and Raleigh, already broke, sank into a quagmire of public debt which would still amount to $148,216.76 ten years later. The spoilers appropriated themselves extravagant salaries and travel expenses. An open bar, called "The Third House," was opened in the Capitol. The building's chipped stairs remain a testimonial to the time when barrels of whiskey, being transported up to "The Third House," did the damage. Unrestrained entertainment at public expense was now licensed, encouraged and again, in the words of Governor Vance, some of the "State House rooms were devoted to the purposes of prostitution." Apparently during their occupation of the building, Union troops never bothered to aim at spittoons and State Treasurer Jonathan Worth, who had been in charge of the odyssey of removing then restoring State archives and records, complained bitterly many times of the desecration. To no avail.

Except for the actual unlocking of the terrible yoke of the slave system, most of Raleigh's former slaves and freedmen fared about as the rest of her citizens during "Reconstruction." Suddenly disoriented, uneducated, they became sharecroppers, went north, stayed on with their "families," wandered aimlessly, and were often unscrupulously manipulated into forming themselves into secret terrorist societies such as the Union League and the Red Strings. Striking back, Raleigh organized an equally shocking society, a Klavern of the K.K.K.

RALEIGH RENAISSANCE

Though the War was technically ended, chronic confusion and terrorism continued for a long time in the Capital since the occupation forces would not be officially withdrawn until 1870. And so reciprocating by the only means possible, Raleigh subtly became more defyingly "southern" than southern. Backs would quietly turn when Yankee accents were heard in the locals' presences. Recalling the South's classic plantation houses, citizens who had any means left began to add white columns to otherwise modest houses, where no columns had been there before. Strangers and out-of-towners were patently suspect. And, for example, according to one newspaper, the crowd was composed of two-thirds military and Negro which gathered at Raleigh's depot on June 1, 1867, when President Andrew Johnson, accompanied by Lincoln cabinet member Seward, arrived to unveil a monument to Johnson's father.

Slowly Negro citizens began to feel that the community was theirs, too. And generally, as white people were freed of northern exploitation and fear of being suddenly

"Africanized," and as Raleigh's people of color began to disbelieve the carpetbaggers' re-enslavement propaganda, Negroes responded in kind to become an important part of the City's revitalization.

The Raleigh Institute which later, by act of the General Assembly, would become Shaw University was founded with northern money in 1865, the first co-educational college for Negroes in the Nation, perhaps in the world. And through both State and National Protestant Episcopal Church efforts, St. Augustine's Normal School and Collegiate Institute for Negroes came next. Incorporated in 1867, it was opened in 1868 with seventy-five of its 110 acres being reserved for farming so that students, by planting, harvesting, and canning, might subsidize their own boarding fees. "The farming became part of our education," one alumnus wrote.

After their re-opening, grade schools up to the mid-seventies had been taught in small houses in different parts of Raleigh Township, without supervision except for a local school committee. In 1876 the Centennial Graded School, the second in the State, with $6,500 coming from contributions, public funds, and grants, opened with a new objective. Every child was to be taught "at least the usual elementary branches of education."

For housing, the Centennial School fell into a piece of luck in that the "Governor's Palace" was abandoned in 1865 as a place fit for the gubernatorial residence. And so classes for the School's 240 enrollees were begun in what was left of the "Palace." The principal was Civil War veteran Captain John E. Dugger, who also took up residence in the "Palace." To increase classroom space, a log corncrib left on the grounds was moved up to adjoin the building. And again to make room, Principal Dugger finally had to buy the Kemp P. Battle lot between Salisbury and Fayetteville and move out. Shortly afterward, buildings were bought for the Washington and Garfield Negro schools and by 1892 there would be 1,900 students in Raleigh.

The City was now beginning to bootstrap its way back into a new world it had not really gotten to know before. In point of time it had been unmanacled in the middle of a vast industrial evolvement. The business of cleaning up old things, old ways, getting out of its stunted pattern was at hand.

NOW YOU CAN'T THROW MUD IN THE PUBLIC WELL

By way of splinting its bones, on April 8, 1870, Raleigh's Board of Aldermen ordered in their new City Ordinances that, "No person shall be allowed to throw filth or rubbish. . .into a public well, cistern, or in any manner injure a public pump" on pain of forfeiting five dollars.

Citizens would henceforth not be allowed to "Feed any horse, mule or other animal on any street except in the vicinity of the railroad depots" nor should he "hitch either of said animals to any shade tree in the City or any post within four feet of the footway." Fine, five dollars.

And one wonders what happened to this 1870 injunction when looking for Raleigh's vanished bowers of public trees which touched their arms to make street shade: "The citizens may plant trees in front of their lots at a distance of twelve feet from the line of the street. If any person shall cut or destroy such a tree he shall forfeit twenty dollars."

Further, it was ordained that "No brick, stone, wood, or other substance obstructing the streets shall be suffered to lie in the streets of the City. . .no produce, merchandise, cooked provisions, poultry, fruit or vegetables. . .shall be kept exposed for sale in or upon any sidewalk, alley, or gulley in the City. . .violator shall forfeit five dollars for each offense."

And "No tan-yard or slaughter house shall hereafter be established in the City. . . .No person shall be suffered to convey out of his or her kitchen, dish water or other slops into any of the City streets on pain of forfeiting four dollars."

Nor were there to be any more auctions on Fayetteville Street, no more guns or even firecrackers shot off within city limits, and no future stealing of sand from the Capital's streets. Finally, it was so ordered that "No hog shall be permitted to run at large in the City."

With all such new-fangled regulations the proscenium during the 'seventies began to frame such things as a castle-copied State Penitentiary which promised humane treatment for those who were unfortunately incarcerated, 1870. A Board of Trade was established in 1872. The money panic of 1873 did not seem to slow up the goings on and by 1879 Raleigh had a real telephone exchange, a loan association, a Y.M.C.A., and on Hillsborough Street a revival of that architecture "Americana" was begun anew for the enterprisers.

EXCELSIOR!

Onward and upward chorused louder than ever in the 'eighties and 'nineties. With census figures totaling 9,265 in 1880, collective public conveyance was urged. And answering the demand on Christmas Day of 1886, a grand parade heralded Raleigh's first mule-drawn street cars. Called the Raleigh Street Railroad Company, its power source improved from mules to horses the same year but electricity would not pull its little coaches until after 1890. That would be six years after the old Raleigh and Gaston Railroad first electrically lighted its Raleigh shops.

On October 3, 1889, all the sweat and cerebration of Leonidas L. Polk, who had been our first State Commissioner of Agriculture, came to fruition when the North Carolina College of Agriculture and Mechanic Arts opened its Main Building to fifty students. The edifice, built by prison labor, had no running water, no electric lights. But it did house all College activities—"workshop, kitchen, dining hall, store room, and gymnasium were in the basement; offices, classrooms, and library on the first, with dormitories on the second and third floors." At that, the City was lucky because money for the school had aggregated so tardily.

Subsidies had come finally from various sources including "The direct donations of the City of Raleigh in money, $8,000." And under terms of the Federal Hatch Act of 1887, which augmented the land-grant legislation of 1862, a total of $300,000 was provided. Polk, too, who must surely have been an eloquent persuader, successfully solicited, with the aid of the Watauga Club, various other funds. The site had been a gratuity from R. Stanhope Pullen.

Pullen divided his land philanthropies between Raleigh City and the College; the dividing line between Pullen Park and the campus was then determined when "Mr. Pullen walked ahead of a plow, held by a small Negro boy, and Mr. J. S. Wynne led the mule over the lines indicated by Mr. Pullen."

By 1892 older citizens were concurrently carping and bragging about Raleigh's too fast and too many changes. There was quite a grand, new Governor's Mansion on Burke Square, a fine City Hall, three cotton factories, yards, and compresses. Streets had been extended in every direction to accommodate the wares of busy carriage and wagon manufacturers. Cotton seed oil mills had been added along with an ice plant, an electric fire alarm system, three daily newspapers and eleven weeklies. And excelsior, an opera house was abuilding!

IT WAS BEULAH LAND

For both fun and charitable causes throughout the 'nineties, Raleigh's people were fund-raising with concerts, lectures, church bazaars, elocution performances, ice cream lawn parties, musicals, box suppers, and drills by the local National Guard, called then the Governor's Guards.

Messrs. Barnum and Bailey usually brought their tents to the City in November and only the State Fair, now moved from east to a west Raleigh location just north of the University campus, could compete with it for popularity. It brought performing horses and elephants, a calliope, spectaculars such as *Nero or the Destruction of Rome* in which gladiators fought and horses pulling chariots galloped around the circus maximus.

Some called the State Fair even grander with its spelling matches, exhibits, sulky and horse races. Greatly featured at times was a balloon ascension during which a parachuter daringly leaped out of the gondola. One got to these wondrous happenings by taking the train at Union Depot or by surrey, buggy, a public hack, a wagon, or horseback.

Train excursions out of the City were in vogue. So were soirees and costume balls at the Yarborough and the Capital Club. Hayrides were altogether the surest way for the young to "get acquainted," and often on a warm evening picnickers coming back into town from the Falls of the Neuse, from Penitentiary Woods, or maybe Cary, could be seen, their wagons covered with spring's wild flowers and dogwood. Sometimes they harmonized with "Slide, Kelly, Slide," as they rode.

Road shows, vaudeville, even burlesque of an innocuous variety entertained citizens of the 'nineties. And in our own Metropolitan Hall during the wintertime, everybody was duly edified by plays having heavy villains and built-in moral lessons. Prices were an astronomical dollar for the orchestra, twenty-five cents for the "groundlings."

In the parlor, around the piano, people were singing "Throw Him Down, McCloskey," "Beulah Land," "Father Was Killed by A Pinkerton Man," and "Bringing in the Sheaves." The bustle had long since replaced the hoop skirt and gentlemen had shaved off their flourishing beards in favor of well-waxed mustaches.

These tonsorial changes were all the better for the more popular Raleigh dances—the German, the Yorke, the rock schottische, Saratoga, the lancers, and the North Carolina polkas. Indeed, the City of Oaks was as gay as an ingenue all through the decade but the century was waning. And as it closed, alas, some of that innocence would vanish into an oft-recalled sweet, violet limbo.

218 North Wilmington Street

Hogg-Dortch House
Built 1850 - Demolished 1962

Reproduced here are the exterior and an interior detail of the Hogg-Dortch House, photographed just a hundred years after it was built, 1850, at North Wilmington between Jones and Lane streets.

Originally the place had only eight rooms. Ceilings were fifteen feet high, their mouldings, characteristic of the whole place, were a series of lateral forms, meaningfully undecorated. First floor windows were all full length French, opening onto an embracing ve-

randa. The exterior had taken its inspiration from the residence of New Jersey Governor Pennington's mansion in Princeton, New Jersey, where the owner had once gone to school; and with time's changing needs, successive wings were added in 1855 and 1919. These additions increased the floor space to sixteen rooms.

The house stood on a four-acre plot dominating its various outbuildings which included a smokehouse, stables, servants' dwellings,

Hogg-Dortch House

cobbler's quarters, and an icehouse which was stocked, in the winter, with imported ice from Chesapeake Bay, the pieces stored in sawdust.

Dr. Thomas Devereux Hogg, whose grandfather and father, Attorney Gavin Hogg, had come from Scotland in 1797, went to the Episcopal School of North Carolina on Hillsborough Street, to Princeton University, and took his medical degree from Jefferson Medical College in Philadelphia. After graduation he practiced in New Orleans for a short while and returned to Raleigh where, in 1848, he married Janet Bryan, daughter of Mr. and Mrs. John Bryan of Plymouth. And though he did not practice here, he became a stockholder in the Raleigh and Gaston Railroad, a major in the Confederate Army's Quartermaster Corps, and a shareholder in the Raleigh Gas Company.

Janet Bryan Hogg died in 1855, leaving three small children. Lucy, the youngest of these married Isaac F. Dortch of Goldsboro and it was the oldest of their eight children, Sally Dortch, who lived with her grandfather, Dr. Hogg, and her aunt, Sally Hogg, in the Raleigh family place. Others of the clan continued living in Goldsboro while making this house their summering place until 1910, at which time they moved here permanently.

After the Civil War the property was occupied by Union officers, and soldiers in blue populated the grounds with their tents. Both Army and family treated one another with civility. And the place was not only spared but handled with respect by the Yankees.

Dr. Hogg, born in Raleigh on October 1, 1823, died in 1904. His granddaughter, Sally Dortch, died in 1951 and the residence was sold to the State, 1957, by the Hogg heirs. At this time chandeliers in the old place were given to the North Carolina Museum of Art and the residence was demolished in 1962, the land to be used as the new site for the North Carolina Department of Archives and History and the State Library.

The North Carolina Museum of Art transferred the chandeliers to the State Department of Administration, which restored them and then installed them in the auditorium of the 1898 building used as a dormitory for the State School for the Blind and Deaf when it was located on West Jones Street. The building is now used for state government offices.

Fayetteville Street opposite Courthouse

Yarborough House
Built 1850 - Burned 1928

In 1850, with a $20,000 capital, four investors opened the Fayetteville Street establishment which became and remained for three-fourths of a century, Raleigh's finest hotel, the Yarborough. Its original stockholders were Jerry Nixon, Major Moses A. Bledsoe, Architect Dabney Cosby, and Hotel Manager Edward Marshall Yarbrough.

The place was already well patronized at the beginning of the Civil War and by 1865, when there was neither food nor servants for home entertaining, Yarborough House superceded the private residence as its collectivized social counterpart. And at the War's

end the hostelry continued gaining stature. It came about because the Governor's "Palace," having been poorly constructed originally and having been occupied by Sherman's officers, was never again used as a home and several succeeding North Carolina Governors, between 1865 and 1889, lived in the Hotel.

This being so, one can imagine the importance of political meetings and social traffic which the walls of the old place embraced. Yarborough House became the backdrop for so many introductions which culminated in marriage that a Raleigh axiom grew from the fact, "I met your father at a Yarborough House Ball."

And it was here that Josephus Daniels was placed under "house arrest" for his stinging *News and Observer* criticism of certain people who were "trying to steal the Atlantic and North Carolina Railroad from the State."

A typical 'nineties Thanksgiving Day menu at the Hotel is revealing: "Oysters, Lobsters, Consomme Imperial, Sheepshead Hollandaise, Potatoes a la Maitre, Quail au Champignons, Chicken Liver Patties, Orange Fritters, Glace au Rhum, Roast Sirloin, Lamb with Mint, Stuffed Turkey, Roast Canvasback Duck, Plum Pudding with Brandy Sauce, Vegetables, Pies, Fruits, Raisins, Cheese, Spanish Olives, and Jelly a la Russes." And if one cared for "strong drink" before, during, or after such a meal, available were "Gin Fizz, Eggnog, Shandygaff, Alabazam, Brain Duster, Catawba Punch, Hannibal Hamlin, Old Nick Rye, and Sitting Bull Fizz."

New wings were added to either end of the Hotel and in 1904, under direction of proprietor Howell Cobb, the place was completely renovated, "modernized," with new furniture installed. This accompanying 1875 pen sketch was made after there had been major changes in the original building, and is a little misleading in that the name, probably superimposed, is misspelled.

There was so much local grief and consternation when Yarborough House burned in 1928 that firefighters were hampered in their work of trying to save the structure.

Additional information from Elizabeth Reid Murray's book, Wake, Capital County of North Carolina, tells that "The longtime Fayetteville Street landmark, the Yarborough House, underwent a series of changes in the spelling of its name. Opened in 1850 by Edward Yarbrough, it was known by that name until about 1870, when its then proprietor, George S. Blacknall, apparently changed the spelling [to Yarboro] at the time he remodeled and enlarged it. This sketch was used on Blacknall's hotel stationery in the 1870s. Under later owners until its destruction by fire July 3, 1928, it reverted to the familiar Yarborough House." And in the 1990s the spelling of proper names continues to be "pluralistic" and a nightmare for researchers.

Geodetic Survey Stones
Implanted 1853

Reminiscent of Stonehenge in miniature and still ground-anchored in the southeast corner of Union Square, these granite Geodetic Survey Stones were installed in April of 1853. According to Florence Jones' scrapbook in North Carolina Archives and History Private Collections, here was the point at which "The United States Coast and Geodetic Survey made its reckoning of Raleigh's geodetic latitude, 35 degrees 46 minutes and 46.67 seconds north, and longitude 78 degrees, 38 minutes and 19.44 seconds west. The stones are situated barely northeast of the exact geographical center of the State."

The point is presumed to be, as it was in the beginning, precisely fifty-eight point sixty-seven meters east and sixty-six point ninety-four meters south of the center of the State Capitol and it continued, until recently, to serve as an exact survey reference, along with some 2,500 later-designated North Carolina ones.

The Raleigh Astronomic Station, as it was called in 1853, was one of the first in North Carolina and was located here by permission of 1851-1854 Governor David S. Reid, construction being completed by the United States Coast and Geodetic Survey.

Especial purpose for its installation was the establishment of telegraphic longitudinal connections between Washington, D. C., Raleigh, and Charleston, South Carolina, inasmuch as earlier attempts to do this, had failed.

Those concerned with organizing the first observations were F. F. Pourtales in Washington, D. C., Dr. B. A. Gould in Raleigh, one Professor Gibbes in Charleston, and G. W. Dean who was chief-of-party and active at more than one place. This personnel must have experienced their share of reverses because, as documentary evidence indicates, progress was difficult and demanding. "Several conditions had to be met before work could proceed. . . .First, the weather had to be favorable at both points. . .second, the telegraph line had to be available. . .third, the telegraph operator had to be in condition to work."

And here, a quoted line from mid-nineteenth century notations concerning the installation's early performance, quality of work, and the vagaries of human behavior, is in itself succinct: "No further observations can be made because of the condition the operator is in."

Christ Church

Cornerstone 1848 - Consecrated 1854
Raleigh Historic Site 1969, National Register Property 1970
National Historic Landmark 1987

Christ Church, across from the northeast corner of Capitol Square, stands on land which was bought from William Boylan with funds from the largess of Mary Sumner Blount, in 1826. On this property the first Episcopal church was built in 1829. It was in this frame structure that an organ was installed which was so highly criticized, as being too worldly an instrument for a house of worship, that there was talk of removing it.

It remained, however, and the Church prospered with two side galleries being added about 1834, to accommodate a growing congregation. Shortly afterward, as the Church and the City continued expanding, a new and more permanent building was planned. And for the design of the proposed granite building, Architect Richard Upjohn of New York and the founder of the American Institute of

Architects was commissioned. His neo-Gothic design, it must be assumed, was completed before 1848 since the cornerstone of the Church was laid in that year.

When finished, the Church's cost, exclusive of its tower which was constructed later, was $18,000. This indebtedness seemed exorbitant but was summarily defrayed in December of 1851 when sanctuary pews were "sold" to individuals at prices ranging from fifty to five hundred dollars each.

The stone steeple-tower was begun in 1859, completed in 1861, and in 1869 a frame chapel and Sunday school combination was added to the site. This latter building was demolished in favor of a new parish house and chapel in 1913. The replacement was designed by Hobart B. Upjohn, grandson of the original architect, and was built of granite taken from the same quarry as the first stone structure.

It was feared that the new addition would dwarf the Church since it was some forty feet longer than that building. But by careful proportioning and by joining it to the Church, with a cloister element, the result was successful. It was finished in 1921 at a cost twice that of the 1854 Church.

Altogether, the landmark, growing piecemeal as it did, and including the old "State Bank-Rectory," forms a consonant and beautiful complex and is admirably related to the State Capitol.

The stone steeple-tower is surmounted by an emblem which carries warning to all, this emblem being of that fowl which gave Saint Peter the warning which changed his life; for it was the crowing cock which brought home to him the fact that he had denied his Master thrice.

The "crowing cock" placed on the belfry was according to the plan of Hobart Upjohn and was a common practice in England, but rare here.

In addition to its original bell, the belfry now houses five large bells which were cast in England, a memorial added in 1987. These are played regularly by a select group of well-trained bell ringers.

The "State Bank-Rectory" was sold in 1968 to North Carolina National Bank which moved it to enable the construction of a new and larger Parish House. The entire complex continues to complement the State Capitol.

Christ Church

127 East Edenton Street

Richard B. Haywood House

1854

Raleigh Historic Site 1969, National Register Property 1970

The Richard Bennehan Haywood house is another Raleigh residence which today remains in its builder's family. Moreover, much of the original embellishment such as mirrors, bookcases, piano, breakfront, and desk survive in spaces first intended for them. And of special distinction is a medallion of George Washington. Ordered to hang in the new State Capitol, it was thought, on arrival, to be unsuitable for that building and was bought by Richard Haywood for his own home. It is still among the other heirlooms in the old place.

Though a medical man and one of the State's leading practitioners, Dr. Richard Haywood designed, supervised construction, and completed the house, 127 East Edenton Street, in 1854. Its bricks were fired by slaves on a family plantation south of Raleigh and were laid up in American bond. The east and west bay windows were carried out in deference to requests of the builder's wife, Julia Ogden Hicks of New York.

Basically the dwelling is a simple rectangle and, like many others of this plan, was symmetrically divided by a central hallway, since blocked to accommodate an inside kitchen. Treated with quiet restraint, the porch's columns and pilasters are Doric and the modified dentil mouldings, triglyphs, and fluting are reminiscent of those seen in the State Capitol.

Dr. Haywood, later a major in the Confederate Army, was graduated from Philadelphia's Jefferson Medical College and did graduate study in Paris. He practiced both in Pennsylvania for a while and in Raleigh. Yet he had time to serve as president of the North Carolina Medical Society, chief physician to the State School for the Deaf, Dumb, and Blind, and to act as one of the commissioners whose duty it became to surrender the City before the advance of General Sherman.

In fact, reliable sources of the period indicate that it was while standing in the Blount Street door of this house that Dr. Haywood, General Sherman, and Union Major General Francis P. Blair who was using the place as his headquarters, drank a toast to the War's end. On that occasion, while the silver service remained weighted down by andirons in the back well, General Blair explained that, in his experience, the well was always a prime target of his men when searching out valuables. The silver was therewith removed and was buried in the garden.

Julia Hicks Haywood, educated in Switzerland, and Dr. Richard Haywood became the parents of ten children. One of them, Marshall De Lancey, born in 1871, inherited the property. He died in 1933 and his wife, Mrs. Marshall De Lancey Haywood, currently retains the home.

After Mrs. Haywood's death in 1969 her son, Marshall De Lancey Haywood, Jr., inherited the house; he and his wife, Margie, continue to live here. This is the only antebellum house in the City of Raleigh still lived in by the family that built it.

The Rogers-Bagley-Daniels-Pegues House*
Circa 1855
Raleigh Historic Site 1979, National Register Property 1979

The Rogers-Bagley-Daniels-Pegues House is a frame Greek Revival style house that stands on a knoll at the northwest corner of East South and South Blount streets, facing Shaw University. Thought to have been built around 1855, it is one of the diminished collection of antebellum buildings surviving in Raleigh.

Prior to the Civil War, Raleigh was mostly a residential city with houses sited on generous lots. The Rogers-Bagley- Daniels-Pegues House conformed to this pattern with its roomy lot that contained, in addition to the house, a separate kitchen, a woodshed, a stable, a dovecote and a privy. The restrained Greek Revival style of the house with its Italianate accents probably reflected the mood of Raleighites of the time—conservative but with a wish to be modern. The details within the house reflect those of the exterior and are distinguished by a beautiful wooden screen that divides the down-

stairs hall. Although the house has been occupied by four different families, it remains in an essentially unaltered state and is a valuable example of antebellum domestic architecture.

The families that have occupied the house since it was built have contributed much to the city, the state and the nation. Its builder, Sion Hart Rogers, purchased the lot in 1853 and started construction of his house shortly thereafter. He was an attorney who served in the 1854 session of Congress and as solicitor for his judicial district. He was a Confederate officer from 1861 until 1863, North Carolina Attorney General in 1864, and again a Congressman in 1872.

Rogers died August 14, 1874, and the house was sold to Major William Henry Bagley. Prior to the Civil War, Bagley was editor of *The Sentinel*, a newspaper in Elizabeth City. During the War, he rose to the rank of Major. After the surrender in 1865, President Andrew Johnson appointed Bagley to the office of Superintendent of the United States Mint in Charlotte, but Bagley refused to take the required "iron-clad" oath and thus, was unable to accept the post. From 1865 to 1868 he served as private secretary to Governor Jonathan Worth, and in 1866, married Adelaide Anne Worth, the governor's daughter. The Bagleys had several children, among whom was Worth Bagley, the first American killed in the Spanish-American War and whose statue is on Capitol Square. William Henry Bagley completed his career as clerk of the Supreme Court of North Carolina, a post he gained in 1868 and held until his death in 1886.

Adelaide Worth Bagley, daughter of William and Adelaide Bagley, married Josephus Daniels, editor of the *State Chronicle* and later editor and publisher of the *News and Observer*, on May 2, 1888. The couple boarded with the bride's mother until 1913, when

Daniels began an eight-year appointment as Secretary of the Navy under President Woodrow Wilson. In 1933, he was appointed ambassador to Mexico by President Franklin D. Roosevelt and remained in that post until 1941. He then returned to the editorship of the *News and Observer*, a position he held until his death in 1948.

In 1919, Mrs. William Bagley sold the house to Albert W. Pegues, the Dean of Theology at Shaw University, an institution established in 1865 for the purpose of educating newly liberated slaves. Professor Pegues, a graduate of Bucknell University, came to Shaw University in 1887 and in 1892 was author of the book *Our Baptist Ministers and Schools*. He remained there until his death in 1929. His daughter, Ernestine Pegues Hamlin, widow of James Thomas Hamlin, a pharmacist, presently owns and occupies the house.

* *Site added for 1992 edition*

Photographed from South Blount Street

Photographed at 515 North Wilmington Street

Now located at 515 North Blount Street

Lewis-Smith House

Circa 1855
Raleigh Historic Site 1973, National Register Property 1972
Moved to 515 North Blount Street 1974

The first, central part of this 515 North Wilmington Street house was constructed about 1855 by Dr. Augustus Lewis, a member of the General Assembly from Wake County, 1854-1856. The mansion's original core contained the basic elements of the two floors, a basement, attic, and the portico, as it is shown here. The property also included an entire city block of gardens, lawns, and dependencies. These have disappeared with time and the place's greenbelt has been diminished by the sale of land parcels.

The portico might have been taken *in toto* out of a Greek Revival architect's handbook. Its first story is Doric, the shafts of the columns being tapered slightly for an easy visual transition upward to the entablature frieze of triglyphs, undecorated metopes, cornices, and finally to the smaller Ionic columns of the upper story. Here the more ornate volutes, consoles, and pediment seem to resolve into a pleasant contrast to the simpler forms below. Fluting of the pilasters, both on the portico and the house proper, are restrained and rather

elegant. The pediment is peaked by a decorative, tin- and-wood ridge tile and the roof is of slate.

The interior is far less imposing by way of embellishment than the outside but is nonetheless pleasantly arresting what with its myriad first-floor reception rooms and its four generous bedrooms above. The upper-floor ceilings are ten feet high, the lower, twelve feet. An inside kitchen was added and other changes were made at the beginning of this century.

In 1912 the dwelling was sold to "patron of the arts" Charles Lee Smith in whose family the title currently lies.

After his death, his widow continued to live here. Because the house stood in the way of the Halifax Street Mall, informally called the State Government Mall, the State acquired the property in 1974 and moved the house to its present location in order to preserve it. Presently the structure is being used adaptively for state government offices.

St. Mary's Campus, 900 Hillsborough Street

Saint Mary's Chapel

1856

Raleigh Historic Site 1969, National Register Property 1970

Saint Mary's early religious services were held in the parlor of the Main Building, Smedes Hall, on the campus. Later they were moved to the lower floor of a building known as East Rock and were held in a room which had been fitted for such a purpose with pews and an organ.

Then in 1856, in his message to the Diocesan Convention, Reverend Aldert Smedes, principal of the school at the time, reported that, "To meet its growing demand for room, immediate arrangements will be made. . .for a chapel of such expressive, tho simple architecture that it will be a constant witness to the religious character and object of the School, and add much to the interest and efficiency of the services."

The little chapel, a current part of Saint Mary's college campus on Hillsborough Street, had actually been started in the summer or spring of 1855 with money given by the Cameron family who lived near-by and owned the property. And it was the Reverend Smedes who gave the chapel its steps, front door, stoop, and stained glass, medallioned windows above. The architect was Richard Upjohn of New York City.

The original neo-Gothic church had only one architectural component, the nave. But in 1905 it was enlarged, through alumnae efforts, to include transepts, decorative windows, a carved altar, and a new pulpit.

Montfort Hall

1858
Raleigh Historic Site 1969, National Register Property 1978

Before the Revolutionary War an Irish orphan named Aaron Boylan, in order to get away from an unkind guardian uncle, stowed away on a ship bound for America. Apprehended, he was sold into commercial bondage by the ship's captain, to pay for his passage. His freedom was later redeemed by the remorseful guardian uncle.

Aaron's son, John Boylan, married Eleanor Hodge and by 1776 they had settled in New Jersey and had become a prosperous merchant family. It was Eleanor and John's fourth son, William Boylan, born in 1777, who was brought to Fayetteville, North Carolina, by his uncle, Abraham Hodge. Uncle Abraham had also brought along his Valley Forge printing press.

In the new State the printing business succeeded and in 1799 William removed their publication, the *Minerva*, to Raleigh. From then on everything that William Boylan, dour and serious, attempted turned into good civic work and wealth. It is said that he planted the first cotton in Wake County, underwrote the Raleigh and Gaston Railroad when it was failing, and personally subscribed money to help build the 1840 State Capitol. In 1850 he was well-directed toward becoming a millionaire.

His several plantations included most of what is now southwest Raleigh, the Central Prison site, the land which became North Carolina State University, and beyond. Meantime, he had married Elizabeth Stokes McCulloch, bought the Joel Lane house, Wakefield, from Peter Browne, and fathered eleven children. He died, rich and respected, in 1861.

William and Elizabeth's youngest son and heir, William Montfort Boylan, had been born in Wakefield in 1822 and was as lively as his father had been grave. He kept a fine stable, bred his own horses, rode to hounds, drank good whiskey, cursed eloquently, and represented all that went with inheriting an antebellum fortune in the South. He continued the tradition of being a good planter and a kind master to hundreds of slaves.

Around mid-century, William Montfort Boylan imported brick from England, hired for its design Architect William Percival of Petersburg, Virginia, and built Montfort Hall, pictured here. In the place pumps were installed for three inside bathrooms, among the first in Raleigh, and ornament for the interior of the house was brought from Italy.

Immediate grounds around the mansion reached to the present intersection of Boylan Avenue and Hillsborough Street, where the carriage gate stood. And family records say that when this gate was closed in the evening, "Marse Buck," as the owner was called, en-

Montfort Hall as Boylan Heights Baptist Church

joyed visiting, in his nightshirt, among his folks, to whom he'd given home sites. Apropos, once a little granddaughter who was with him remonstrated, "Grandfather, it wouldn't be so bad to go around in your nightshirt if you only wouldn't carry a lantern." "Marse Buck's" reply was, "No difference—nobody around here for miles but Boylans anyway."

After the Civil War the garden of Montfort Hall became a camp site for Yankee soldiers and the front porch of the mansion was used as their barber shop. Food, prepared in the outside kitchen, was speared off platters, by the invaders, before it reached the Boylan dining room.

An extended portico with grandiose columns was added to the house, by a new owner, in 1910 and the place is presently occupied by the Boylan Heights Baptist Church, a body which made other, more recent changes.

The mansion has been through additions and adaptive uses. After the church vacated the property, it remained empty until Mr. and Mrs. John Jadwick purchased it in 1980 to restore as their residence. Restoration continues to both the outside and the interior.

Photograph from Saint Mary's Street

Northeast corner Hillsborough and Saint Mary's streets

Tucker House
1858
Demolished 1968

Born April 5, 1829, Rufus Sylvester Tucker was only twenty-nine when he built his "palace," off the northeast corner of St. Mary's and Hillsborough streets, in 1858. Constructed by the firm of Thomas Briggs and James Dodd, it was modern in every aspect and the owner, when the residence was finished, was so eminently pleased with his contractors that he is on record as having written them his heartfelt approval.

Besides the obvious reasons why the residence is memorable is the fact that the building's two towers, so subtly integrated architecturally into the main structure, were purposeful. They housed the original water tanks for indoor plumbing and it was from a near- by pond that Tucker slaves hand-pumped the water which filled them. Too, the place was one of the first in the City to be illuminated by an acetylene gas lighting system.

Rufus S. Tucker was a younger son of Ruffin Tucker who, with another son named William H., conducted a successful Raleigh dry goods store in the first block of Fayetteville Street, 1851. After the father's death, Rufus Sylvester and his brother, William, as partners under the name of W. H. and R. S. Tucker, carried on the business and it is said that the brothers' relationship was so close that neither ever questioned the other as to disbursements from their joint checking account.

During the Civil War, Rufus Sylvester Tucker was appointed by Governor John W. Ellis to serve as quartermaster for the post of Raleigh and other than carrying out these duties he is said to have raised an independent company of cavalry in 1861. He was commissioned major.

Returning from the War, Major Tucker re-entered the clothing business. As well, he became a director of four railroad companies and the Raleigh National Bank. He incorporated the Rescue Fire Company, organized Raleigh's first Chamber of Commerce, and for thirty-one years was successively director and president of the State School for Deaf, Dumb, and Blind. He retired in 1883 and died in 1894.

Mrs. Rufus Tucker, with some of the thirteen children, continued living in the residence until her death in 1909. The house was later converted into six apartments, suffered abuse and neglect and has been vacant for some years. The land on which the mansion stands is currently offered for lease. But before the landmark is destroyed and in good civic conscience, Raleigh citizens might ask one another why the place could not be leased, restored, and used in some manner by an agency, school, person, organization, or by the Municipality since it remains the City's best example of that flamboyant, all-but-vanished, and romantically free architecture Americana.

Among others, the place has so charmed local writers that at least one published poem honors it in a piece which insists that the mansion's great carriage house has forever been the nocturnal abode of Greek mythology's winged horse, Pegasus.

Sadly, in spite of attempts by Raleigh preservationists to save it, the Tucker House was demolished.

114 Saint Mary's Street

Tucker Carriage House*
Second Half Nineteenth Century
Raleigh Historic Site 1976, National Register Property 1975
Restored 1989

The Tucker Carriage House is unexcelled in a number of ways. First, it is the only building known to survive that had a connection with Rufus Sylvester Tucker who was one of Raleigh's wealthiest post-Civil War merchants. His mansion, begun in 1858, was designed by William Percival who designed Montfort Hall, the First Baptist Church on Salisbury Street and the Carter B. Harrison House.

Second, the Carriage House is an unusual example of a later nineteenth century outbuilding, with its ambitious scale, irregular form, and rich surface treatments of patterned shingled walls and slate roof. It is likely that the firm of Thomas Briggs built this structure since the firm of Briggs and Dodd had built the main house.

The estate was purchased from the Tucker heirs by Dr. James A. Rogers, a prominent Raleigh physician. In the 1940s Dr. Rogers'

Tucker Carriage House restored

daughter removed parts of the horse stalls and used them in the stables at her home, Tatton Hall.

And lastly, this property is a true study in preservation perseverance. In 1973 the Raleigh Housing Authority began planning for its second highrise structure for the elderly, and around 1975 acquired the remaining Tucker House property for its location. At that time the Housing Authority entered a Memorandum of Agreement with the Division of Archives and History to actively seek a preservation solution for the Carriage House. For the next ten years preservationists helped seek the right tenant, but no concrete solutions came to fruition although a number of projects were proposed.

Then, in 1985, Arts Together, a non-profit community arts school, leased the building from the Raleigh Housing Authority for one dollar and a promise to restore it. Armed with the lease and

bound by the agreement, the Board of Directors engaged the architectural firm Clearscapes to produce plans to convert the Carriage House into studios and administrative offices for the school. It then raised nearly $500,000 to implement those plans with generous support from the Raleigh City Council, the North Carolina General Assembly, the National Trust for Historic Preservation, the Preservation Foundation of North Carolina, Inc., and from many of the state's leading businessmen and the general public.

On January 28, 1989, a longtime dream came true as Arts Together moved into the 7,000 square foot Carriage House. Today the old building is an example of its era's architectural legacy. And it is said that when the students and teachers leave the building, Pegasus can be heard relaxing in his eternal nocturnal stable.

* *Site added for 1992 addition.*

209 Ashe Avenue

Cox-Wynne House
*Circa 1858 - Demolished 1967**

Known generally as the Cox-Wynne house because of its late nineteenth century owners, the earlier history of this most elegant residence at 209 Ashe Avenue has been obscured by the fact that its 1859 deed was lost. The first documentable owner of the place was William Boylan who sold the original twenty-two acre site and the building to T. E. Sheppard, November 14, 1859. Apparently Sheppard shortly needed money since, within the purchase year, he mortgaged the property to William S. Mason who foreclosed the mortgage and took title by quit claim deed.

Mason kept the place ten years then sold it plus three and a half acres of its surrounding grounds to General William Ruffin Cox, June 22, 1869. It was perhaps because of General Cox's prestige that his name, more than any other, has been associated with the residence. He was born March 11, 1832, in Scotland Neck, grew up in Tennessee, and was admitted to the bar in 1852. Coming to Raleigh in 1859, he became at various times a judge, solicitor, Confederate General, and in 1892 was elected Secretary of the United States Senate. He was wounded five times at the Battle of Chancellorsville and led the last charge against the enemy, before Appomattox.

It was General Cox who laid out Raleigh's Cox Avenue as an alternate entrance to his property, the lawns and pastures extending north all the way to Hillsborough Street. Finally he sold the residence to Henrietta P. Martin on December 2, 1886. After her death, the property was acquired by the R. N. Wynne family. It was bequeathed to and was more recently occupied by the Wynne descendants, Eliza Wynne and her sister, Lois.

There would seem to be a certain magnificent serenity implicit in the architectural resolution of this building, called by some the most beautiful house in Raleigh. Obviously, as seen here, the detailing both of the interior and exterior was done with restraint mixed with a touch of allegro. The sturdy, spiral stairs led from the second floor to the widow's walk.

As a continuing, visual joy to Raleigh citizens, the house needs to be gently restored and maintained by some architecturally sensitive person, agency, or institution.

* A sad postscript must say that the last paragraph is no longer appropriate as the house is being demolished, September, 1967.

Cox-Wynne House

15 East Peace Street

Peace Institute

1861

Raleigh Historic Site 1969, National Register Property 1973

Establishing a young ladies' Presbyterian seminary in the Capital was talked about as early as 1847. But the founding action was not taken until 1857 when the Reverend Joseph M. Atkinson, who was minister to Raleigh's Presbyterian Church at the time, inaugurated a fund subscription drive for the undertaking. It was mainly through his efforts that prosperous Raleigh merchant and elderly bachelor, William Peace, contributed $10,000 plus eight acres of land to the purpose. Other investors brought the cash figure up to an initial $20,000 and in 1858 this, the Main Building and the Institute's first, was begun at Wilmington and Peace streets.

The facade is obviously dominated by the three galleries and four great Doric columns. The columns rest on rectangular, brick bases which terminate at the height of the building's first floor. And looking on upward, the three tiers of lacy banisters, rather than the medallion-centered pediment, seem to unite the whole neo-classical approach. The doors of the balconies are each fanlighted and are all repetitions of the same treatment. The consoles are used in pairs.

The structure was almost ready for classes in 1861 when the Civil War intervened to halt the entire operation. But the unfinished school did not lie vacant. It was used for three years as a Confederate hospital and at the War's end was commandeered by the Union forces for the Freedmen's Bureau.

Eventually the Institute's directors regained possession of the property but found the building so dilapidated that it seemed inexpedient to try to raise restoration and completion money, this time from a destitute populace. The directors then offered the premises to Shaw Institute, a Negro co-educational body which had been organized in the old Guion Hotel and was then searching for a permanent building.

It was only at the last moment that the Reverend Atkinson and some of his colleagues raised a few thousand dollars, mortgaged the property, and began completion of the building as well as its renovation. In 1872 the directors, including Reverend Atkinson, D. G. Fowle, W. E. Crow, T. McGee, and R. Stanhope Pullen, announced that the institution would be ready to receive students the following autumn.

After restoration, the ground floor housed the recitation rooms, music department, and dining hall. The second floor was given over to parlors, offices, private apartments for the principal, and the chapel. On the third floor was dormitory space for students and faculty. Drawing, painting, and calisthenics took place on the top floor.

After completion and refurbishment, Peace Institute was leased to the Reverend Robert Burwell and his son, John B. Burwell, who had been connected with the Charlotte Female Academy. And from then on to the present, except for more financial troubles in 1878, the school prospered under various presidents and faculties. It was bought in 1907 by the Presbyterian Church and in 1930 the name was changed to Peace, A Junior College for Women. In 1940 the name was again altered to Peace Junior College; and finally, in 1943, it became officially known as Peace College.

On campus, in front of Main Building, is the fountain given to Peace in 1922 by the Andrews family. It originally stood near the south corner of the Heck- Andrews House on North Blount Street.

For a number of years, Peace College has conducted an ongoing development program, with new buildings including a library, music building and dormitories. Additional nearby property has been acquired for expansion and the wrought iron and brick fence has been extended. With this expansion, the streetscape of the Blount Street Historic District from Peace Street to East Franklin Street has changed from late nineteenth and early twentieth century residences to landscaped parking lots and a dormitory.

Carter Braxton Harrison House
1861 - Demolished 1962

Colonel Carter Braxton Harrison's American classic, shown opposite, was made possible by the terms of his father's will, probated in September, 1829. "To my son. . .a tract of land 1,840 acres about Davis Creek. . .and the following Negro slaves Ralf, a blacksmith, Arthur. . .Celia. . .and all her children. . .Dale, Alfred, Needham, Anders, Calvin, Penia together with all their future increase to him and his heirs forever. . .signed William Harrison, Esquire. . .Franklin County."

Though a minor at the time, young Carter grew up to continue the role of landed gentry, to acquire stock in the Raleigh and Gaston Railroad, and to be cited for bravery in the Civil War, both at Chattanooga and Chickamauga.

In 1857 he bought from Thomas Pollock Devereux the seventeen-acre Raleigh site of this property and engaged Architect William Percival of Petersburg, Virginia, for the mansion's design. Within its predilection for the new freedoms in form and a disdain for planning in the old neo-classical and Colonial idioms, Percival had already designed other exciting buildings in the City. This one, however, built at eighteen Seaboard Avenue, reflected the most sensitive interpretation of this rare and short-lived architectural period and clearly stated that the designer was one of the Nation's finest practitioners of the mode.

As the details suggest, little by way of flourish and comfort was left out of this interior. Its statuary-niched rotunda presented a three-way view— north, south, and up through the skylight. The trim was solid mahogany and the floors were variously laid with marble and matched oak. There were two symmetrically bilateral, cantilevered stairways leading upstairs from the grand hallway and hardware, including doorknobs, was plated with silver. The marble mantels were imported from Italy.

Colonial Harrison had built the house for his beautiful bride, Margaret McKnight Jeffreys, belle of several counties, but perhaps because of the owner's failing health or maybe his financial reverses,

Carter Braxton Harrison House

18 Seaboard Avenue, North end of Salisbury Street

they sold the place to Joseph Gulley, Sr., for $50,000 in 1875. The Gulleys, in the early 'nineties, re-sold the house to General Robert F. Hoke of Lincolnton. Tradition, however, insists that his wife, Lydia Van Wyck Hoke, felt that the mansion was too far out of town. And so within a year they moved nearer to the center of town.

From that time on the house was leased, rented, or sold to various Raleigh families. It was reconditioned by John O. Ellington in 1912, and in 1930, responding to the creeping neighborhood deterioration plus the diminished greenbelt of its land protection, the inevitable vivisection was performed. The carriage house was demolished in favor of a filling station on Peace Street. And at this time an owner with a heavy hand chopped rather than rearranged the castle into five apartments. The left flying stairway was ripped out, the rotunda sealed off on the second floor, the promenade porches sliced to enclose more apartment space. Five elementary kitchens were splashed throughout, one of which was expediently placed in the library, for the purpose of making pot and pan repositories out of existing mahogany book shelves.

Efforts to save the building were made by the Raleigh Historic Sites Commission, Incorporated, but, severely vandalized and neglected, it was dismantled by the 1962 owner, the land at that time being taken over for commercial use within the Raleigh Redevelopment Commission's Smoky Hollow project.

Raleigh and Gaston/Seaboard Coast Line Building

Circa 1862
Raleigh Historic Site 1973, National Register Property 1971
Moved to North Salisbury Street 1977
Restored 1988

The Raleigh and Gaston/ Seaboard Office Building, above, must have gone through several kinds of changes. For example, it is sketched into Drie's 1872 bird's-eye map of Raleigh but without the ornamental ironwork on its west elevation. This must have been added in the late 'seventies or 'eighties since the treatment was popular in that period.

Also, the brickwork and fenestration of the upper floor are slightly different from the lower three which suggests that the upper level was added before 1872 to existing first, second, and ground floors. It is known that in 1847 the Raleigh and Gaston Railroad owned lot number 272 where the building stands at North and Halifax streets, and two other contiguous lots, numbers 273 and 259. They appear on Johnson's map of Raleigh which is dated that year. And there are a few who feel that a part of the building is as old as the Raleigh and Gaston's completion, 1840.

Augmenting that projection, the Annual Report of the Raleigh and Gaston of 1865 says: "The warehouse at Raleigh, which was owned jointly by the Raleigh and Gaston and the North Carolina Railroad had been burned. . .the remainder of the buildings were intact and were reported to be ample for the immediate needs of the company. The buildings were reported to be of the most permanent kind."

"Most permanent kind" would indicate brick and so it is presumed that at least a part of this building was indeed constructed on the site between 1840, the aforesaid date of the Railroad's opening celebrations, and the 1865 date of the above report. It has been known as the Seaboard Office Building since 1871 when the Seaboard and Roanoke Railroad gained control of the Raleigh and Gaston.

The straightforward and beautiful structure, the elegant cast-iron

tracery of porches and galleries (details shown), the contrastingly baroque consoles, all conspire to place it in the sphere of one of Raleigh's meritorious buildings.

Further research determined that the Raleigh and Gaston/Seaboard Coast Line Building was constructed circa 1862 as a two-story building that in 1875, according to The Daily News, was "to be adorned with a beautiful iron porch running the whole length of the front. When completed, it will add great beauty to the building."

In 1886, a single-story wing was added to the south side of the building and in 1891 a third story was added to the main part of the structure. Changes continued even into the 1940s when a second story was added to the wing which was in turn lengthened. The building was purchased by the State and moved, without the two-story wing, to its present location in 1977 to make way for the Halifax Street Mall, informally called the State Government Mall. Vacant for a number of years, it has now been restored by the State for adaptive use as offices for the Division of Occupational Safety and Health of the Department of Labor.

The Seaboard Half Roundhouse, pictured next page, is a crescent. Its turntable is just outside the semicircle and several pairs of tracks flange out from the turntable pit into the shelter. Probably built in the latter quarter of the nineteenth century, it is a documentary delight. Its structural members are solid timbers held together with iron straps. Two fat, cast-iron stoves with their fluted, iron chimneys are intact and are still used since the turntable and Half Roundhouse today serve train number Seventeen going to Portsmouth, Virginia, and number Eighteen returning.

Nonetheless, vines and stalks of wild flowers now creep through the siding of the clapboard shell which follows the contour of the solid masonry walls, a walkway in between. And speaking of the age of this building, it surely could have been the inspiration for the famous, old lines—"Run for the roundhouse, Nellie, he can't corner you there."

The unique structure was demolished in 1968.

Raleigh and Gaston Railroad Office Building, circa 1870   *325 Halifax Street*

Seaboard Half Roundhouse   *South of Peace Street and east of Capitol Boulevard*

Late Nineteenth Century
Demolished 1968

501 Rock Quarry Road

Confederate, Oakwood, and Federal Cemeteries

Located on Rock Quarry Road and shown above, the Federal Cemetery, sometimes called the National Cemetery, has not always been so designated. It was originally one of the burial places of Confederate soldiers, those who could be brought home from battlefields, and as well, since the site was conveniently near Raleigh's James Johnston Pettigrew Hospital, it became the resting place of the wounded who died in that building.

Soon, however, the Rock Quarry cemetery, as it was called, showed need for attention. The ladies of Raleigh were first to recognize this and on May 23, 1866, met and organized the Ladies Memorial Association of Wake County, whose purpose was to care for Confederate graves and to select a "suitable and permanent resting place for the heroes of crushed hopes."

And according to the Memorial Day special of *The Daily Call*, 1889, "Miss Sophia Partridge first conceived the idea of having a collective place of interment for the dead boys in gray, and to her belongs the credit of suggesting and mainly organizing the first Confederate cemetery. . . ." At this time several shaded acres at what is now Oakwood Avenue were proffered by Henry Mordecai, great grandson of Joel Lane, and were accepted as the new site.

However, the Association had to act before it was ready for "Early in January, 1867, or perhaps December, 1866, the Federal government sent an agent to Raleigh to select a location for a Federal cemetery. He selected and confiscated the Rock Quarry cemetery where both the Federal and Confederate dead were resting. . .he had not the patience to wait until the new place for the Confederate dead was in a state of readiness. . .and ultimately threatened that if they were not removed by a certain day they would be dug up and thrown into the public road."

And so on February 22, 1867, both old and young men of the City organized into pick, shovel, and wheelbarrow crews and the women sustained them with coffee and beer as they went about their macabre task. The difficulty of the labor had been compounded by Union soldiers as they robbed the graves, looking for loot. Almost overnight then the old Rock Quarry Road place, former burial ground for the Confederacy, became the Federal Cemetery and the more distant, oak-grove acres were thereafter associated with the "Gray." More land was added to this site and it was incorporated as Oakwood Cemetery, reproduced bottom next page, in 1869.

During the re-burial changes, no prayers, memorial services, or consecration ceremonies had been allowed at Oakwood. Nor were the citizens of the Ladies Memorial Association, under pain of being shot, allowed to go in a procession to their new cemetery. So, in order to care for the place, the women met in unobserved twos and threes at Raleigh street corners, each bearing an obscure bouquet or object for a grave. Harboring pictures of General Lee and any show

501 Rock Quarry Road

701 Oakwood Avenue

of a Confederate flag carried severe reprisals.

For a while both factions continued to bury their exclusive own in the separate places. And on August 28, 1871, the City closed down while 103 open graves at Oakwood received the remains of that many who were brought home from Gettysburg. And from 1869 to the present, Raleigh's citizens, as well as its military, have been buried at the site.

The Federal or National Cemetery, as it is sometimes called, is now partially financed by Federal funds and continues as a resting place and memorial for veterans of all wars.

The Federal Cemetery is now filled. Between the Confederate Cem-etery (1867) and Oakwood Cemetery (1869) is a small Hebrew Cemetery with the earliest grave that of Max Erlanger (1869). The O'Rorke or old Catholic Cemetery, located on North Tarboro Street, was established in 1858 on land donated by John O'Rorke. Later used by the city as "potter's field," it is now under supervision of Raleigh's Parks and Recreation Department and is often referred to as the Tarboro Road Cemetery.

When the section for blacks in the City Cemetery was filled by mid-1871, the city acquired land off Fayetteville Road, and Mount Hope Cemetery was established for blacks in 1872. Additional land has recently been purchased and lots continue to be sold.

123 Fayetteville Street

Tucker Hall

Dedicated 1867 - Razed in the 20th Century

According to Raleigh's August 28, 1867, *Daily Sentinel*, Tucker Hall, pictured here, had just opened. Fronting the east side of Fayetteville Street's first block, it was described: "Width of front 43 feet, 4 inches running back 120 feet, with an area in front 6 feet, covered with Hyatt's patent light work to give light to the basement . . . . The store floor is the entire depth and width of the building . . . . The walls are hard finished with ornamental plaster cornices. . . .In the centre there are eight iron columns of the Corinthian order. . . in a style that would do credit to any Northern City. There are two counting rooms at the back end of the store. . . .The Hall includes four rooms at the front end, parlor, saloon, dressing and ante- rooms for musicians. . . .At the back end there is a stage extending across the width of the building. . .including private boxes. The width of the Proscenium is 23 feet, with a height of 16 feet. There is a complete set of eleven scenes and 26 wings. . . .The entire auditorium will seat 1,200 and the whole building is provided with the handsomest gas fixtures."

Apparently there were two entrances to the store space and a center door which led to the second or "Hall" floor. The windows were plate glass and the "composite" iron of the facade presented "a most imposing appearance." The architect was B. F. Warner of Broadway, New York; the contractor, Thomas Coates of Raleigh. Others who worked on the structure were "Scenic Artist–R. S. Smith, Chestnut Street Theatre, Philadelphia, State [Stage] Carpenter–Chas. A. Brown, lately employed at Niblo's, N. Y., Gas Fixture Makers–McKenzie & Clan Ranald, West 4th Street, N. Y., Painter and Grainer–Alex Hardie, Raleigh, Plaster and Cornicer– J. H. Hamall."

Here was Raleigh's finest commercial building, one in which the brothers, William H. and Rufus Sylvester Tucker successfully purveyed clothing, whiskey, theatre, toiletries, and offered a "meeting place of the best atmosphere," for many years. It was razed, or partly so, in this century. This "partly so" is not altogether conjecture. It is thought by some that the Wilmington Street end of Tucker Hall

Tucker Hall (back portion)
Demolished 1969

123 South Wilmington Street

was extended and remains standing as Ivey's shipping room. This theory is supported by close examination of the general characteristics, roofscape, and brick dating of that building, reproduced above. In fact, inside this building, as if marching out of a late nineteenth-century parade, may still be seen several of what must surely be the same fluted "iron columns of the Corinthian order," those structural members which held up Tucker Hall.

The last remaining vestige of Tucker Hall was razed in 1969 and the site has been used since then as a parking lot.

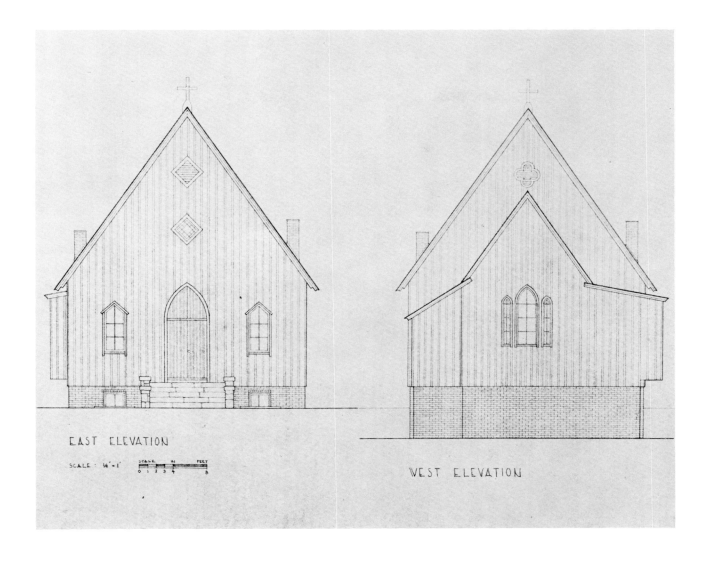

EAST ELEVATION

SCALE ¼"=1'

WEST ELEVATION

Saint Ambrose Church
Built 1868 - Razed 1965

Saint Ambrose Church, seen here, was built at the northwest corner of West Lane and Dawson streets in 1868 and was, at that time, called Saint Augustine's. It was the official place of worship for students from Saint Augustine's College and on Sundays parades of students could be seen marching from the campus to services in the little chapel. It seated only 175.

The 1896-1897 Raleigh City Directory lists the church as Saint Augustine's. The name was changed to Saint Ambrose about the turn of the century, after Saint Augustine's College built a new church on its own campus, 1895.

Saint Ambrose then remained on the Lane and Dawson site until it was moved, about 1901, to South Wilmington Street. There it was razed in 1965. A new church, replacing it and built on Darby Drive in Rochester Heights, still retains all the salvaged appurtenances from the old church—communion vessels, altar, and brass.

Peaked with a tiny crucifix, the building represented neo-Gothic architecture reduced to its simplest and most basic elements.

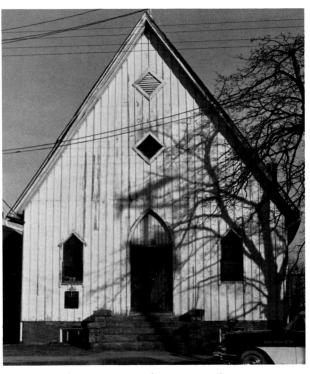

Northwest corner North Dawson and West Lane streets

2008 Hillsborough Street until 1962, 2813 Mayview Road

Wynne House Tower
Circa 1870 - Salvaged 1962

This tower originally stood atop the second floor of the old Wynne residence, built circa 1870, at 2008 Hillsborough Street. When the house was demolished in 1962, Mr. and Mrs. Ben F. Williams bought the cupola Americana, had it salvaged whole by crane and hauled to their property at 2813 Mayview Road. Here the new owners replaced some of the fancy, wooden shingles, re-cut and adjusted the slate of the conical roof, and "implanted" it with landscaping—shrubs, flowers, and a pebble-brick, circular walkway.

They also flagged the cone with a saucy, metal pennant and made doors out of the two keyhole or mosque windows.

This tower, as designed in the house from which it was taken, had no access stairway and was obviously a purely imaginative accent added to the building, for flair only. It is now functional. More, it has been transformed into what is probably the most distinctive potting house in Raleigh. It has become the *piece de resistance* within an urban garden of rare interest.

Heck-Andrews House

1870

Raleigh Historic Site 1972, National Register Property 1972

Specifications written for Colonel and Mrs. Jonathan McGee Heck, owners, by Architect G.S.H. Appleget for this freely imaginative, French-inspired mansion, now standing at Blount and North streets, seem more descriptive than any other material. The architect's spelling is his own. "Stairs in front hall to run to the third Story to begin with one Pannel Newell Post, 12 in. Octagen Mahagany with Butter Nut Pannel as good as is made Balisters Oak, or Chestnut, or Ashe, 2 l/2 in. in diameter Octagen, and fluted 5 in. Black Walnut Rail of the latest style. . .All to be of first quality . . .Cornice on Main Building according to Plans, with a good snug gutter finished up neatly. Cornice on Manchard Roof the same . . . .All Sideing 5/8 thick 6 inches wide all heartt and Rabeted on the bottom edge so as to sett tight together. . . .All floors for Building to be 1 1/4 in. thick and not Moore than 6 inches wide and of Good Material. . .for Pizzas the same thickness and not More than 4 inches wide, and all flooring well seasoned."

Started in August of 1869, the residence was finished by contractors Wilson and Waddill about 1870. During the building months, however, Colonel and Mrs. Heck found that the original time estimate and cost calculation for construction had been too low. Although the owners had already agreed to furnish some materials, they entered into another contract on April 11, 1870, one which specified that the contractors agree to keep "not less than ten hands employed constantly upon the building until its completion." They advanced more money, on a monthly basis, to these workmen.

Colonel Heck, a lawyer, lived in Morgantown, (West) Virginia, before coming to Raleigh in 1865 and was, during Civil War years, responsible for raising and equipping the Thirty-first Virginia Regiment. He was said to have been charmed with the City, from earlier visits, and lived here to become Chief Marshal for Raleigh's 1892 Centennial celebration, "In the history of Raleigh, a great event, which he had shaped to its notable success!"

After his death in 1894, the residence remained in the Heck family until about 1916 when it was sold to A. B. Andrews who lived there for over twenty-five years. Upon his death, 1946, the house was sold.

Although seriously neglected and deteriorating, the mansion remains proudly unembarrassed at its inherent pretentiousness. Nor is it preoccupied about ill treatment. Its romantic personality seems not to fade with time and thus, being alive, it might shock no one to see an 1880 guest of the place ascend the cupola stairs and take a midnight stroll around the widow's walk.

This once elegant Victorian house had a handsome fountain which is now located on the campus of Peace College. Fine stables were to the rear of the house.

At the present time the State is in the process of acquiring full title to the house. How appropriate it would be if during Raleigh's Bicentennial year, the home of the Chief Marshal of Raleigh's 1892 Centennial celebration could be restored to its original grandeur and used adaptively as part of Raleigh's future.

Heck-Andrews House

309 North Blount Street

137 South Wilmington Street

Heilig-Levine Store
Circa 1870
Raleigh Historic Site 1978

The commercial property seen here seems to be sketched into the famous 1872 C. N. Drie's aerial map of Raleigh and is therefore presumed to have been built before that date. It stands at 137 South Wilmington Street and has housed, among other establishments, a hotel, grocery store, and at least three furniture companies.

Typical within its period, a corner of the first floor was sliced off to make the main entrance to the three-story structure open at Wilmington and Hargett streets. Twenty-four, tall, eight-paned windows lighted the upper two floors, a row of six chimneys accented the store's south side, and the roof line extended to form a deep, bracketed overhang. The structural members were, and still are, iron-stropped heart pine pillars.

Between 1875 and 1876 the Carolina House, a boarding establishment, occupied the building. Next, from 1880 to 1897, it became the Central Hotel.

The building's 1899-1906 occupant, Royall and Borden furniture wholesalers and retailers, was a name familiar "to the citizens of this city, not only for low prices, reliability and fair dealings, but as well for prompt service and the large stock they carry. The business has been established here for over ten years, and incorporated under the present title for over seven years. . .the building and annex. . .is 45 x 90 feet. . .and the finest line of house furnishings that could be desired are carried therein. The business done requires employment of a force of ten people, and every attention is paid to their customers, and prospective purchasers, and every article to complete the modest home or most palatial mansion can be found here." From 1907 to 1927 Maurice Rosenthal, grocer, used the building and another grocery store, Morgan Grocery Company, 1928-1935, took over the premises.

The building has been since 1936, and continues to be today, the emporium of furniture purveyors, Heilig- Levine. A contemporary photograph of the building is reproduced here (1991).

Heilig-Levine Store is located in the National Register Moore Square Historic District.

316 Fayetteville Street

300 Fayetteville Street

United States Post Office
Cornerstone Laid 1874
Raleigh Historic Site 1972, National Register Property 1971
Wake County Courthouses

Raleigh was indeed proud, so records indicate, of its new United States Post Office and Courthouse Building, *completed in four years and occupied by the Post Office in 1878. It would be 1879 before the Courts used this new home at the corner of Fayetteville and Martin Streets.* It was a substantial structure, costing about $400,000, and was the first Post Office to be built in the South after the Civil War. It was designed within a certain tradition of late nineteenth-century institutional buildings. And as such it seemed to state a feeling of reaching back to the Renaissance for forms and inspiration.

By 1883, Raleigh had letter boxes and qualified for free mail delivery service which had to be delayed until all the streets and houses and businesses could be numbered. Free delivery service began in 1884 with four city carriers, George W. King and Jeff Denton, white, and Charles N. Hunter and Arthur Gorham, colored.

After only thirty-five years of use, however, the building was extensively remodeled in 1913. And again, in 1938, changes were made which included additions to the west side of the building.

After that improvement it continued to serve its purpose until the present. This structure has also housed certain other Federal offices.

The old Wake County Courthouse appears in the background of this turn-of-the-century photograph.

When the Post Office was remodeled in 1970-71, it was designated the Century Station and is now one of many branches in this growing city. The Main Post Office/Federal Building opened on the 300 block of New Bern Avenue in 1970. Its construction closed one block of East Morgan Street. And today, plans are underway for another move—this time across the street into a building that will house only the Post Office and its auxiliary services.

When Raleigh was established as the Capital, the Wake County Commissioners resolved to remove from the log courthouse to within the City of Raleigh, then just on paper. By September, 1792, they took action to plan for a "large and elegant courthouse." By June of 1793, Theophilus Hunter, Sr., and James Bloodworth of New Hanover County agreed to donate halves of the selected property. Bloodworth's half was conveyed with the condition that the courthouse always continue on this half-acre of ground or it would revert to James Bloodworth or his heirs.

Thus, the second courthouse of wood was constructed and resembled an old-fashioned country meetinghouse. A special tax was levied to pay for the structure.

By May of 1835 a new "fireproof" structure of brick was underway from a plan by Alexander Bragg and William White, a Raleigh builder and construction superintendent. The wooden building was moved to the edge of the property and used until the fireproof structure was ready in 1837. The wooden structure was then declared surplus and sold. It was moved where it continued as a residence and rooming house.

The courthouse was remodeled and greatly enlarged in the 1880s, as shown in the picture with the Post Office.

By 1915, a modern cut stone structure, designed by P. Thornton Marye, with ten classical columns decorating the front exterior, replaced the "fireproof" one. And by 1970, as Wake County's growth continued, a highrise stone structure of exposed aggregate concrete panels had replaced the 1915 building. All four of the "new and modern" courthouses had one thing in common—they were all on the same site because of James Bloodworth's restricted deed.

1915 Wake County Courthouse

Shaw University Campus

100 Block East South Street

Estey Hall

1874

Raleigh Historic Site 1973, National Register Property 1973

In the early 'seventies Henry Martin Tupper, who had been a chaplain in the Union Army, approached former slave and later bank cashier, Charles N. Hunter, concerning establishing a seminary for Negro girls at southeast Raleigh's "Shaw Collegiate Institute." Enthusiasm for the idea crystalized into an immediate affirmative. But there was no money.

Tupper, Shaw's founder and first president, continued Elijah Shaw's ingenious notion of selling brick, made by student labor on the campus, to finance the structure shown here. Construction was begun at once; but even though Raleigh was having a general building boom, the sale of brick did not return sufficient capital for the job.

Tupper had also suggested to his friend Hunter that a "Jubilee Troupe of Singers" be trained here and sent to the North for concerts, the money to be used for the building's completion. And

Hunter, speaking on May 10, 1916, said that during Dr. Tupper's absence with the singers, "he requested me to have charge of the building operations. . . .Captain J. H. Jones was foreman of the brick work and Mr. A. J. Byrd. . .was in charge of carpenterwork. . .that he would send money each week to make payments. . . .In the meantime, I had borrowed enough money to pay the workmen for two weeks. . . .After this the funds came regularly and Estey Seminary became an assurance."

Other than from those efforts, $8,000 toward construction funds came from the Brattleboro, Vermont, firm of Jacob Estey and Sons, for whom the building was named. An annex was added around 1882.

The "Seminary" became Estey Hall in the early twentieth century, was renovated between 1937 and 1940, and has been used as an on-campus dormitory. Unfortunately, this building, a landmark of both human perseverance and exemplary period architecture, is scheduled for demolition.

Estey Hall remained in use as a women's dormitory until 1968. In 1970 the building was abandoned. In 1976 the Estey Hall Foundation was established to make plans and raise money for its rehabilitation. The Raleigh City Council voted an initial grant of $14,000 to fund a feasibility study for the project and this study, once completed, launched an ongoing effort supported by government and corporate grants to stabilize and restore the building as a human resources center. The perseverance of the original builders of Estey Hall is echoed in the members of the Estey Hall Foundation, and the restored building will complement the adjacent 1932 Memorial Auditorium and add historical flavor to the ongoing plans to redevelop the nearby Civil Center complex.

Shaw University was not only the first co-educational institution for blacks in the United States, but it also had a Law School and its Leonard Medical School was the first four-year medical school in North Carolina.

Born a slave, Dr. Edward A. Johnson received his law degree from Shaw University and later became Dean of the Shaw Law School. An educator, businessman and author, who was the first black to publish a North Carolina textbook, he moved to New York in the early 1900s, had a successful law practice and became a member of the New York General Assembly.

At his death in 1944, his will provided that a trust be set up to aid the Negro blind in Raleigh and Wake County. The City Clerk of Raleigh continues to administer those funds.

Leonard Medical School   Shaw University Campus

T. H. Briggs and Sons

1874

Raleigh Historic Site 1969, National Register Property 1973

Thomas Henry Briggs I, grandson of Joel Briggs and Elizabeth Joiner Briggs of Scotland Neck, and the youngest son of John Joiner Briggs and Elizabeth Utley Briggs, was born October 23, 1821. He married Eveline Norwood and started working in his father's shadow at carpentering and contracting for anything Raleigh citizens needed—houses, horse troughs, pumps, coffins, outhouses. And with James Dodd, about 1850, he went into the mill work business.

On an unlikely date, August 15, 1865, Briggs and Dodd opened a small store on the same site as the one pictured here. They sold "plaster, wax candles, homemade soap. Tobacco was taken in trade at 50¢ a pound and resold for 60¢ . . .nails, sugar, dishes, gun powder, anything to get started until the flow of merchandise from the North could arrive."

With everybody else destitute, Raleigh people wondered where the merchant got his enterprise money. And it was soon learned that Briggs, remembering how his Loyalist father had had everything confiscated during the Revolutionary War, had wisely converted all of his considerable wealth into gold and silver coins, just before the City was garrisoned. He had then sealed the money in lead pipes and buried the pipes on a hill overlooking Devereux's pond. He had identified the spot by marking trees. But, unfortunately, the Union officers had chosen the place for a campsite and cut all the trees for firewood. And after the occupation army had moved out it was only by trial and error, digging and probing that Briggs had been able to recover his fortune.

The establishment prospered and in 1874 there was enough capital to build this red brick structure, "the tallest building in east Carolina and Raleigh's first skyscraper." It replaced the earlier store. And not long after the opening, James Dodd retired from the partnership leaving the business to become known as T. H. Briggs and Sons.

When Thomas Henry Briggs I died, August 4, 1886, all businesses in Raleigh closed to honor him and a public memorial service was held in Tucker Hall.

This building, after almost a hundred years of successful operation by Thomas Briggs' descendants, is one of the few downtown structures to remain proudly and honestly as it was built. No street-floor mask of carrara glass, phony-cut stone, or aluminum has replaced the original. There has been no overlay of paint, no shave-off of nineteenth century decoration to alter the facade's fidelity.

This building, 118 years later, still stands proudly and relatively unchanged on its original site. The fourth generation of the T. H. Briggs family still owns and operates the 127-year-old business.

220 Fayetteville Street

Heck-Wynne House   *511 East Jones Street*

The Heck Houses*

Between 1871 and 1875
Raleigh Historic Sites 1979, National Register Properties 1973

Colonel Jonathan M. Heck, a West Virginian, came here in 1865 and by 1870 was building his own Second Empire style townhouse, designed by G.S.H. Appleget, at 309 North Blount Street. In 1871 Colonel Heck purchased 25 acres of land and had it divided into lots, three of the lots being those which these houses occupy. These three houses are smaller and more modest than Heck's own townhouse, but the similarities between the structures suggest that Heck's home, or Appleget himself, inspired the design which was sometimes facetiously called "Steamboat Gothic." Evidently the structures were completed about the same time as the house at 218 North East Street was sold to Caroline S. Pool on April 8, 1875; the house at 503 East Jones Street was sold to Jennie L. Lee and the one at 511 East Jones Street to Elizabeth W. Wynne on April 9, 1875.

Captain James W. Lee, the 1880 Chief of the Raleigh Police Force, is in the City Directory of 1881 as the owner-occupant of 503 East Jones. At one time he was employed by the "overseas" division of the American Tobacco Company and upon retirement bought land in Johnston County. From this tract he cut the long-leaf heart-of-pine which was used in the construction of his house. Perhaps he and Colonel Heck had an arrangement, for this type timber was used in the construction of the other two houses also.

In 1882, Gray's Map of Raleigh shows the other two houses belonging to J.M. Heck and to G.W. Wynne. The Heck-Lee House was inherited by the owner's daughter, Jenny Lee Brady. L.G. Bullard purchased it in 1933.

About these houses, many Raleigh citizens of today retain memories of having played in the cupolas or "pilot houses" and document their claims by initials carved into the towers' frames.

* In the 1967 edition of this book, these houses were listed as the James W. Lee Houses.

Heck-Lee House   *503 East Jones Street*

Heck-Pool House   *218 North East Street*

526 North Wilmington Street

The Merrimon House or Wynne Hall

1876

Raleigh Historic Site 1976, National Register Property 1975

This house seems to have captured, in composite dress, the evolutionary story of Raleigh architecture. Its shutters and siding turn back to Colonial forms, its cornices and the obligato of its consoles suggest the 1840 neo-classical, while the delicate woodwork of the porches and fenestration reflect the whimsical, sometimes beautiful, decorative license of the period in which it was built, 1876.

Still standing and superbly preserved at 526 North Wilmington Street, the place was originally designed and built by Judge Augustus Summerfield Merrimon who put up the frame and left the wood "to season" for eighteen months before adding the clapboard and interior finishing. Much of the inside trim, including the vault-like doors and stair rail, is solid walnut. The original floors were heart pine, the ceilings fourteen feet high, and among the elegant fireplace mantels, one is of Florentine marble. The residence remains, except for addition of bathrooms and closets, without substantial change. None was needed.

Judge Merrimon was born September 15, 1830, in Transylvania County, North Carolina. And with only eight months of formal schooling, his reading, throughout life, must have been prodigious

inasmuch as he was admitted to the bar in 1853. He became solicitor for the Eighth Judicial District, a Superior Court Judge, a United States Senator, 1873-1879, and Chief Justice of the North Carolina Supreme Court, 1889-1892.

As solicitor, he was often in grave personal danger during the Civil War, because of divided loyalties of the people in his District. Later he resigned the position of Superior Court Judge rather than enforce military laws of Reconstruction. Merrimon was one of the prosecuting attorneys who conducted the impeachment proceedings of Governor W. W. Holden. He died November 14, 1892.

Toward the end of the century the house was bought by the father of famous Walter Hines Page. The senior Page had bought the place from the Merrimon family and later Mrs. Page married J. Stanhope Wynne. It was bought by Peace College in 1919 and between 1935 and 1965 it was used as the residence of the College's president, Dr. W. C. Pressly. Presently the fine house is maintained as a Peace College dormitory and is called Wynne Hall.

In 1973 this property was purchased by the State and is being used adaptively for government offices.

330 Hillsborough Street

Dodd-Hinsdale House

1879

Raleigh Historic Site 1969, National Register Property 1972

At 330 Hillsborough Street, the townhouse Americana, pictured here, is thought to have been built by Thomas Briggs in 1879 for one of Raleigh's mayors, William H. Dodd. From owner Dodd it was bought in 1890 by John Wetmore Hinsdale and has remained in the Hinsdale family since that time.

The house is one of the finest examples and, thanks to the owners, one of the best preserved of those left standing in the City, from the era called Victorian. And as such, it might well be perpetuated. Its facade is bilaterally symmetrical, which is rare for this type of residence. And its bold, "Eiffel Tower" cupola, topped with a tiara of metal tracery, is as surprising as it is gay. The chimneys present themselves as crenelated battlements and the heavily but simply bordered windows, plus the plain surfaces of the pressed brick, rather rest the vision by contrast to the building's multiple decorative elements.

The guttae, hanging from the "capitals" of the entrance portico, are repeated across the east and west wings of the porch and seem to read with a separate, ornamental meaning of their own. The consoles of both floors are also placed in a different series of mod-

ules to offer variation.

The interior has been as well cared for as the outside and with its thirteen-foot ceilings, engaging plaster mouldings, deep bay windows, double parlors, and pretty staircase, it might well be an 1879 dramatic cyclorama. The only major changes in the whole place have been the addition of bathrooms, inside kitchen, and a frame apartment to the house's left rear.

After the death of John Hinsdale, Jr., in 1971, the house fell on hard times. While family and preservationists sought funds and appropriate usage for its salvation, the structure suffered from a number of minor fires and vandalism, and an expected renovation fell through. Then in 1982, it was purchased by businessman Thad Eure, Jr., with a vision for its future — a very fine restaurant. For the past six years a master craftsman has lived on the property and is meticulously restoring the interior details. A magnificent staircase has replaced the vandalized one. Central heating and air-conditioning and plumbing are all now up-to-code.

But the untimely death of Mr. Eure has put any ultimate use plans on hold. The property remains in his estate. And the Dodd-Hinsdale House eagerly awaits its future.

140

16 North Dawson Street

Dr. James W. McGee House
Circa 1880
Demolished 1971

Concern for the north and west porches of sixteen North Dawson Street, reproduced here, seems to have pre-empted all of the unknown architect's attention. The house appears to be an extremely plain person who has just enmasked himself for a ball. The baroque, repetitive forms comprising the square columns' "capitals," the fancy acorn drops, fans—all are masterpieces of the skilled jig saw artisan and document, as well as any house in Raleigh, the era's intrigue with the new sawing blade.

The verandas' balustrades are suggestively neo-classical and, against the house's simplicity, they become major decorative components. The four-pane windows are generously large, their trim slightly arched at the top, and the facade's small gable, with its center medallion, reads rather as a miniature pediment to the protruding room above the front porch.

Owner-builder James William McGee, M.D., who came to Raleigh from Duplin County in 1878, built this house around 1880. His son, James W. McGee, Jr., also a medical doctor, added a new kitchen with a room above it in 1920 and for many years the residence has been used as doctors' offices and apartments. And, as one may see, the house is slowly dying of suffocation since Dawson Street was made an automobile thoroughfare.

The automobile thoroughfare made the site more valuable for a commercial structure, and this masterpiece of the skilled jigsaw artisan was demolished in 1971.

3 East Edenton Street

William Worrell Vass House
Circa 1881
Demolished 1971

Here is the more picturesque and history-worthy of the only two residences remaining on Capitol Square. At number three East Edenton Street, it was built around 1881 by Major William Worrell Vass. And since a biographical note about him has been included with the Vass-Speight House, treated elsewhere in this book, it is sufficient here to say that he is identified in the Raleigh City Directory as being the occupant of this house in 1883.

Such three-story places, usually built where land values have so increased for commercial or institutional use as to prevent their survival, are being erased at an alarming speed from the local as well as national cityscapes.

The house's extravagant exterior with its decorative chimneys,

1895 photograph from Halifax Street

cupola, patterned slate roof, and wooden ornamentation has seen only one major change in its long existence. Earlier in this century the roof of the main, south porch was extended to the east for use as a carport. Otherwise, the interior and exterior are a unique perpetuation of that particularly American building vogue which was characteristic of the 'eighties and 'nineties.

Inside, the original frosted glass and brass gaslight chandeliers, now electrified, depend from ceiling medallions which are of heavy plaster relief. Brass door knobs, and hinges, as seen when opened, are ornamentally embossed. Doors themselves are arched by cutting off the two top corners of the rectangle and scrolled woodwork frames them. The room right of the main hall has a neo-Renaissance fireplace and was used as Major Vass' study. To the left are the parlor, with its black marble mantel, and dining room. The kitchen and pantries are at the end of the wide hallway. The curving stairway, located well to the rear of the hall, is especially handsome.

Still owned and lived in by Vass descendants, portraits and family furniture all intact, the residence seems to further complete its image, also its actual position, as a documentary gallery, both inside and out. As such, and situated so splendidly, the place is, without change, a living example of its era.

And all "eras" come to an end at one time or another. When the State razed the W. W. Vass house in December of 1971, the "era" of private residences facing Union Square, or Capitol Square as it is called today, came to an end. Miss Eleanor Vass, descendant of the builder, who had sold the property to the State, died the same day the house was demolished, at age 94 years. When completed, the plaza of the new Museum of History will occupy the site and a new era will begin.

709 Hillsborough Street

Joel Whitaker House
Circa 1882
Altered 1972

Standing at 709 Hillsborough Street, the red brick Joel Whitaker residence is one of the few nineteenth century houses remaining on a thoroughfare which was full of mansions in the latter part of that hundred years. The place, architecturally, is rather unusual in that its simplicity places it out of the vogue of its time, nor did its inspiration come from any well-defined school of the day. The slate roof line varies with parts of mansard, pitch, and cone; the two-panel beveled glass, main entrance has great charm and sheltering it, the little portico, again, shows the jig saw artisan's preoccupation with the machine. Outside window sills are six-inch-thick rectangles of solid pine.

A central hall divides the house and an elegant, spiral stairway rises from it. Two parlors, one of them pentagon shaped, dining room, kitchen, and work rooms comprise the first floor; bedrooms are on the second.

The house was built by Joel Whitaker, Sr., around 1875, for his first wife. He was, among other things, a brickyard owner and in 1869 he had bought Whitaker's Mill, then located north of Raleigh, on Crabtree Creek.

The house was partially burned and then rebuilt about 1885 and it is known that both Dr. Andrew W. Goodwin and a family named Castlebury lived in the place after it left the Whitakers. It has more recently been used to house a dance school, a beauty shop, et cetera.

Additional research indicates that the Joel Whitaker House was built around 1882 and partially burned in 1883. Mr. Whitaker had good neighbors for most of the furnishings, including the piano, were saved and stored by the Tuckers across the street and by Captain Ashe of Elmwood. Whitaker then rebuilt the house of red brick and oddly enough, after such a precarious beginning, it is one of the few remaining nineteenth century houses that once lined Hillsborough Street.

Brantley's Drug Store, which many older Raleigh families remember as being located at 135 Fayetteville Street and then in the 500 block of Hillsborough Street, was moved to this house in the 1970s by John Brantley, Jr., who was one of the Castlebury heirs. The wooden portico was removed and an awning hung in its place. The drug store is no more; however, the marble fountain has been given to the Museum of History and when it is displayed, it will evoke many fond memories of homemade ice cream and ice cream sodas on a Saturday afternoon.

835 West Morgan Street

Central Prison
1884
Demolished 1978-1984

There were legislative efforts to establish a State prison as early as 1815, but nothing was accomplished until the General Assembly of 1869 provided for construction of "a penitentiary with a stockade and buildings to contain 500 cells." Shortly, temporary log-cabin detention blocks were provided, 1870, while this building, designed by Ohio architect Levi T. Schofield, in imitation of a Medieval, Gothic bastion, was built.

Its construction contract, however, had been given to a private builder and with only foundations completed, the appropriation was exhausted. The State then assumed construction responsibility and the first block of sixty-four cells was finished in 1875, though the original complex was not completed until December of 1884—at a cost of $1,250,000.

Before 1931 the compound still had only one well and spigot for all convicts' bathing; sanitary facilities were extremely limited; buildings' roofs were of wood and were not removed in favor of fireproof concrete slabs until the general 1931 renovation. Other roofs were fireproofed in 1952 and at various times since 1931 many

145

Central Prison

additions and subtractions, within the whole area, have been made.

Architects Wiley and Wilson, for example, were authorized to add an industrial building, 1939-1941; and Bernard Crocker, architect, built a new shop and main building, 1952-1953. And between 1960 and 1965 the architectural firm of Holloway and Reeves built hospital and honor grade facilities for the prison.

The exterior of the old building and its confining granite wall remained for many years as they were constructed; and when one tower was removed in 1946, a State historical society objected so formidably that the tower was replaced as before. But in 1954 all of the original turrets, battlements, spires, and pointed cupolas were condemned by the building inspector and removed, one by one, until none remains.

Today a modern prison complex replaces the "Medieval, Gothic bastion" which was demolished over a period of six years.

Graves-Fields House*
Between 1884-1891
Oberlin Village
1866

The Graves-Fields House, located at 802 Oberlin Road, is a Queen Anne style landmark in Oberlin, a Reconstruction village settled by freedmen following the Civil War. Built between 1884-1891, the large stylish house is an architectural testimonial to the determination and success of Raleigh freedmen in the last quarter of the nineteenth century.

In 1866 Lewis W. Peck, a commission merchant, divided his farm into lots, approximately 1.75 acres in size, and sold them to Negroes. Other landowners in the area followed suit. Named after an Ohio school and station on the Underground Railroad, Oberlin was the manifestation of the freedmen's desires to own land and provide educations for their children. By 1869 it was the location of a graded school that predated the city school system by seven years. In addition to the graded school, Oberlin boasted Latta University, an institution of higher learning founded in 1892 by the Reverend M. L. Latta. Reverend Latta was indefatigable in his search for funds for his school and sought them as far as Paris and in London, where he had tea with Queen Victoria.

The Baptists and Methodists both established churches in Oberlin Village. Oberlin Baptist Church, founded circa 1880, stands next to the Graves-Fields House. Wilson Temple United Methodist Church, founded in the mid-1860s, stands across from the site of the graded school. The community cemetery, which was behind the school, is still there.

Oberlin Cemetery

Among the early residents of Oberlin were James Shepard, Alonzo Peebles, Grandisen Turner, Andrew Hinton, Thomas Williams who was a carpenter for Thomas H. Briggs, and Andrew Andrews who received a Confederate pension because he had helped build the earthen breastworks around the city in 1863. Before the end of the 1870s, Oberlin had a population of 750.

The first recorded post-bellum owner of the property at 802 Oberlin Road, formerly called Hillsboro Road, was Jacob S. Allen. On January 21, 1884, he sold it to Willie M. Graves, a brickmason who later was a Justice of the Peace. During the late nineteenth and early twentieth centuries, brickmasonry was a skilled trade dominated by black artisans.

And in time, Graves built this two-story house with a high hip roof and tower. With its center hall plan, the house still retains its original front porch and stained glass panes in the upper sashes of the windows on the first story. The stained glass window still remains in the gable.

On May 10, 1922, the house became the property of Christine Graves Harris and Mildred Graves, who were daughters of Willie Graves. On December 1, 1938, the Graves House was purchased from the Home Owners' Loan Association by John Graham, a railroad fireman, and his wife Alice. Finally, in 1945, the house was purchased by Mr. and Mrs. Spurgeon Fields, its present owners and occupants. Fields was the chauffeur for Josephus Daniels, editor and publisher of the *News and Observer*, and, after Daniels' death in 1948, was custodian in the newspaper offices.

* *Site added for 1992 edition*

Hawkins-Hartness House

Circa 1885

Raleigh Historic Site 1972, National Register Property 1972

This grand, pressed-brick residence, at 310 North Blount Street, was never supposed to have been built. It was all a mistake. The misunderstanding happened when Martha Bailey Hawkins fell in love with and bought the Bryan House which had been on the same site. Then, since Martha Hawkins and her husband, Dr. Alexander Boyd Hawkins, were shortly leaving for a Florida vacation, they asked Dr. Hawkins' brother, Dr. William J. Hawkins, to have the Bryan house restored for them during their absence.

Returning, the owners found that the brother had not only removed the Bryan place to the corner of Tarboro Road and Hawkins Street but had replaced it on the lot with a new house of his own design, the same reproduced here. Nor had brother William spared the smallest detail in his effort to create comfort, durability, and a feeling of affluence in his plan. Remembering his and his brother's medical-training days at Jefferson Medical School in Pennsylvania, he recalled that Philadelphia cabinetmakers were famous for their skills. So, from there, he hired and had brought to Raleigh a master craftsman who measured the drawings and, under supervision of Dr. William himself, fabricated the woodwork for the entire house, in Philadelphia. Solid-wood trim of mahogany, walnut, and pine, polished exclusively with olive oil, was used throughout. Bathtubs and lavatories were in walnut frames, copper lining the tubs, marble, the lavatories. Door and window sills were marble slabs.

The exterior had distinctly displeased Mrs. Alexander Hawkins who disliked the facade's severity, especially since a "Southern-summer porch" had been excluded. It was she who added the ninety-two-foot veranda, a feature rather out of scale with the house and one which seemingly mitigates the design's architectural intent.

On the grounds originally were croquet and tennis courts, servants' quarters, a stable, later moved to the corner of Oakwood Avenue and Linden Street, and a carriage house. A windmill in the back yard pumped water from a well into a tank located in the residence's attic. This water was used for utilities. A 6,000 gallon cistern in the north garden furnished drinking water for both this house and for the Governor's Mansion just to the south. For transporting the water, "Uncle David," a servant attached to the Governor's home, came with his cedar bucket three times a day.

In 1924, after the death of Dr. and Mrs. Alexander Hawkins, the house was bought from their heirs by Williams Erwin, for $40,000. The fifty pairs of shutters were, at that time, removed and stored on the top floor.

Again the place changed owners when it was sold, around 1928, to James A. Hartness, Secretary of State between 1929 and 1931. And at this time Mrs. James Hartness lives in and maintains the property.

By May of 1883, the designs for the Governor's Mansion had been accepted. The room configuration and the style of woodwork in the Hawkins-Hartness House lead to strong speculation that the builder of this house was familiar with the plan of the Governor's Mansion.

The State acquired the property from the estate of Mrs. James Hartness in 1969 and uses it for offices. In the last few years, descendants of the Hawkins family have given some of the original furnishings to this property.

1914 photograph   *310 North Blount Street*

Three Elm Street Houses

Pullentown

Between 1881-1896

These three late nineteenth-century residences, unusual for their simplicity, were built between 1881-1896. They are located at 408, 410, and 416 Elm Street in east Raleigh and represent some of the earliest "developer" houses in the City.

Their realtor-builder, Richard Stanhope Pullen, was born in 1827 and was the same who donated part of the land for the now North Carolina State University and all the ground for Pullen Park. Indeed, the area around which these buildings stand was known as "Pullentown." A bachelor, the builder is said to have constructed the houses for his sisters.

The philanthropist and developer was quoted as saying that he never wanted a wife, a slave, or a dog. It is known, however, that he did keep one body servant, Washington Ligon, whom he called "Wash." And Pullen was often seen in Raleigh, carrying his inevitable umbrella, with "Wash" and the servant's dog following behind. This little frame is important because of the fact that Mr. Pullen used the point of his umbrella to indicate the spot where he wished a tree

to be planted. "Wash" would then dig the hole and plant the sapling. In this way Richard Stanhope Pullen is credited with having added five thousand trees to the cityscape of Raleigh. He died in 1895.

Pullen built five other houses in the area, 401, 404, 411, and 415 Elm Street and 519 Oakwood Avenue. All were brick, but 401, 404, and 416 were stuccoed.

Sawnwork, as seen on 408, was a typical feature of these houses, along with flat-paneled brick ornament and French doors. These houses form one of the most cohesive streetscapes in Oakwood.

Pullen, considered today as the originator of the "greenway plan" for Raleigh, bequeathed 404, 408 and 410 to nieces, two of whom were sisters, the third his greatniece. Today's owners have adapted these residences for contemporary living.

On the northwest corner of Oakwood Avenue and Elm Street is an identifying marker for "Pullentown," which is located in the Oakwood Historic District.

Raleigh Water Tower

1887

Raleigh Historic Site 1969, National Register Property 1971

Various local newspaper accounts for September, 1887, pridefully recorded progress and completion of the City's Water Tower. Located at 115 West Morgan Street, its cost was published as "about $14,000," and "The last bolt was riveted. . .by Little Robert Wynne, the seven year old son of Mr. J. S. Wynne. He was swung up a distance of over 100 feet and struck the last blow." On September 16, it was reported that "A number of buildings on Fayetteville Street were connected to the Water Works yesterday." And at four o'clock in the afternoon of September 29, "The Water Works were tested . . .every requirement complied with. Civil Engineer Arthur Winslow, general manager M. M. Moore, and Mayor Thompson officially witnessed the test. The Rescue, Capital, Independent, and Victor Hose Companies managed the nozzles and Master Fred A. Olds pulled the lever that placed the works in motion."

Raleigh Water Works built the Tower and held the franchise for public supply. In 1901, Wake Water Works took over the property, operated the plant until it went into receivership in 1913. The City then purchased it and shortly afterward, 1924, the place was abandoned, the iron tank removed from the Tower's top.

In 1938, the landmark was bought from the Municipality by a Raleigh architect, for use as his offices and at that time the exterior and interior were adapted to the needs of an architectural facility. Sensitively and farsightedly, the original walls and major openings were left intact by the purchaser. The plain, utilitarian form of the Tower itself and the rear building, which housed the original shops and offices, were retained, decorative Georgian details being added.

The Tower's first thirty feet were constructed of granite, brought from Rolesville Quarry. The remaining fifty-five feet were of handmade brick. Walls were three feet thick and the octagonal shaft was twenty-four feet in diameter. It was built primarily to support the tank.

It is fortunate for the City that on May 27, 1963, twenty-five years from the date of private purchase, the structure was conveyed to the North Carolina Chapter of the American Institute of Architects to be used as their State Headquarters with assurance, in writing, that the property should be held as an historic site without substantial change, in relative perpetuity. This arrangement represented one of the first occasions in which the Raleigh Historic Sites

Raleigh Water Tower

Commission was able to effect an important preservation transaction, William Henley Deitrick being both owner of the Tower and an early member of the Commission.

 The idea for the publication of the 1967 edition of this book was Wil- *liam Henley Deitrick's, who served on the book's Editorial Committee.* *Mr. Deitrick is considered the "Father of Historic Preservation" in* *Raleigh.*

Labor Building
(Old Supreme Court and State Library Building)
Occupied 1888

Authorized by the General Assembly on February 25, 1885, as a new, two-story building to "provide a suitable room for the Supreme Court and the State Library," the building photographed here is at present, after successive alterations over a period of eighty years, generally known as the Labor Building.

The original appropriation for the L-shaped structure, constructed on land acquired by the State in 1881 at the northeast corner of Edenton and Salisbury streets was $10,000, a figure which was earmarked only for such skills and materials as those which could not be furnished by the State Penitentiary. Another $16,000 was authorized in 1887 in order to install plumbing, finish the building, and add to the basement a central heating plant which was to be used for the Capitol, the new Supreme Court offices, and one other State building.

Colonel W. J. Hicks, who was an architect as well as superintendent of the Penitentiary, drew the plans and the "old red brick building," as it came to be known, was formally dedicated, with due ceremonies, on March 5, 1888.

In 1914 the two stories were converted into four by simply inserting flooring between the high-ceilinged first and second floors.

And at this time the State Library, the Supreme Court, and its Library were moved across Union Square into their new quarters on West Morgan Street. In 1940 the red walls were painted gray, a change which was made to bring the building into closer "harmony" with the stone ones surrounding it.

In 1942 the first floor housed the Department of Labor; the second, Banking Commission; third, Insurance Department; and the fourth, various other State bureaus and commissions. (Repair shops of the General Services Division were included by 1957, in the basement.) Still a sturdy building in 1952, the center portion was architecturally renovated and fireproofing was added.

The cupola, rather like a foolscap, reads today as if it had been put on as an afterthought of the original plan. It remains to date the building at a glance, and to lend interest to the facade.

A. G. Bauer was the assistant architect for this building. As part of an overall rehabilitation plan to update the structure, the State had the gray paint, which had been on the building since 1940, meticulously removed to restore the exterior brickwork as close as possible to its original 1888 appearance. The Department of Labor now occupies the entire structure, which is the second oldest extant State building in Raleigh.

North Carolina State University Campus

Holladay Hall
1889
Raleigh Historic Site 1969

Holladay Hall, originally called Main Building, was North Carolina State University's first and for some time its only academic structure. When built in 1889, out of State Penitentiary-made brick, it contained everything which transpired at the school, even to sleeping quarters on its upper two floors for the institution's entire enrollment, seventy-two students.

Designed by Charles L. Carson and built by W. E. Ashley in a not-too-inspiring era of American architecture, the building would seem to have gained a patina of dignity with time's passage. Nor have successive renovations in this century disturbed its proportioning. Actually, it had been planned to withstand whatever destiny the years might bring, a fact gained from William J. Peele's cornerstone-laying address of August 22, 1889. "In its walls are nothing but North Carolina brick and her still more solid sandstone. It is a goodly and worthy structure. . .I would say in the language of the Latins, itself an emblem of immortality, *Esto perpetua.*"

Alexander Quarles Holladay, for whom the building was later named, was the son of an eminent Richmond, Virginia, lawyer and member of Congress, Alexander R. Holladay. The son was trained in ancient and modern languages, both abroad and at the University of Virginia. On the date of Virginia's secession from the Union, he married Virginia R. Bolling and joined the Nineteenth Virginia Regiment. He became a colonel, survived the War, and returned to Virginia to practice law, farm, and serve in his State's Senate.

Eventually he was chosen president of Virginia's Stonewall Jackson Institute and subsequently head of Florida Agricultural College. And on August 30, 1889, he became the first president of North Carolina College of Agriculture and Mechanic Arts. His office was in this building, the same which houses the 1967 Chancellor of North Carolina State University.

In 1992 the Chancellor's office continues in this, the original building of North Carolina College of Agriculture and Mechanic Arts.

Raleigh Cotton Mills

614-618 Capital Boulevard

Pilot Mills
Circa 1890
Raleigh Historic Site 1990
National Register Property 1989

Raleigh Cotton Mills
Circa 1890

The first unit of Pilot Mills was built circa 1890. Its original president was William H. Williamson and the building has had at least twelve additions.

Raleigh *Illustrated* indicates that in 1904 the factory was operating "with an output of 1,250,000 yards of cotton plaids..." per year. By 1910 it was manufacturing shirting and chambray, had 425 looms, 11,000 spindles, employed about 300 people, used 5,000 bales of cotton annually, and turned out a yearly 8,000,000 yards of cloth.

About 1920 the mill was sold to Consolidated Textile Corporation and re-sold to a group of Raleigh citizens in 1931. In 1966 it was bought by Crompton Incorporated of New York, a company which is now manufacturing fine combed cottons and synthetics in the building.

It is surprising to know that in the early days of this mill its labor union treasurer absconded with all collected dues and the factory has not had a union since that time.

Raleigh Cotton Mills, shown above, is located near the terminal of the Seaboard Airline Railroad. Like Pilot Mills, it was also built around 1890. Of it the 1904 Raleigh *Illustrated* says: "Raleigh now has in successful operation a large spinning factory, the Raleigh Cotton Mills, that consumes 1,750,000 pounds of cotton annually making hosiery yarn."

The old building was originally adorned with two imposing towers, earlier removed, and the building is now painted gray. It is currently used as a Philco products center of distribution.

Pilot Mills responded to change, accommodated to it and mirrored the development of the textile industry in Raleigh. However, since it closed in 1982, Pilot-Crompton Mill, as it is now called, has changed hands several times. It is located at 1121 Haynes Street. Hopes for restoration and adaptive use have not materialized and at present its future is dim. But hope springs eternal. Raleigh Cotton Mills is used as a distribution center and for several small businesses.

122 South Harrington Street
Circa 1890 - Demolished 1967

The sensitive and discriminating balance between plain clapboard surfaces and highly ornamental trim of this house made it one of the better Raleigh examples of the residence Americana, circa 1890.

As in the case of many frame houses of the period, the pilasters and columns of the porch here seem to be a try at being descendants of the Corinthian order. Obviously, they miss and instead resolve themselves into "new" and differently romantic adaptations. This would seem to be true of the dentils and the carefully modulated consoles.

The unusually simple wood crescents over the eight- paned windows lend further contrast to the jig saw decoration and thematically the house could hardly have done without the ventilating medallions centered in the eaves. Brickwork of the boldly patterned chimneys was apparently never pointed up and with encroaching commercialism from all directions, the whole place was allowed to deteriorate. A sturdy house, however, the place was used for professional offices until quite recently.

The Raleigh City Directory of 1905 indicates that Frederick F. Harding, foreman and later superintendent of the old Raleigh Iron Works, lived here at that time.

The house was demolished in 1967 and 25 years later the site remains a parking lot.

200 North Blount Street

Governor's Mansion

1891

Raleigh Historic Site 1990, National Register Property 1970

The Governor's Mansion, shown here, was finished on Burke Square in 1891 and was financed, for the most part, by the sale of State-owned property. The $10,000 proceeds from sales, however, fell far short of the needed figure for completion of the residence and an additional appropriation of the same figure was authorized during the 1885-1889 tenure of Governor Alfred M. Scales. Still the money was inadequate and Superintendent of State Prison, W. J. Hicks, who was in charge of construction, commandeered all kinds of methods for stretching the funds. He used native pine rather than an imported material throughout the interior, boosting at the same time North Carolina products. He employed prison labor for brick making and some of the convicts' initials on the brick remain as testimonials to their labor.

Governor, 1879-1885, and Mrs. Thomas J. Jarvis pressured the ground swell for erection of the Mansion since, after post-Civil War abandonment of the old "Palace" at the end of Fayetteville Street, several Governors had been obliged to live either in rented Raleigh property or in a hotel. Mrs. Jarvis strongly felt that necessary and fitting hospitality could not be dispensed from a public hostelry. And shortly, Samuel Sloan of Philadelphia and his assistant, Adolphus Gustavus Bauer, were chosen as architects to begin the work in 1883.

The residence was designed within the American architectural idiom of the latter part of the nineteenth century and with its freely flamboyant verandas, gables, chimneys, and patterned slate roof, was castigated in this century as being ridiculously over-ornamented, baroque, rococo, old-fashioned. But those critics, who were championing razing the building in favor of a "modern" one, have since

Governor's Mansion

recognized the Mansion's worth in its proper perspective—as a livable, valid, beautifully rare link in the State's chain of historical and architectural continuity.

Generally, the interior, having been renovated and redecorated periodically, has not been greatly changed from the original concept except with the addition of baths and the division of the second-floor ballroom. As well, some modifications have been made to better accommodate both the private and public aspects of the Governor and his family's living.

The broad, main hallway with its sixteen-foot ceilings, the fluted, Corinthian columns and pilasters, the freestanding stairway toward the rear, all would seem to project the try of the architect to capture in dignified form the official purpose of the building. And traditionally each Governor and First Lady who have lived in the place have added to its stored-up legacies.

In 1965 Mrs. Dan K. Moore, wife of Governor Moore, appointed an Executive Mansion Fine Arts Committee to help preserve, furnish and maintain the mansion as an historical asset to the State. In May, 1967,

the legislature gave the group statutory commission status through an act passed by the General Assembly.

However, only four years later the General Assembly created another commission to bring forth plans for a new residence for the Governor. After extensive travel, perusal of submitted plans and evaluation of the present residence, the Executive Residence Building Commission recommended, and the General Assembly in 1973 concurred, that it was more appropriate "to Renovate the Governor's Mansion and to Make It Suitable as Both a Public and Private Residence for the Governor." Thus an extensive renovation began: new heating and electrical systems, installation of air-conditioning, construction of a fire tower, repointing the brickwork, and the like.

But the most intriguing part of the renovation was the uncovering, under approximately 12 coats of paint, of the beautifully handcarved staircase, made of native North Carolina heart-of-pine, which originally had been stained and varnished. And that is how the staircase is seen today.

In 1991 the Governor's Mansion celebrated its Centennial.

Leonidas L. Polk House

1891
Raleigh Historic Site 1976, National Register Property 1977

Leonidas LaFayette Polk, the son of Andrew and Serena Autry Polk, was born in Anson County April 24, 1837. He attended Davidson College a short time, married pretty, seventeen-year-old Sarah Pamela Gaddy in 1857, and settled on the homestead of his father.

His plantation life and marriage were interrupted by the Civil War and, wounded at Gettysburg, he wrote his young wife whom he called "Sallie," "I was wounded on the 1st in our last charge upon enemy lines. . .a shell burst immediately in my front. . . .I was struck to the ground but, recovered and went through the charge. . .not sensible of the wound. . . .I stayed near the battlefield until the 3rd when all who could travel had to leave. . . .I have some money, but no clothes, the Yankees having captured all my clothing except what I have on."

Leonidas Polk survived the conflict to become the farmers' champion of North Carolina, serve in the General Assembly, become the father of our State Department of Agriculture, assist in founding the predecessor of North Carolina State University, head the National Farmers' Alliance and Industrial Union, help create a Baptist school for girls, establish and publish the *Progressive Farmer*, become North Carolina's first Commissioner of Agriculture, and "had he lived four weeks longer, would surely have won the nomination of the People's Party for President of the United States in 1892."

Destitute after the War, he singlehandedly set about building the town of Polkton when, in 1873, the Central Carolina Railroad transversed his Anson County plantation. In that hurried effort he laid out lots, converted one room of his home into a post office, another into a general store, set up a printing press, and by 1880 the census of Polkton numbered 183 people.

He lived in his new town only four years inasmuch as he was already an important State figure and was needed in the Capital. In 1878 he removed to Raleigh where "Sallie" and he and their six daughters, whose ages ranged from four to twenty, occupied the house shown here. It was built as having "all modern conveniences, such as bath-rooms, water-closets, hot and cold water and gas."

The residence, sometimes described as "gingerbread Gothic," was located at 565 North Person Street but was moved to the rear of a property at 612 North Blount where it remains in good repair as an antique shop.

Additional research indicates that it was not until April 8, 1890, that Sarah G. Polk, wife of Leonidas, purchased a lot on the west side of Person Street "as extended beyond the limits of the City of Raleigh." And it was on this lot that they built their home, 1891. Previously they had resided at 542 East Jones Street.

The house, shown here, is now rental property. However, plans are currently underway by the Wake County Historical Society, Inc., to move the structure to an appropriate location and preserve it for an adaptive use that can also recognize one of Raleigh's most important nineteenth century residents — Leonidas L. Polk.

Behind 612 North Blount Street

The Park Hotel
1893
Demolished 1975

The Park Hotel, finished in 1893, and seen here as it appeared in 1925, was built by A. F. Page. And according to the Raleigh *Illustrated* of 1904, Howell Cobb, who was also proprietor of the Yarborough Hotel, "has recently purchased the Park Hotel, a comparatively new house, of one hundred rooms, beautifully located, on Nash Square, and will remodel and convert it into a hotel of the very best class, and cater to the best element of winter tourist travel."

Before 1905 the hotel, indeed, had been remodeled by Architect William P. Rose, at a cost of $25,000, renamed The Raleigh, and its policy changed from accommodating winter guests only to that of taking all-year travelers. At this time the building is described as having seven floors, each 135 by 160 feet, a dining room for 100 guests, and otherwise reported as being lighted by electricity and having steam heat. Further, "Every comfort and convenience is provided, including up-to-date elevator service. The office, writing rooms, lounging room and lobby are handsomely decorated, have mosaic tiling and marble wainscoting. The house is conveniently situated a block from the business center of the city, a block from Union Station. . . .This makes it a favorite stopping place with travelers and tourists." Again, in 1912, the structure was remodeled and converted into apartments and Raleigh had its first apartment house.

The building, cast precisely within the design mold of its time, perhaps represents the latter days of the romantically eclectic. And it continues, in 1967, to serve again as one of Raleigh's downtown hotels, now called the Park Central.

The Park Hotel was designed by A. G. Bauer, who provided the working drawings for the Governor's Mansion. In 1975 it was demolished to make way for a parking lot.

Fourth Dorm

North Carolina State University Campus

Fourth Dorm
Built 1894 - Demolished 1964

Primrose Hall
1896

In the early thinking of those concerned with founding the North Carolina College of Agriculture and Mechanic Arts, now known as North Carolina State University, emphasis was especially upon agriculture. But with the growing concern for diversification of Southern industry, stirring at the same time, two founding protagonists merged to write a compounded resolution on January 18, 1887, and "The Board of Aldermen of Raleigh suggested that the proposed Industrial and Agricultural schools be combined." Raleigh's Watauga Club had been the main proponent of the mechanical faction and was led by William S. Primrose, Josephus Daniels, Walter H. Page, and others while Leonidas L. Polk had been spokesman for the farmers.

About 1893, four years after the school had opened its "Main Building," other needed structures were quickly added—a model dairy and four small brick dormitories, First, Second, Third, and Fourth, named in order of their completion. The square, doll-like Fourth Dorm, photograph above, took its architectural inspiration from the eighteenth-century French. Its walls were made from the

1,500,000 bricks which the school's first Board of Trustees had requested, along with a supply of labor, from the State Penitentiary. The little building's reputation grew and it became known as "Bloody Fourth" because of so many students' fights within. The last of these early campus dormitories, Fourth, was taken down to make land for School of Design expansion in 1964.

Primrose Hall, pictured on next page, was so named to honor earlier-mentioned William S. Primrose and started the precedent of naming buildings for the school's benefactors. Constructed during the summer of 1896, it was originally used for instruction of botany and general horticulture and in 1904, after "Agriculture Hall" was built, it housed the Department of Civil Engineering.

One must hope that this tiny, yet pompously towered, little landmark, which preserves the scale of the early campus, may be kept and cherished as one of the four early remaining buildings, Holladay Hall, Watauga Hall, named for the Watauga Club, and a piece of the 1897 infirmary being the others.

Primrose Hall

North Carolina State University Campus

Capitol Square

Confederate Monument
Unveiled 1895

This unusually fine photograph of the Confederate Monument, on Capitol Square, is a contemporary one and was taken from the iron-balconied west portico of the Capitol. The monument, earlier criticized as being a view obstruction to the Capitol Building, has since been felt to be an inseparable part of the Square's milieu and of its history. It was dedicated "To Our Confederate Dead" and was unveiled May 20, 1895, amid addresses, a parade, and other formalities.

The shaft is seventy-five feet high, made of Mount Airy granite, with three bronze figures of uniformed Confederate soldiers, one atop and one each at the north and south sides of the column. And although these statues were modeled, according to some reports, from a photograph of Raleigh veteran W. R. Dicks, and cast in Munich, the entire feeling of the monument is much like other Confederate memorials to be seen throughout the South.

The thirty-two pound naval cannons, at ground level, beside the monument, were originally mounted at Fort Caswell within the Cape Fear River defenses and were dismantled when Confederate forces abandoned the fort in 1865. They were turned over to the Norfolk Navy Yard and later given to the State by the War Department in 1902.

Women of the State raised money for the memorial and these funds were added to by legislative appropriation.

Saint Augustine's College Campus, 1315 Oakwood Avenue

Saint Augustine's Chapel

1895

Raleigh Historic Site 1969

Saint Augustine's College Campus, National Register Property 1980

The little Episcopal chapel, pictured here, was built in 1895 on the Saint Augustine's College campus in northeast Raleigh on land which formed part of Willie Jones' summer estate, "Welcome." Jones is remembered here because, as noted in the text of this volume, he was one of the original commissioners chosen to site the City of Raleigh.

The church was designed by Henry Beard Delany, a Negro clergyman who served as Suffragan Bishop of North Carolina; the labor was done by students. Perhaps for reasons of economy, native stone, quarried in the vicinity, was used both inside the building and out, even for the altar, lectern, and support for the altar rail. Interior walls have had no plaster or other kind of visible "finish" and their mortared, local-stone texture conveys an exciting and primitive honesty.

Because many students were not of the Episcopalian persuasion and were converts to a faith requiring baptism by full immersion, a baptismal pool and granite font were installed in the back of the church. Unusual, too, is the fact that this chapel has a lych gate or roofed ante-entrance in which, in early ecclesiology, the bier was placed to await the coffin of a deceased minister or church member.

The church, especially with its later added transepts, is reminiscent of small Norman chapels seen outside of London and in the Cotswold Hills of Gloucestershire.

The campus of Saint Augustine's College was placed on the National Register in 1980. The building housing Saint Agnes Hospital, and located on the southwest corner of the campus, was constructed in 1909 and was not only a hospital, but also a nurses' training center for blacks. The college students quarried the native stone for the building. Though no longer a hospital, but still an integral part of the campus, Saint Agnes Hospital was designated a Raleigh Historic Site in 1979.

Northwest corner of Fayetteville and Martin streets

Tucker Building
Built 1899 - Demolished 1966

Major Rufus S. Tucker acquired part of the land, at the northwest corner of Martin and Fayetteville streets, on which this building was later constructed, in 1883. When he died in 1894 the property was willed to his wife, Florence P. Tucker who bought adjoining footage and in turn conceived the notion of erecting a "modern" office building on the lots.

Plans were drawn by C. M. Cassels of Norfolk, Virginia, and the building was completed in September of 1899. It was one of Raleigh's first office buildings but word circulated that the new structure would never be completely occupied because it was too much "office" space for Raleigh with sixty-six foot Fayetteville Street frontage, seventy-two foot Martin Street depth, and rising five stories high.

In any case, when completed, with its interior iron balustrades reaching to the second floor and its marble steps, the pressed brick building was thought to be a skyscraper though not Raleigh's first inasmuch as the four-story Thomas H. Briggs building, seen far right in this Albert Barden photograph, had been built more than two decades earlier.

Contrary to the doubters' opinions about full occupancy, the building became popular at once and a variety clientele rented its spaces. Corner space on the ground floor, leased by Dr. James McGee, was called the Tucker Building Pharmacy and was later taken over by Gilbert Crabtree and Henry Hicks. Next to it, fronting on Fayetteville Street, was Cross and Linehan's, a men's clothing store. And on the upper floors professional people, tradesmen, and businessmen took offices.

Of Cross and Linehan's, the Raleigh *Illustrated* for 1904 reports that, "This concern has been established for a period of some fifteen years. . . .The house deals in an excellent line of all kinds of clothing, furnishings, and hats—in fact everything that a man wears. All goods are guaranteed to be of the best make and the highest quality, while at the same time they are sold at the lowest prices. Terms are strictly cash."

The building was sold to Wachovia Bank and Trust Company in 1927 and was used by that institution until 1966 when it was demolished.

102 North Blount Street

Baptist Female University
Opened 1899 - Demolished 1967

The Baptist Female University was born old. Its founding had been talked about by the Baptist State Convention for more than a half century before the first students matriculated, 1899. The delay in its beginnings was explained by Richard T. Vann, early mentor and second president of the school. "The reason assigned was poverty, but Wake Forest. . .accumulated $100,000 in endowment before the Civil War. I fear, therefore, we must admit that the longstanding assumption of superiority by men over women was responsible."

After multiple financial reverses, matched by equal perseverance, the last note and mortgage of this building, at Edenton and Blount streets, was canceled and burned on February 10, 1904. A "joyous celebration" then ensued.

The five-story landmark was designed by Architect A. G. Bauer who also did plans for the present Governor's Mansion, and it would appear that his high C on the "fluff and filigree scale" was no better representative in his work than here. The old building was relinquished as the school site during Christmas vacation of 1925-1926 and the enrollment moved into nine new buildings on property that

had been known as the Tucker Farm, then located three miles west of Raleigh. Meantime, the school's name had been changed, 1904, to the Baptist University for Women and again in 1909 to Meredith College, so re-named for Thomas Meredith who was the originator and editor of the *Biblical Recorder* and one of the founders of the Baptist State Convention.

The towered and altogether fanciful structure, however, did not yet die. It was then converted into what was known as the Mansion Park Hotel, later changed into apartments, and finally bought by the State in May of 1951 for $165,000. It is now being demolished, 1967, in favor of using the land for State office expansion.

Baptist Female University was chartered in 1891; but three concerns delayed its opening: raising enough money, whether or not Baptists would support the education of women, and the location. In 1991 Meredith College celebrated its charter's Centennial year and unfortunately, 100 years later, there are still some who will not accept women as equal under God.

In 1992, the site of the 1899 campus is still used as a state government parking lot.

The State Capitol, detail

Part III
1900-1992

Figure by Gutzon Borglum, Elmwood Garden, 1967

Part III
1900-1992

ONCE MORE UNTO THE BREECH, DEAR CITIZENS

The new century counted 13,643 people living in Raleigh, fifth largest city in the State. But of these, literacy reports for 1900 reveal that almost fifty percent of the Negro population and twenty percent of the white remained illiterate. And so with the sure knowledge of these figures, educational changes were promptly proposed by Governor Charles Brantley Aycock in his inaugural address of January 5, 1901. "We are prospering as never before—our wealth increases, our industries multiply, our commerce extends. . . .Gentlemen of the Legislature, you will not have aught to fear when you make ample provision for the education of the whole people. . . ."

Obviously, the City could go no further without a proper high school facility. Called Raleigh High School, it opened on West Morgan Street in 1908 with two hundred and fifty students, eight classrooms, an auditorium and extensive basement. Straightaway the enrollment leaped to five hundred, many of whom tasted wonderful divertissement on occasions when the City Water Tower, just west of the school, overflowed.

As measured by luxuries which it could and did support, Raleigh was indeed prospering. It was considered, in the early part of the century, "the best theatre town for its size in the Nation." As early as 1903 the City had seen its first "talking" picture. Exhibited in Metropolitan Hall on the second floor of Fayetteville Street's Market House, the "talkie" impresarios always brought along their own screen, projection machine, and phonograph. Unfortunately, action did not always fit the dialogue. And often the hero's big mouth moved while the voice was that of the squeaky heroine, pleading for help in saving the old home place.

The Revelry opened some time later on Fayetteville Street and was the first and only exclusively motion picture parlor in the City. It made a specialty of showing Biograph reels and was equipped with "improved type projection machinery. . .electric fans, heating system, modern opera chairs and all other comforts for its patronage. . . ." Employed regularly here was a five-piece orchestra. Though it all sounded commodius enough at the time, the Revelry was completely refurbished in 1908, renamed the Almo, and was operated continuously until it burned in 1925. Across the street was another theatre, the Superba.

The Grand, in a building constructed solely for theatre purposes, opened its 115 Fayetteville Street doors in 1910. It advertised a "six-piece orchestra for afternoon and evening performances and a balcony provided with orchestra chairs." Alack again, the Grand burned in January of 1928. At five-cent admission charges, other Fayetteville Street theatres came and went. There were near the Capitol both the Airdrome which was a tent affair, and the Gaiety which featured dancing girls and two-reel thrillers. "Nice" people turned up their collars and pulled down their hats when attending the Gaiety.

It was the old Academy of Music, however, built at the corner of Martin and Salisbury streets in 1893, which was entertainment's aristocrat. It was magically fitted out with *deus ex machina* and often played, among other things, two to four original-cast New York shows a week during the season from October to March. Here were seen Dustin Farnum, Geraldine Farrar, Schumann-Heink, Will Rogers, Irene Castle, Madame Melba, W. C. Fields, Ethel and John Barrymore, Maude Adams, and as a special attraction, Jim Corbett of heavyweight fame.

The City enjoyed all of this and yet in 1910, with a population of 19,218, it was only now building a "large" municipal building and auditorium combination. Truthfully, in March of 1909, Raleigh had been mortally scared into hurriedly authorizing the $125,000 bond for the building. The fright and then the pressure had come about earlier when lack of an adequate auditorium caused Democratic State Conventions to meet in Charlotte and Greensboro—and a House bill providing for the Capital's removal to Greensboro passed a second reading. As one local historian paraphrased Shakespeare about the affair, "It was once more unto the breech, dear citizens, to save the Capital for Raleigh." And here must be added the too-frequent addendum—the auditorium burned October 25, 1930.

BUSINESS AS USUAL IN REFRESHING BEVERAGES

Beginning with the first decade of this century, Raleigh yet encompassed only four square miles and would expand city limits again in 1907 and 1920. Paved now, though, were seventy miles of its streets, macadam and stone being the favorite surfacing. Most of these thoroughfares, too, enjoyed accessibility to the Street Railway Company with its thirty-five tram cars and eleven miles of track.

Manufacturing had now added hosiery, underwear, iron castings, plows, boilers, engines, structural ironwork. As well, says the 1910 Raleigh *Illustrated*, "Raleigh's fifty manufacturing plants turn out medicines, cigars, roofing, stoves, fertilizers, and aerated waters." These "aerated waters" were none other than Coca-Cola which was bottled at 115 South Wilmington and Pepsi-Cola, dispensed from an establishment at the corner of Davie and Salisbury streets.

The uniquely American drug store had come to the City, one at Fayetteville and Morgan, the other at Fayetteville and Martin. They were owned by the same proprietor and purveyed, among other things, Cardui, Creomulsion, Black Draught, Lydia Pinkham, Carter's pills, five-cent cigars, and Castoria. In both stores advertisements noted, "Soda water departments are conducted and an extensive business is done in refreshing beverages." It was just as well that soda water was plentiful since the font for anything stronger had, at least overtly, dried up all of Raleigh's "spiritous" parlors back in 1908 when a State-wide referendum had been called. Nonetheless, apparent prosperity continued with water from twenty-five public mains.

In the century's early teens the Capital was beginning to boast about such figures as 3,640 pupils in public schools, $3,250,000 in bank deposits, and 1,200 miles of telephone lines. At the same time it was a quasi-town of part livery stable, part automobile garage. Woodall's Stables had been opened for business at the corner of Blount and Davie and offered "The best- lighted, ventilated and most sanitary stables in the South. . .well protected with ready outlets against fire. . .this firm invites everyone whose horse needs a holiday to send him here."

The other half of things found the Carolina Garage and Machine Company, at 109-113 West Hargett, described as the largest such plant in the State. It had "A completely fitted garage and one of the best-equipped machine shops for auto repairing in the South." It was the agent for both Carolinas and Virginia for "the best known and more reliable cars— the Buick, Franklin, Waverly, and White." Commercial "progress" had begun in earnest, that which would mortgage the City's sight and soul for the next fifty years.

A few of the more sensitive did protest at what was happening. The Woman's Club of 1913, for example, sponsored Charles Mulford Robinson's *A Plan for Raleigh* in which he rather pleaded: "It is a great pity that wires of the business district were not put underground before recent pavements were laid. But perhaps this waste will be worthwhile, considering the limited extent of the paved district, if the lesson be thus conclusively taught. . . .It is just as reasonable and necessary to require that wires be placed in conduits before a street is permanently paved, as it is to require that sewers and water mains shall be constructed in advance. . . .They are a serious menace in case of fire. . .they lead to the beheading and mutilation of trees."

Mr. Robinson and the 1913 Raleigh women also challenged raising commercial signboards and the practice of painting advertisements on buildings' walls. "They are dangerous (owing to high wind, faulty construction) or from obstruction to fighting fires. They shut off street views. . .disfigure architecture. . . .Shall the City grant the right to make Raleigh streets ugly and unsafe for the sake of a doubtful advantage to individual merchants, the profits from such action being directed chiefly into the pockets of the electrical and advertising interests?" But, blowing in the wind against privileged license, these voices were never heard.

THE SIXTH CONFLICT

Declaration of war "to save the world for democracy," on April 6, 1917, seemed to be the catalyst for mitigating left-over "Reconstruction" bitterness. For the first time, an American flag was flown above the Confederate Soldiers' Home in the City and some sixty veterans of the Civil War volunteered for service.

Back in 1861 a white handkerchief had been dropped from a State House window, signifying for the waiting crowd below, the secession decision. In 1917, pervasive word from Washington into Raleigh homes was as instant as the telephone. Contingents of Boy Scouts, National Guardsmen, Confederate soldiers, and citizens, both Negro and white, paraded from the Capitol to the auditorium. Bands of the Third Regiment played and patriotic rallies were held all over the City.

In less than two months the Capital had registered 2,558 men for selective service and in all, nine military organizations were formed here for this War. On September 25, 1918, Camp Polk, a 16,000-acre tank corps training center, was established just off Hillsborough Road. Raleigh's women made hospital supplies, set up canteen arrangements for meeting and serving "the boys" as their troop trains passed through on one of the four railroads now serving Raleigh. And North Carolina State College offered all of its facilities for soldier training.

Governor and Mrs. Thomas Walter Bickett installed cots on the second or ballroom floor of the Burke Square Mansion and kept open house for transient service men. Nor, according to the Governor's open letter, datelined Raleigh, June 11, 1918, was he prepared to countenance slackers. "I have instructed our police officials to rigidly enforce vagrancy laws. All men. . .who refuse to work five days in the week, after having been given notice by the County Council of National Defense, should be prosecuted for vagrancy. . . .This will reach the idle rich as well as the idle poor."

By May of 1918 Raleigh and Wake County had sent 775 soldiers to France and at the armistice, November 11 of the same year, the State as a whole had paid more than its price with casualty numbers at 5,799, third highest in the Nation.

To greet the survivors home on March 24, 1919, church bells rang to call worshipers and thanksgivers together. "Automobile horns, cowbells, bugles, and stentorian whoops" filled the air with victory. "False alarms kept the fire department busy. . .and Meredith girls, in their blue skirts and middy blouses, made an effigy of the Kaiser, banished him. . .and did a serpentine march around the Capitol."

PLANLESS PROSPERITY

Although the 1918 influenza epidemic had closed schools, public institutions, and taken 238 lives, our soldiers came home to an otherwise prosperous town of 24,000 people. There had been myriad changes and the City was expanding in every sphere except that of taste and order. "Growth" continued to be evaluated in terms of more people, dollars, payrolls, smokestacks, automobiles. Rampant commercialism was still holding the saddle horn and would jealously, lobbyingly guard it until our own time when public awareness would finally call "halt" to licensing demolition of worthy, historical buildings and replacing them with jerry-built potential slums—"halt" to garish signboards, indiscriminate tree destruction and to pollution of our air, land, and water.

Meantime, the unheard few kept trying to retain what had been good in the old cultural continuum while striving to inject a modicum of discrimination into the leaping new. Illustrative is Raleigh Mayor T.B. Eldridge's January 18, 1922, entreaty. "Had a city planning board been operating in Raleigh a century ago the railroads would not have been allowed to cut across street extensions. . . .Observe what happened to Edenton Street and Lane. Take a position on Blount near the Governor's Mansion and look northward. The County Home is in full view and Blount Street ought to lead right up to its doors; but two railroads are found to cut off progress in that direction as effectually as though the space were occupied by a river with neither bridge nor ferry."

He goes on to say, "Take another instance of misdirected municipal development viz., Hillsboro Street westward from the Oberlin Road. The greatly decreased width of the street at this point is an ugly disfigurement of the City's most important avenue. . .consider what might have been if the State Fair had been located somewhere other than Hillsboro Street. . . .Behold the crazy-quilt patches that have been stuck on the sides and hung on the corners of the original city plan. . . .Give the kaleidoscope another turn. . .see streets that were laid off for no earthly purpose but to sell building lots. . . .The acquisition of additional park areas will be a stroke of real municipal statesmanship. Nash Square today is little more than an open space and an opportunity. Moore Square is a network of bypaths and a convenient place for the display of secondhand wearing apparel. A City Planning Commission would win its way to the hearts of the people by rescuing these squares from their state of neglect and misuse . . . .Zoning exists in Raleigh today only in the restrictions applied to construction of buildings in what is called the fire district. But zoning should go a long way beyond that. . . ."

A 1924 survey indicates that these "crazy-quilt patches" stuck on the City's sides, which the Mayor referred to, were Hayes Barton, Mordecai Place, Boylan Heights, Cameron Park, Country Club, Roanoke Park, and College Park. These then, plus the old, comprised the 1924 City. And though the beginnings of modern city planning were being aired by the more alert, few yet understood or foresaw the ultimate necessity of channeling the desecrating course of the private automobile. Instead, in the 'twenties it was encouraged and, with the City's blessing, crowned first queen of the May. Its restrictions mainly covered automobile handling. *Traffic Ordinances of the City of Raleigh*, 1924, begin: "Whereas the increase in the number of motor vehicles and congestion of traffic. . . .has made it necessary. . . .to prescribe. . . .regulations upon streets and thoroughfares of said city. . . .It shall be unlawful. . . .to drive a vehicle propelled by gasoline. . . .at a greater rate of speed than ten miles per hour in the Business District of said city and twenty miles per hour in any portion. . . .lying outside."

In passing, it is revealing to note that the 1924 speed limit had increased two miles per hour over that specified in the 1916 Ordinances. It is known, too, that the 1924 "Business District" was defined as enclosed by Morgan, Blount, Cabarrus, and McDowell. Finally the Ordinances prescribed that "Every person driving a motor-driven vehicle. . . .shall pass to the right, and upon coming up from the rear of another vehicle, pass to the left. . . .all shall be driven to the right of the center of the street. . . ." And so the machinery was in place for the physical deterioration of the old "one square mile" and its approaching residential streets, Person, Hillsborough, New Bern, Glenwood, and later many others. With so few to say nay, filling stations began their "beautification" of most choice corner sites.

MAKING DO WITH DOUBLE THE PEOPLE

Like the rest of the Nation in the 'thirties, Raleigh floundered in the wake of the great depression. Six of the City's banks failed as relief rolls multiplied. And inasmuch as Raleigh's population had nearly doubled in the 'twenties, to 37,379, real suffering from food shortages jarred old timers into recalling the desperation of Civil War days.

There were, however, a few depression-inspired compensations. Citizens and businesses were making do with far less or no buying power and survival techniques showed rare ingenuity. The April 30, 1933, *News and Observer* demonstrated a case in point when it offered a free trip to Chicago's "The Century of Progress" to any person who would sell $392 worth of the paper's subscriptions—paid in advance, of course. Flappers had stopped flipping and instead were seriously using their relatively new voting enfranchisement. And on May 1, 1933, three-point-two percent wine and beer became legal again, a fact which shortly and sharply diminished Raleigh's flourishing prohibition demimonde.

In terms of "made work," artificial respiration by the Federal Government plus all the citizen self-help succored the depressed town back into orbit, along with many of its old mistakes. The new Memorial Auditorium was dedicated on January 19, 1932, less than two years after the first one had burned. It was a hurried enterprise but nobody wanted to hear again the wail to move the Capital. In a copper box, buried in the building's cornerstone were items characteristic of the Raleigh personality: a sketch of the old Governor's "Palace" which formerly had been on the site, a photograph of Robert E. Lee, a Confederate battle flag, a copy of the Old North State song, a current newspaper, and a reproduction of the 1792 William Christmas map of the City. That done, the structure, which the architect had designed as "compatible" with the Capitol, forever confined and embalmed Fayetteville Street into a few north-south city blocks.

Paving the City's way for more refuse absorption of the combustion engine, the first six public transportation buses were unleashed on March 1, 1933. Their routes covered Roanoke Park, Hayes Barton, and other parts of northwest Raleigh. And City Hall ceremonial records for the occasion tell us that they were home-state products, their components being manufactured in Henderson and Wilson. Unfortunately, on March 13, 1933, Raleigh's last trolley car pulled "into local oblivion at midnight, nearly a half century after the first street car. . .started its career while a band played and people cheered."

A different architectural feeling, philosophically generated in the latter part of the nineteenth century and ambiguously labeled "contemporary," came to Raleigh in the late 'thirties and early 'forties. At that time it was generally characterized by simplified, utilitarian designs which were easily adaptable to commercial, institutional, even residential needs. And within the framework of its evolutionary changes in adaptations, vogues, professional interpretations, it continues to modify Raleigh's physical profile. Early public housing illustrated the beginnings of the new design philosophy at about the time the City's Housing Authority was established. Having acquired money from the Federal Government, bond sales, and private investors, the new City agency began, 1939-1940, construction of Halifax Court and Chavis Heights. Both of these complexes were plain rectangles, some of them sited in parallel tiers, a considerable departure from older architectural modes. In these beginnings, Raleigh was devilishly trying in the direction of slum clearance and public housing. But even in 1940 the effort was only a raindrop in the barrel inasmuch as the City's population had risen another hundred percent in just the one preceding generation.

CAME THEN ANOTHER WAR

For a while we had called ourselves the "arsenal of democracy." Then, on December 7, 1941, happened Pearl Harbor to suddenly electrify the Country into sending men and women to all global fronts. North Carolina's Capital responded to this seventh war feverishly. Hollywood figures swept through town to glamourize war bond rallies and sales. United Service Organization canteens mushroomed. Most people worked from sunrise to dusk. And again the Governor, J. Melville Broughton this time, entertained soldiers, sailors, and marines in the Mansion. North Carolina State College students gathered scrap metal for the cause and Raleigh-Durham Airfield became a military installation.

With normal farm output being shipped overseas, Raleigh school children and adults had planted, by 1945, four thousand victory gardens, on back and front yards, even curbs. And when it was over Wake County, as ever, numbered its casualties. Killed in action had been 114, sixteen had later died of wounds, fifty-seven non-battle deaths had been recorded and eleven others were presumed dead.

METAMORPHOSIS

All the while, war's booming and its parallel, inflationary prosperity, were being heard and felt in every sector of the City's life. Raleigh settled into a paroxysm of necessarily hasty changes and in an assay toward handling the metamorphosis, the municipal government reorganized itself in 1947 into a Council-Manager system. The new structure must have succeeded inasmuch as it had inherited a city debt of $50,000 and at the end of one year, June 30, 1948, had come up with a $166,000 surplus.

City Hall was so delighted with its accomplishments that it published a purring booklet, a little tome which indicated that, "All personnel for the City, under new procedure, is being paid by check instead of cash. . .all city officials handling any money or real responsibility, have been put under bond."

During the year there was "Increased rental on city properties such as $6,000 for Devereux Meadow. . . ." and included among twenty-six other innovations mentioned were: "Salary adjustments in Police and Fire as well as all other divisions in order to bring our employees up to the standard of other cities. . .a sick and annual leave policy has been adopted. . .the city has a pension plan, effective January 1, 1949. . . .During the year the city devoted much time in an effort to improve one of the worst conditions, namely traffic and parking. . . .One way streets were put into service, traffic lanes were painted on streets, new traffic lights were installed and $21,000 was expended to synchronize lights on Hillsboro Street. . .additional parking meters were installed. . . ."

Further, "Provision has been made to have two garbage collections weekly. . .water and sewer line extensions have been extended and by 1949 sewer and water will be available to every home within the city limits. . . .Police Department was divided into. . .Traffic, Detective, and Street Patrol. . .the City of Raleigh contributes now a truck, two dog catchers and $75 a month to the Wake County Society for the Prevention of Cruelty to Animals."

Then at last, "The city has provided funds to employ a Planning and Zoning Engineer. . .to revamp our Zoning Ordinances and prepare a city plan. . .a city without a plan is like a ship without a rudder."

WHO SHOT RALEIGH?

Surely enough, as Raleigh had been so often forewarned in the early part of this century, the next decade saw the old City suffer for many reasons, especially because of the uncontrolled, one person per one super-powered automobile. "Downtown" seemed to be dying, like thousands of others in the United States, of slow strangulation. Empty "loft" spaces appeared, some business firms moved out, along with efficient public transportation and customers began to howl, "there's no place to park my car." And so, in a futile effort to keep private-car shoppers coming, sound, often historic and architecturally significant buildings were razed, the land forfeited to parking lots. These places then were soon to put up, sometimes by mid-day, their movable signs, FULL.

Various workable nostrums were offered including a tree-and-flower-bowered mall for Fayetteville Street in which private cars would be excluded and the pedestrian might again become king and queen. But the plan was turned down as a cure too visionary. Too expensive.

City buses continued their empty routes as personal automobiles pre-empted their service and cars increased their course of perfuming, lacerating, and dismembering not only "downtown" but the rest of the City with their accommodating freeways. Yet only the minority citizen was aware that freeways had long since been negated by better planners, as passe in other cities, outmoded, no solution because these eight-laners, too, would be car-gorged before they could be paid for.

Experienced international city planners had many times said that the cohesive, good-living city size should not exceed about 80,000 people; that public transportation must bring people into business complexes; that "growth" should not be measured in numbers of people and concentration of industries and their payrolls. But understandably, few were prepared to relinquish the privacy and comfort of individual conveyance. Nor did many, in their inevitably busy lives, look at the evils of megalopolis in order to understand the merits of a static census within a confined area. Raleigh, it was said in retrospect by the experts, was eating its two cakes throughout the late 'forties, 'fifties, and early 'sixties.

Schools were being built to which more classroom space had to be added before their new doors were hung. Trailer classrooms, using up erstwhile playground areas became common. The City overflowed into hurriedly built residential subdivisions and all annexable ones were soon added in an effort to defray rising municipal expenditures.

By 1960 "downtown" had already splintered and deployed into a dozen or more not-too-pretty shopping centers—their asphalted sites clean shaven of existing trees. Still, it did not appear that any end was in sight since it was true that as late as July, 1964, some who held the "big" philosophy were on record with the slogan "Raleigh wants two hundred thousand people by 1980."

It was really not until the 'sixties that most average citizens began to look around at their City and not entirely endorsing what they saw, asked—who shot Raleigh?

BIRTHDAY CITY

And yet, as spoken in the beginning, "Always on its back, Raleigh has to be looking up." It is looking up, and out. In this year of its 175th birthday, 1967, the City finds itself at the crossroads. Without blinders, it is seeing in all directions. There are in the wind now beginnings of people vigilance, citizen pressure, concern for order and elegance, disdain for the ugly, and respect for inheritance. Afoot at present are forces which hope and work to see that one day all utility poles will be flattened and their wires put in underground conduits.

Somewhere along the way the notion that Raleigh was to be a governmental, educational, and cultural center in particular, got lost; and unlimited industry was sought out, invited, and came, but without preparedness on the part of the City. Now, however, resulting, further pollution of our water and air is being studied. Industry itself is becoming more conscious of and willing to cooperate in directions which favor stoppage of air-water defilement, the building and maintenance of more sightly plants, the retention of natural-growth trees. The regurgitating smokestack is slowly losing its past image as the symbol of "progress."

Considered now are master plans for the Research Triangle Park and its contiguous land which are perhaps to be zoned toward avoiding further waste, shoddiness, and old mistakes. All of this planning, if executed, will possibly spread throughout the whole region, involving for the better, not only Raleigh but Chapel Hill, Durham, and the enclosed Triangle as well.

Raleigh now requires of the heretofore largely unrestricted "developer-builder" long-forgotten sidewalks. Walkways, also, are being demanded around school locations. In new subdivisions land must be left free a specified length of time, for City option, to the purpose of insuring space for schools, fire stations, playgrounds, parks; and the Municipality, whenever possible, hopes to exercise these options quickly. People, their elected representatives, their planners, are concerning themselves with the wisdom of saving and restoring the best of our physical past.

The more sensitive of Raleigh feel, at present, that ending the spoilage and reviving aesthetic values have only begun, that there is much to do. The work of those citizens who would regenerate the City's taste consciousness has embattled them, in latter years, over a course of self-interest, apathy, often greed. But they feel that these fights are healthy for both factions, certainly for the City. In any case they have seen the renewal started with a certain rational proposition of reversal and many feel that it will continue. That is, they sense that Raleigh has begun to do something about outmoded city-growth philosophies.

Raleigh is now studying feasible, efficient, collective transportation as other cities have been doing. And in easy stages the City plans to rid itself of the aforesaid tree-destroying wires, a matter pushed along by that wider awake populace. Elected and appointed City officials are looking for ways to reverse the strip blight slumminess of all approaches coming into the City, changing them into well-ordered avenues. Raleigh planners and a progressively greater number of citizens are becoming vocal in seeking of the new shopping centers that they reserve a modicum of their asphalt oceans in favor of more green spots, fountains, public benches, shade, safe pedestrian walkways. And they feel that existing centers might then follow the leaders to jackhammer up a little of their own black surfaces for other kinds of shopper accommodation.

Local leaders in all these spheres are thinking in terms of a more orderly evolution for the whole region. And they hope it will be possible to inaugurate, giving it teeth, some kind of public body which, with popular endorsement, will codify standards and forbid further debasement in all areas. Also, they continue the running battle to regulate billboards and neon eye- offenders, just as the Federal Government is doing on some of its highways. And finally, in keeping with national trends, new and specific legislation is being contemplated, that which will prevent indiscriminate destruction of Raleigh buildings designated historically and aesthetically worthy of retention.

While all of these things are in ferment, the torch-bearers and others continue to ask the question— are correcting the old faults and controlling the new of our environment interfering with the inalienable prerogatives of the individual, with private enterprise especially? To answer this, most have long since decided that minding their own air, water, and what they have to look at is everybody's business. They feel that the good and bad of commercialism birthed most of our cityscapes and these innovations will only augment a rewarding direction shift in attitudes of business concerns—for the sake of all, the touring visitor, for the present and future progeny.

Many feel that completion of these proposed and actualized changes are within reach. And if they can be accomplished with a sharpened sense of civic ecology, historical continuity, with remembrance of the original, planned Capital concept, and with a new thrust at preserving the good of what belongs to the citizens— chances are that some of the fine Raleighness of the City's personality will survive with dignity for another hundred and seventy-five years.

ANOTHER BIRTHDAY — ANOTHER CENTURY
1992

Raleigh, twenty-five years ago, blazed new trails in preservation for municipalities throughout the State when it became the first in North Carolina to purchase an historic site for development as an historic park. It is still blazing trails for preserving the city's heritage with its monetary backing for the development of the City Market/Moore Square area. But even with these pluses, Raleigh, twenty-five years later, still faces many of the same problems enumerated when the 1967 edition of this book was published. However, with the support and assistance of an enlightened populace, the City Council is doing something about some of them.

The 1991 General Assembly, at the urging of Raleigh and Wake County officials, passed a bill allowing up to a five-dollar tax per vehicle for Wake, Durham and Orange counties to be levied so that mass transit for the Research Triangle can be addressed, not just with talk, but with funding. For these years of growth explosion have called for regional planning as well as city and county planning.

In Raleigh itself, "tree-destroying wires" are at last going underground in parts of the downtown area. Mr.

Charles Mulford Robinson's *A Plan for Raleigh*, sponsored by the Woman's Club in 1913, is at long last beginning to come to fruition. And in new subdivisions in Raleigh , wires are going underground right at the start.

Today, new shopping centers must have a certain amount of green space and trees within their parking lots to negate seas of asphalt. But unfortunately, shopping centers are still being approved by the City Council to spring up like mushrooms along major approaches to the city; this in spite of City Council approved "entryway-corridor-plans" that seek to put an end to "strip blight slumminess" and seek to create "well-ordered avenues."

Over the years many plans with both professional and citizen input have come and gone. The Raleigh City Council is continuing to develop "Master Plans" for its downtown area and an Urban Design Guide which would lay the ground work for compatible new development in the area.

Since 1979 Raleigh has had a Comprehensive Plan, which is updated quarterly. This plan will guide Raleigh's growth, but only if it is followed. Raleigh citizens need to understand this plan and its scope in order to "watch dog," for too often exceptions are made and too often regulatory ordinances are set aside, and the plan is violated. An addition to the Comprehensive Plan was made in July of 1991 when the City Council included a preservation element which recognizes Raleigh's heritage, yet includes a growth strategy that provides a way development and preservation can work hand in hand. For after all, Raleigh's heritage should embrace the development of its built environment as well as its trees and parks and open space planned in the beginning by William Christmas.

Raleigh now has sign ordinances which regulate "billboards" and "neon-offenders." The ordinance regulating billboards has been tested and upheld by the Supreme Court of North Carolina as well as by the United States Court of Appeals.

Raleigh's Historic Properties and Districts Commissions, with stronger State-enabling legislation and local ordinances, have gone a long way in recognizing and designating our tangible historic resources. And Capital Area Preservation, Inc., is plowing new ground for preservation in the non-profit sector. But even with all these positive actions that have taken place during these past twenty-five years, it is still possible for a First Citizens Bank Building, a designated Raleigh Historic Site, to be imploded and replaced by yet another parking lot.

There are still mountains to climb and valleys to cross, but in the words of Elizabeth Waugh, author of this book and a prophet in her own time, there is still that continued need for "a sharpened sense of civic ecology, historical continuity, [and] with remembrance of the original, planned Capital concept, and with a new thrust at preserving the good of what belongs to the citizens — chances are that some of the fine Raleighness of the City's personality will survive with dignity for another [two hundred] years."

Roy Gussow Sculpture, NCSU Campus

112 South Salisbury Street

First Presbyterian Church
Dedicated 1900
Raleigh Historic Site 1969

Cost of the original Presbyterian church, $17,000, to appear on this 112 South Salisbury Street lot was met by a public auction of its pews, an endorsed custom in 1818. That "brick building of Colonial design" was removed about 1897 to be replaced by the church seen here. The cornerstone of this structure, the First Presbyterian Church, was laid in 1898 and the building, free of debt, was dedicated in September of 1900.

Major changes in the physical aspects of the building complex were made between 1951 and 1957 at which time offices were remodeled, the Sunday school annex redesigned into a small chapel, class and choir rooms added, and the sanctuary refurbished. Cost of these alterations was $235,000.

The interior of the sanctuary is particularly rich in that symbolisms—the Word, *Manus Dei*, Lamb of God, Fire of the Holy Spirit, Star of Epiphany, Calvary, Lily of Resurrection, Harp of Praise, and others, are seen in relief on the lectern and elsewhere.

The quality of the church's chancel windows, planned and manufactured by Willet Studios of Philadelphia, is also unusual. The

designs were created in sheet lead which was then "flown" with gold leaf, the figures being superimposed later upon colored glass.

Here, the use of rounded brick in the towered belfry, the heavy masonry, round arches, narrow openings, and stubby columns with their heavy capitals, all derive from the Romanesque whose heyday was enjoyed in western and southern Europe between the ninth and twelfth centuries. These characteristics, along with the simple cornices, patinated corbels, and projecting buttresses, represent one of Raleigh's subtler examples of masonry technique.

Organized in 1816 with the Reverend William McPheeters as its pastor and a congregation of 29 members, one of whom was Nancy Holmes, a free black, the First Presbyterian Church celebrated its 175th anniversary in 1991. Though the church complex has increased in size with several additions, its sanctuary still stands on the same site of that first brick church building in Raleigh, the cornerstone of which was laid on July 4, 1816. In the rear of the present sanctuary is a signed Tiffany window, dedicated to the memory of the Reverend McPheeters.

Dr. Andrew Watson Goodwin House

1903

Raleigh Historic Site 1980

The owner-builder of this 220 Hillsborough Street mansion, Andrew Watson Goodwin, was born in Wake County September 15, 1863. He went to school locally, was later graduated from medical college in 1887, and returned home to practice medicine. In 1902 he was elected to the Chair of Anatomy in Raleigh's Leonard Medical School, became chief physician for St. Agnes Hospital, and built this residence in 1903. He was married to Love C. Haughton.

A title search to this property indicates that in 1868 the land and

whatever improvements were on it before the Goodwin house was built, were bought by John W. Hutchins for a tax default of $28.74, in a sheriff's sale. On July 6,1881, transfer was made to Edward H. Lee and it was from him, on October 1, 1902, that Dr. Goodwin bought the property for $10,000. Again in 1939 the Goodwin heirs sold the land and residence to Fannie Smith and from her estate it was bought by King's Business College in 1953.

The place would seem to be the resolution, the last significant ploy of Greek revivalism in the City. Its bold ostentation obviously

tells part of Raleigh's story. From the plinths and architrave of the four Ionic columns to the bas-relief garlands on the entablature, up to the dentil forms, cornices, and pediment, there is for the eye a succession of exuberant surprises. Even the front windows and main entrance are variously treated. Inside, the plan follows the classic pattern of this vogue with a wide, central hall and double parlors, one on either side.

The Raleigh *Illustrated* for 1904 says of the architect who designed the elaborate residence: "Wm. P. Rose—Architect, Rooms 310-311-312 Tucker Building. Mr. Rose has been located in this city for five years, and is one of the best known men in his profession in the Southern country. . . . The works done by Mr. Rose. . .in Raleigh and surrounding country are the best testimonials of his skill, namely, among the fine residences he has built in this city is the

home of Dr. Goodwin."

Raleigh's Leonard Medical School, where Dr. Goodwin was Chair of Anatomy, was located on the Shaw University campus and was the first four-year medical school in North Carolina.

Many Raleigh residents remember 220 Hillsborough Street as the Reinlyn House (ca 1949-1953), purveyor of fine food, warm hospitality, and a perfect setting for bridal luncheons, family festivities or just a quiet evening out.

In 1979 King's Business College sold the property to the North Carolina Democratic Party for use as its state headquarters. The North Carolina Democratic Party has given to the Historic Preservation Foundation of North Carolina, Inc., an easement on the exterior of the house, the iron fence and gates, and on certain interior features.

North Carolina State Administration Building
1913

In 1911 the General Assembly established a State Building Commission and authorized it to acquire "a suitable site or sites for an Administration Building or buildings fronting on Capitol Square . . . ." Further it requested, "erect thereon or on land already owned by the State, a fireproof building. . .of such design or finish as in their judgment will best subserve the interest of the State." The structure pictured here, built between Salisbury and Fayetteville streets and facing West Morgan, followed that directive.

When completed, for $325,000, the faintly pseudo- French-Renaissance building was called the State Administration Building and housed not only the Library but the Supreme Court, that Court's library, North Carolina Historical Commission, and offices of the Attorney General. The four-story structure was built of Indiana limestone and the fenestration of each floor was treated differently—arched on the ground level, framed with carved fascines on the second, decorated moulding on the upper floors.

Origin of the Library's collection goes back to a miscellaneous aggregation of books which accumulated in State officials' offices. Some of these volumes and papers, however, were lost in the 1831 State House fire. After that, in 1837, the Secretary of State became

the State's official librarian and fifty dollars a year was appropriated for the purpose. The collection was then contained in the 1840 Capitol where it stayed until 1888 at which time it was moved to what is now the Labor Building. It remained there until the structure shown here was completed in 1913 at which time it was transferred to this building.

At the present time, 1967, the building is being renovated in order to house another branch of State government.

This building also housed the North Carolina State Art Gallery until the 1950s. The State Library moved to the Archives and History/State Library Building in 1968. The name of the Administration Building was changed to the Ruffin Building, in memory of Chief Justice Thomas Ruffin whose statue stands in the lobby; it now houses the North Carolina Court of Appeals.

Philip Thornton Marye of Atlanta, architect of this building, designed at least three other buildings in downtown Raleigh: The City Auditorium 1911, Commercial National Bank (First Citizens Bank) 1913, and the Wake County Courthouse 1915. Sadly, these three structures have now been destroyed.

Photograph from Peace Street   *723 Saint Mary's Street*

Needham B. Broughton High School
1929
Raleigh Historic Property 1990

The original units of Needham B. Broughton High School, built on ten acres of the Smallwood property at Saint Mary's and Peace streets, were completed on September 1, 1929, and at that time the gymnasium, auditorium, cafeteria, and class rooms provided for 800 to 1,000 students. The school was constructed of native granite similar to the Wake County stone used in the State Capitol, except for the finish texture, and was quarried within two miles of the building site.

Architect William Henley Deitrick used overtones of the Italian Lombard Gothic style plus some of the Romanesque motifs. These were then adapted within 1929 design vogues to educational needs of the period. Orange colored, mission clay tile served as roofing material and the four-storied tower provided the main entrance while heavy wrought iron, grilled gates gave access to the auditorium and gymnasium foyers. Floor construction was of web steel joists,

two-inch concrete, and surfaced by linoleum. Roof base was steel plate covered with half-barrel tile.

The three-bay structure, later greatly enlarged by additions and annexes, was 414 feet wide and 236 feet deep and the middle, three-story bay was centered by the buttressed clock tower.

The building was named for Raleigh businessman and school board member Needham B. Broughton. Broughton had been born in Auburn, near Raleigh, in 1848 and was the uncle of J. Melville Broughton, Governor between 1941 and 1945.

An out-of-state American Institute of Architects jury awarded this building the outstanding school prize in 1930. The commission was gained by competition held by the Raleigh City School Board.

Since its completion in 1929, the Broughton High School complex has had five major additions as its student body has continued to grow. The latest addition, 1991, houses the Science Department.

185

Tatton Hall
1935

This town-country mansion was built on Oberlin Road during the great depression of the nineteen thirties when labor, time, architectural care, and supervision were abundantly available. Acquiring the fourteen acres of land which had been earmarked for a housing development, the owners, Mr. and Mrs. Norman Edward Edgerton, engaged the services of New York Architect William Lawrence Bottomley, who was a Prix de Rome winner. The place was completed in one year.

The oversize, yellow brick was fired in Glasgow, Virginia; some of the hand painted wall canvas was commissioned and brought from China; and ornamental woods—mahogany, cherry, and walnut for the drawing room, were imported from various other places.

Interior of the neo-Georgian house follows no particular architectural dictum in that the formal dining room is Greek Corinthian, the cantilevered, spiral stairway of the main hall seems dramatically contemporary in its simplicity, and the drawing room is Chinese Chippendale—all of which variations make each of the large rooms freely fanciful.

There was no natural tree growth on the site when it was acquired and the owners have, over the years, cultivated the magnificent greenbelt of magnolias, hardwood, and shrubbery. A formal garden, swimming pool, and "Dutch" house are also scattered over the grounds.

The place derived its name from the English ancestral home of the owner.

2501 Glenwood Avenue

The Deitrick House
1936

When Glenwood Avenue extension was still predominantly residential, 1936, the neo-Georgian house, shown here, was designed and constructed by its owner- architect, William Henley Deitrick. Neither labor nor material was spared in this building's quality, the great 'thirties depression notwithstanding.

Each element of its interior detailing richly but quietly recalls eighteenth century Southern influences, yet never does it do so slavishly and the whole plan is freely adapted to twentieth century living.

Interior proportioning is divided into relatively small spaces, the dining room being the largest in the house. Library, kitchen, pantry, living room, and main hall comprise the first floor while garages are below grade to the rear. A simple, spiral stairway rises from the hall to second-floor bedrooms. And a rear, arcaded porch invites family privacy away from the street.

For the 2501 Glenwood Avenue residence, a formal flower garden was designed for the back yard. And inasmuch as Mrs. Deitrick had a predilection for exclusively white flowers, this garden, as seen in the moonlight, became a rare fantasy, a ballet blanc.

Today the residence retains its town-country dignity in spite of the usurpation of part of its greenbelt by a "wider" traffic throughway.

Thomas Wright Cooper House
1938

Architect Thomas Wright Cooper planned this house in Budleigh at 1718 Canterbury Road in 1938, as his residence. Though, obviously, the painted-brick structure has many stylistic adaptations inherent in its design, the place was called, when built, "Monterey House." Its second-floor veranda represents one of the first instances, in this area, of using the cantilever principle in this manner. Perhaps for this reason the post-depression residence was considered, at the time it was built, and notwithstanding the eighteenth-century shutters, to be extremely "contemporary."

Architect Cooper was born in Raleigh in 1897, son of the manager of Raleigh Marble Works. He was apprenticed to Raleigh Architect James A. Salter. In 1919 he passed the State Boards, practiced here, and served, for a time, as president of the North Carolina Chapter of the American Institute of Architects.

Amphitheatre, 1967

301 Pogue Street

Raleigh Little Theatre

Dedicated 1940
Raleigh Historic Site 1991

Here pictured is the Raleigh Little Theatre. Located on Pogue Street on the site of the old State Fair Grounds' race track, it has been labeled by some authorities as one of the City's earliest and most successful buildings to be designed within the "modern" architectural idiom.

The idea of a local, live theatre for Raleigh was the notion of Cantey Venable Sutton, the land was donated by the City, and the proposal was sponsored by the Work Projects Administration.

Interior space needs of the building apparently determined its clean, exterior perpendicularity. Originally the fly rose thirty-five feet above stage level and the proscenium was thirty-five feet wide by eighteen feet high. Other spaces included a lounge, workshops, make-up rooms, costume storage, foyer, and offices. The stage was forty by sixty feet and seating for the auditorium proper accommodated three hundred people. Recent alterations have changed both backstage facilities and seating capacity.

The theatre was designed by Architect William Henley Deitrick; working drawings were prepared by Architect Thad Hurd while Landscape Architect R.J. Pearse planned the contiguous three-thousand-seat amphitheatre for outdoor performances, and the landscaping.

A spectacular rose garden, with an original planting of 3,000 bushes, was added to the site in 1948.

In 1989 the Gaddy-Goodwin Teaching Theatre, designed by Brian Shawcroft, was constructed at the rear of the existing theatre and echoes the design of the original building, while more than doubling it in size. The new building is also painted brick.

1411 Jackson Place

Baker Wynne House and Garden
1948
Demolished 1978

At 1411 Jackson Place, the Baker Wynne House, both inside and out, is a tastefully borrowed bit of Colonial Williamsburg. It was built in 1948 as a bachelor's residence, the first floor being divided into kitchen and living room while the half story above is one large dormitory space.

The interior is paneled in Carolina long-leaf pine cut and cured in 1742, and the hardware throughout is from the same period. Exterior and enclosing garden walls are made of eighteenth-century hand-fired brick and are laid up in Flemish bond. Architect Thomas W. Cooper designed the house.

Since Mr. Wynne, the owner, is a plant enthusiast who is internationally recognized as an originator of new hybrid day lilies, the three levels of gardens which surround the place are in themselves a rarity. Here axial paths, both of brick and grass, define rectangular beds of perennials and herbs. Vines and shrubs, strategically planted, lend seasonal interest to the walled patio.

The house and garden are set beneath a 200-year-old white oak, one of the last and finest of the original grove of trees growing in the area.

Only a remnant of the original garden wall, with its carved brick cap, stays today, as the remainder of the site serves the YMCA as one of its parking lots.

Oberlin Road and Clark Avenue

Cameron Village
First Stores Opened 1949

In 1910, from the old Duncan Cameron estate, heirs sold off a 110-acre parcel of land, a tract on which Cameron Park was plotted. However, between 1910 and 1947 what remained of the historically important plantation continued intact except for small pieces which were sold to become Rex Hospital, the Raleigh Apartments, and Broughton High School. By 1947 Raleigh's population growth had all but surrounded the remaining 158 acres, located in the northwest quadrant of the City, about one and a half miles from the central business district.

Then in August of 1947 J. W. York, local contractor, and R. A. Bryan of a contracting firm in Goldsboro, obtained an option on the land. Their development plan called for early landscaping of the property, with potential shade trees, the burying of utility wires, and a built-in consumer population for the shopping center to be gained by siting apartments, residences, and service establishments adjacent to the stores.

The development was to be called Smallwood Village, a name which had been associated with the property through marriage into the Cameron family. But in October, 1947, at a meeting of the City Planning Commission, the proposed name was changed to Cameron Village, and certain other revisions were made in the original proposals. Still more modifications in planning were later arranged in deference to various objections on the parts of some Raleigh groups and citizens.

Chief designer of the buildings was Architect Leif Valand and the first stores were formally opened on November 17, 1949—Rose's, Colonial Stores, The Cradle Shop, the Village Restaurant. By June of 1950 the list of Cameron Village establishments had reached sixteen. It continues to grow in 1967.

This early picture of the development illustrates the first phase of what was to become the original major, planned challenge to Raleigh's central business district.

Cameron Village still continues to grow; its shops now number 77 and it remains one of Raleigh's favorite shopping centers.

The Paschal House
1950

For the design of their new house at 3334 Alamance Drive, Dr. and Mrs. George W. Paschal, Jr., chose James W. Fitzgibbon, an architect who had but recently come to Raleigh as a member of North Carolina State College's School of Design faculty. Fitzgibbon, being dedicated to the principles and philosophies inherent in contemporary design, planned this house within those concepts. And when built, 1950, the place was considered by some to be quite a radical departure from local traditional residential forms and building techniques.

One approaches the house via a generous crescent driveway and enters the north, main door by a courtyard and atrium. The bedrooms, study, and other related spaces are on the left while to the right are utility rooms, kitchen, and dining room. The twenty-one by thirty-one foot living room is opposite the atrium and opens, from its southern orientation, onto a rear terrace. Focal point of this room

is a massive, sunken fireplace, now familiarly called the "conversation pit."

Since the house sits on a knoll just off a heavily used highway, privacy was insured by a large greenbelt of old trees and new, relatively heavy landscaping. An open space was left to the rear for lawn games and athletics and for catching sun through the glass-sheathed, south facade.

The residence is constructed of cypress, glass, native Wake County stone, is solar heated and its owners feel that, through its seventeen years, it has "lived" up to its original design intent, assuring indoor-outdoor livability while at the same time retaining its informal dignity.

Over 40 years later, its owners still feel that it continues to fulfill its original design intent.

North Carolina State Fair Grounds, Hillsborough Street at Blue Ridge Road

Dorton Arena

1952
Raleigh Historic Site 1976, National Register Property 1973

Located on the State Fair Grounds just west of Raleigh, this, the Livestock Judging Pavilion, later named the Dorton Arena after long-time State Fair Manager J. S. Dorton, was completed in 1952. When finished, it was internationally acclaimed by architects and various other critics as "the most significant building of late times." It won "First Honor Award" from the American Institute of Architects and the "Gold Medal in Engineering" from the Architectural League of New York.

The basic design was the work of Architect Matthew Nowicki, a Polish emigre who had been engaged as consultant for the building by Architect William Henley Deitrick. The original and exceedingly simple plan was the combination of the two age-old engineering principles, tension and compression, in a manner never attempted before. Unfortunately, the brilliant young designer did not live to see completion of the preliminary plans nor the model. He died in an airplane accident in 1950. Architect Deitrick then completed the plans and supervised construction.

A more suitable name for the arena might probably have been "The Paraboleum" since it is parabolic in plan, section and elevation. The two great curving arches are supported on thin vertical columns and the roof is hung on wire cables stretching between the arches and the seating stands. The cables are attached to tension springs which in turn are fastened to the side of the arch, thus providing flexibility for the up and down movement of the roof, caused by varying atmospheric conditions. This principle was validly tested when, in 1954, Hurricane Hazel caused fourteen-inch waves in the roof surface without leakage and without damage to the building.

The parabolic plan is 300 feet in diameter in each direction and the arches rise to ninety feet. Seating tiers accommodate 5,500 people while movable chairs on the arena floor will seat an additional 4,000. Roof drainage is at the point of intersection of the arches and is spilled directly into open catch basins. Great steel hinges within the arch intersections afford expansion and contraction of the concrete arches, a factor which eliminates the need for usual expansion joints. The roof of "V" corrugated metal is covered with rigid insulation board and standard bonded roofing. The two arches at either end are tied together by prestressed cables, in an underground tunnel.

The pavilion used the tensile properties of steel in its most efficient form and is possibly the first construction of a roof suspended over a large area, completely on cables.

Consulting engineers were Severud, Elsted, and Kreuger of New York and the contractor was William Muirhead of Durham, North Carolina.

1028 Cowper Drive

Anna Riddick House
1952

At 1028 Cowper Drive, the Anna Riddick house was designed by Architect William Dewey Foster as a modified Georgian-style townhouse. Most of its materials were well-seasoned in advance. The handmade brick came from century-old demolished buildings—the Odd Fellows Orphanage at Goldsboro and Raleigh's Dorothea Dix Hospital. The pine floors were also bought from Dix Hill and the living room's marble mantel was taken from the old Pell Building on Fayetteville Street.

A circular stairway rises from the entrance hall; the small breakfast room space may be enlarged for summer meals by opening doors onto the adjoining high-walled terrace. This arrangement also prevails with the living room which may by made larger by opening it onto two separate patios. These variations help to resolve the house's intent which was to function as both a one-person dwelling and as a place for large-scale entertaining.

On the second floor is the owner's bedroom and another space which was planned to be used as an extra guest room.

Outside, added interest is given to the patio walls by a *brise-soleil* treatment—alternation of open spaces and wall texture—a building medium which insures breezes, privacy, and some sun at the same time. The windowless chimney wall, the small stoop, and the neo-Georgian shutters type the house's exterior character as being traditionally eighteenth century. Yet it is neither strictly nor formally so.

Though ownership has changed, the house remains essentially the same.

Elizabeth Thompson House
1952

The plan of this house, at 1001 Cowper Drive, was the collaborative efforts of its owners, Elizabeth Warren Thompson and Lillian Macon Thompson, and Architect Thomas Herman of Wilson. Many of its decorative elements, including the wainscoting, mantels, and trim, were acquired from first-floor rooms of the Josh Perry House in Warren County, now torn down. The owners kept these materials stored until this house was built, 1952.

As well, the outside iron work, seen here in the balustrade and balcony, was taken in 1942 from the old News and Observer Building at 415 Fayetteville Street, at the time it was demolished. The front door's fanlight came from a house in New Bern.

The floor plan of this residence was in no way a stock formula but was designed by the sisters especially to fit their tastes, needs, and possessions. The library, paneled in old pine, is on the right, living room to the left, and the dining room is entered underneath the curving stairway, at the main hall's end. Bedrooms are on the second floor. And a service wing which contains a laundry, servants' quarters, and garage is attached to the right rear of the house.

Rather a synthesis of Greek revival and Georgian feeling prevails in the house and unusual about its exterior is the detail of painted redwood quoins which lace up the facade and corners of the beaded siding.

At the death of the original owners, the house was sold. Since there were no restrictive covenants to protect its architectural and historic fea-tures, successive owners have been free to change them at will. However, the cantilever staircase remains intact.

1001 Cowper Drive

1520 Canterbury Road

Saint Michael's Episcopal Church
1956

Saint Michael's Episcopal Church, at 1520 Canterbury Road, is the result of close design cooperation between Architect Leif Valand, the church's Rector, and members of the congregation. It is therefore not surprising that almost every architectural element of the building represents ecclesiastical symbolism. The three front pillars, for instance, are used as an expression of the Trinity. And above the main entrance is a Narthex cross, symbolic of believers taking up the load of Jesus as they enter the building.

Inside, the A-frame nave is spanned by southern pine arches, twelve of them, representing the Apostles. Seven steps, symbolic of the Holy Spirit's gifts, lead from the nave up to the altar and all major materials used in the church are repeated in the altar's construction—metal, brick, concrete, and stone. Aggregation of these materials represents the offering up of the building to God.

The church complex has been enlarged since its founding and now includes a columbarium on its grounds.

196

2110 Blue Ridge Road

North Carolina Museum of Art
Opened 1956
New Museum Building Opened 1983

The collection in the North Carolina Museum of Art is the culmination of more than forty years of work on the part of many North Carolinians. It had its beginnings in the North Carolina State Art Society, organized in 1926, at which time the Society began to sponsor annual exhibitions and in general to encourage art activities throughout the State.

In 1927 a substantial bequest was left to the Society by Robert F. Phifer and in 1929 the organization came under State financial patronage and control. In that year the Society began a small exhibition gallery, moving it ten years later into a larger one, and finally into State property. Then in 1947 the General Assembly passed a bill appropriating $1,000,000 for acquisition of art for a museum to be located in Raleigh.

This original appropriation was amended as to be dependent upon available surplus funds at the end of the fiscal year and also upon securing a matching of $1,000,000. Both of these conditions were met. The latter stipulation was satisfied when the Samuel H. Kress Foundation agreed to match the $1,000,000. Its gift, however, came some time later in the form of unspecified works of art valued in excess of two and a half million dollars.

The unique part of these developments was that North Carolina was the first State in the Union to give so much money for a collection and to do so prior to the construction of a building to house it. This housing situation, however, was finally resolved in 1953

when the four-story Highway Building in the first block of East Morgan Street was selected as a temporary showplace for the acquisitions. It was renovated and redesigned to contain ninety-four cubicle galleries, by Architect Edward W. Waugh; and at that time the well-known Rembrandt scholar, Dr. W. R. Valentiner, became its first director. The Museum was opened in 1956.

The original Museum purchases included, among many other masters, the work of Ruisdael, Rembrandt, Hals, Rubens, Van Dyck, Reynolds, Gainsborough, Homer, Stuart, and Murillo. And over the years the Museum's collection has grown through contributions from individuals, families, corporations, and foundations to embrace an outstanding Renaissance collection including Giotto, Botticelli, Titian, Tintoretto, Raphael, and Lochner and more recently a representative group of Impressionists including Renoir, Monet, Pissarro, and Degas.

The value of the Museum's collection is assessed at roughly $10,000,000. A new building is planned for sometime in the future.

The collection has been developed to include Egyptian, Greek, Roman, African, Oceanic, New World, and Judaic works of art. Later acquisitions include works by Bierstadt, Albers, Hartley, O'Keeffe, Speight, Stella, Rauschenberg, and Noland.

Designed by Edward Durell Stone Associates of New York and Holloway and Reeves of Raleigh, the new Museum building, located on a 140-acre tract in west Raleigh, opened in 1983.

George Matsumoto House
1957

The owner-architect designed this two-level house as both a home and an architectural studio. The place was cited on the sharp declivity of a stream bank and from the street it appears to have only one story. It is, however, oriented toward the creek, insuring privacy; thus the lower or studio floor is not apparent from the facade.

Located at 821 Runnymede Road, the three-bedroom house is structurally supported by six twelve-inch wood beams which rest on a concrete block wall. Each of these in turn is held up in the center and on the stream side of the house by six wood columns. The column members are carried through the upper floor to support six

matching, twelve-inch roof beams. The floor and roof joists transverse the structural beams and cantilever at either end for a total of eight more feet of floor space. Outside, these end spaces are covered with vertical wood siding, for textural variation, while other exterior walls are covered in four-foot modules of prefabricated paneling.

The small house, winner of several architectural awards, was designed by Architect George Matsumoto, a former resident of Raleigh, in 1957.

912 Williamson Drive

Philip Rothstein House
1959

The well-planned modulation of this house at 912 Williamson Drive developed for the original owners, Mr. and Mrs. Philip Rothstein, the combination of affording informal interior living accommodation while conveying, on the exterior, a certain chiseled orderliness—a duality which the owners originally specified.

The designers, Architect G. Milton Small and Associates, organized the house into three main sections: sleeping suites at both ends of the structure and unpartitioned, general living areas in between. Within this central open space were the living and dining rooms, their spatial definitions being achieved by judicious furniture arrangement. This flexibility was designed to lend itself easily to varied and impromptu entertaining.

The neighborhood site was one of a series of large, wooded lots, and nearby houses were all built with generous setbacks. These factors assured built-in privacy which was doubly guaranteed since

the house was equipped with year-round air-conditioning. The sharply sloping topography presented some difficulty but this was resolved by placing the building on short columns, compensating for the landscape. Lifting the structure on a columned platform also contributed to a "floating" form which the architects wished to achieve.

Siding for the place was made of tongue-and-groove, vertical pine boards. The interior finish of all main areas included acoustical-tiled ceilings and white vinyl tile flooring. The cabinet work was walnut with a dull finish.

The perimeter of this house was wisely bordered by a bed of washed white gravel, both to add to the place's well-tailored look and to obviate the inevitable grasslessness of open crawl spaces. The residence was finished in 1959.

Isabelle Bowen Henderson's Garden

213 Oberlin Road

Isabelle Bowen Henderson's Garden
Completed 1959
Raleigh Historic Site 1990, National Register Property 1989

Photographed here is the "front planting" of one of the most beautiful and imaginative gardens in North Carolina, that of painter Isabelle Bowen Henderson. Located at 213 Oberlin Road, it is an all-season design and has been called "promiscuous" because of the multiple varieties of flowering plants which the owner shuttles from other garden beds in order to keep it always in color. Still, at tulip time it can turn into prim and planned formalism.

The premises have been elegantly planted on ground nurtured by the Bowen family since the turn of the century. There are now fruit and nut trees, a vegetable spot, herb beds, flowering shrubs. But this high-fenced portion of the grounds was designed about 1959 by Landscape Architect Lewis Clarke in close collaboration with the owner. Its general plan is accented by a broad, curving brick path which is wide enough for two wheelbarrows to pass or for three children to race on it without disturbing the tulips, irises, or whatever else is bordering it in season. For example, in the early fall one wheelbarrow must zig-zag on the walkway to miss the lambs ears,

santalinas, pinks, and blue petunias. Later, myriad colored chrysanthemums, representing the whole spectrum, contend, each with the other, for attention.

An herb house provides space for a collection of Jugtown pottery, harvesting baskets, lawn chair storage, and jars of the summer's preserves. It is adjacent to a shaded patio, complete with hammock.

The "front garden" and indeed the whole place is a rare sanctuary of intrigue and repose in all seasons. The color photograph, looking east, was taken from the studio room of the residence.

After Mrs. Henderson's death in 1969, her sister inherited the property, has cared for it, and has successfully defended it from two condemnation proceedings for the Oberlin/Ferndale Connecter. Students and classes from the architecture, landscape architecture, and horticulture schools at North Carolina State University continue to study the Henderson House and Garden, which is the earliest known example of the Williamsburg Revival design movement in Raleigh. May they continue to have this opportunity for many years to come.

North Carolina State University Campus

Harrelson Hall
1961

To actually achieve "in three dimensions" the circular form of North Carolina State University's Harrelson Hall was not easy for its designer, Architect Edward Walter Waugh, since the building was conceived as a sharp departure from traditional architecture. However, with the close cooperation of the then Dean of the Faculty, John W. Shirley, and others the architect convinced officials that "not only did the campus mall need a focal point but also that a circumferential form enclosed maximum space."

Several semesters were used up in the building's planning and when construction was completed, in 1961, it became the first round classroom structure ever built for a university and was widely publicized.

The prevailing idea in the design was to arrange three slightly concave discs, each above the other, with horizontal levels encircling their peripheries—a form rather like a shallow soup bowl. This plan resolved into two floors, those needed for current student numbers, and allowed for a third floor to be added for projected enrollment increase.

Located on the horizontal rims is a circular hall with faculty and departmental offices opening on to it while the sloping disc spaces accommodate large and small lecture rooms and are also entered from the round hallway. Radial, transverse halls from the building's core give access to this wider peripheral corridor.

The inner, flat center of the structure contains another circular corridor which connects to a spiral ramp. This easy-grade ramp "floats" around a core cylinder containing lounges and lavoratories. At three points around the outer circumference of the building, scissor stairway units drop to the pillared ground floor. Elevators, as well, are provided.

On the grade-level floor all mechanical installations, which are sited in the inner core, are glass exposed for those interested and the remainder of the ground-floor circle is open to students as a shaded, outdoor promenade. The structure is artificially lighted and year-round air-conditioned.

The local firm of Holloway and Reeves, Architects, did working drawings and handled supervision of the building's construction. The classroom and office structure was named for John William Harrelson, Chancellor of North Carolina State College between 1945 and 1953.

Northeast corner Hillsborough Street and Oberlin Road

Branch Banking and Trust Company

(West Raleigh)
1962

Attempt was made in the design of this building, the Branch Banking and Trust Company office in West Raleigh, to preserve the remaining residential character of its location, Hillsborough Street at Oberlin Road. But a consideration equally important to the architects was the preservation of existing, large trees. Both objectives were obviously realized as one may see in the evening photograph of the little bank, reproduced here.

Also in this drive-in bank, a successful synthesis of the work of landscape architect, designer, engineer, and sculpture-painter was undertaken and achieved. The structure was begun in February of 1962 and completed in September of the same year by the firm of F. Carter Williams, Architects. Its designer was Turner G. Williams and landscaping was the work of Richard C. Bell.

For further aesthetic interest a stained glass mural with a patterned grille was added to the building to form part of the west wall. It was designed by Joe Cox of Raleigh and a detail of it is shown here.

The Cox mural has been dismantled to make way for today's modern convenience of automatic 24-hour banking service.

3515 Glenwood Avenue

Northwestern Mutual Insurance Company
1962

Constructed in 1962 on the Glenwood Avenue extension for the Southeastern Department of the Northwestern Mutual Insurance Company, this office building's straightforward architectural statement expresses many of the building techniques and design preferences used in the early nineteen sixties.

An analysis of the structure's proposed function led to providing one large space on the main floor, subdivided only by office spaces, a bookkeeping room, and service area. On the lower level are shipping-receiving, plus employees' lounge and lunch room which open onto an enclosed garden.

The entire perimeter of the main floor is sheathed in glare-reducing, gray glass and porcelain enamel. A ten-foot overhang pro-vides shade and protection for this aluminum-framed glass and also serves to stabilize interior and exterior environmental conditions.

The building is set on a masonry foundation of utility brick fired in four-inch squares. The main floor and basement are structurally of reinforced concrete. Steel bar joists and gypsum deck were used for the roof.

The local architectural firm of G. Milton Small and Associates is responsible for the work.

In 1969 Northwestern Mutual Insurance Company changed its name to Uniguard Mutual Insurance Company, doing business as Uniguard Insurance Group. In August of 1976 it sold the building to the Raleigh Orthopaedic Clinic.

Jones Street between Wilmington and Salisbury streets

North Carolina State Legislative Building
1962
Dedicated 1964

Constructed in 1962 astride Halifax, between Jones and Lane streets, the State Legislative Building is distinguished not only architecturally but also functionally since it houses all legislative processes of the State Government—the only building in the nation devoted exclusively to legislative purposes.

The columned, marble-faced structure was sited on relatively cleared land and was immediately landscaped with multiple varieties of well-grown trees and shrubs. The basement was designed to operate as mechanical and maintenance spaces—for parking, offices, and post office facilities.

On the first floor are four promenade courtyards, legislators' offices, committee rooms, a dining room, and serving kitchen. From the first floor an imposing, axial stairway, which is heavily carpeted in vermillion, rises to the top floor. Here one may look down from spectators' galleries onto the House and Senate chambers or step out to the open-air roof gardens. Five pyramidal roof forms offer spatial volume over the building. They have coffered ceilings, are geometrically patterned, and their designs are outlined in gold.

The building also contains projection rooms and an auditorium equipped with both fixed and movable chairs which seat a total of 550, a library, a chapel, news media spaces, and display compartments.

Architect Edward Durell Stone of New York City designed the building and a local firm, Holloway and Reeves Architects, completed working drawings and supervised construction. Landscape Architect Richard C. Bell was responsible for the landscaping.

On November 20, 1964, Chief Justice Emery B. Denny, on behalf of all the people of North Carolina, dedicated the State Legislative Building "to the Legislative processes of our State Government, to the End that we shall forever have a government of laws and not of men."

Over the years more space requirements by the legislature have not only called for reworking some of the interior space in the basement and on the first floor of this building, but have necessitated the construction of the Legislative Office Building on the Halifax Street Mall for additional space for legislators.

Geodesic Dome
As Seen in 1964

A world "premiere" was ascribed to Raleigh in 1953 when a thirty-one-foot diameter hemisphere was lifted off a hill above Pullen Park, as the first fully erected building to be flown by helicopter.

Following that, early in 1954, Geodesics, Incorporated, and later called Synergetics, Incorporated, with its beginning inspiration coming from R. Buckminster Fuller, was established as a design prototype development concern. And in 1956, under contract with the United States Department of Commerce, a hundred-foot diameter trade fair pavilion dome was designed and test erected here, then dismantled and flown from Raleigh-Durham Airport to Kabul, Afghanistan. This dome was later used by United States trade fairs and expositions in South America, Africa, Europe, and the Orient.

Other thinking, experimentation, and construction, using untraditional architectural principles, followed and several hemispheres ranging up to 125 feet in diameter were designed and built in Raleigh for the United States Government. One of these was constructed for Elizabeth II, Regina, when she visited Ghana. And different ones went also to the Air Force Academy, the New York and Seattle World Fairs, to Cleveland, Saint Louis, New Orleans, and Niagara Falls.

Architect James W. Fitzgibbon, for many years, headed Raleigh's Synergetics, Incorporated, and the illustrative 120-foot dome, shown here, was designed by the firm in 1964, to be used as a pavilion throughout the world.

The Geodesic Dome continues to be used throughout the world as a temporary structure.

Aycock Street at Glenwood Avenue

Our Savior Lutheran Church
1964

Our Savior Lutheran Church, the A-frame building shown here, was built at Aycock Street and Glenwood Avenue, in 1964, and was a winner of the North Carolina American Institute of Architects' Honor Award in 1967.

The $80,000 church was proposed when it was found that the congregation's existing building could not be expanded for a growing membership because of an earlier classroom addition. This sanctuary was then constructed on the limited remainder of the church's property. The older structures were thereafter used for educational and kindergarten purposes.

In this building the exposed steel, scissor trusses of the nave's interior create the single *piece de resistance* of the whole church while the narrow, stained glass windows and the two tiers of drop lanterns offer perpendicular contrast to the criss-crossed steel beams. The floors are concrete, the roof is of asphalt shingles, and the building's sides are brick, cavity walls.

Both the church and its furnishings were designed by G. Milton Small and Associates and the crucifix, symbolic of Jesus' death, resurrection, and ascension, was created by Robert H. Kinmont.

By 1989 the church had added a new education building, enclosed areas leading to the sanctuary, and a new landscape plan for this enlarged complex on the corner of Aycock Street and Nash Drive, facing Glenwood Avenue.

207

Exchange Plaza as photographed in 1967

Exchange Plaza
Completed 1965

1890s Market House

Corner Fayetteville Street and Exchange Plaza

Here is Exchange Plaza. Its revitalization work was completed and accepted on behalf of the City from its donors, Wachovia Bank and Trust Company and Raleigh Savings and Loan Association, March 27, 1965.

The little cut-through, from Fayetteville Street to Wilmington Street, was not always so elegant nor so wholesome. For a long time it was not even a properly dedicated street but was rather a lane where the market place stood and where chickens and ducks ran at will in the mud. And in part of the nineteenth century, because of its liquor shops, tobacco parlors, gambling rooms, fist fights—it was known as "Grog Alley." In the 1890s the Market House, as shown here, was located on the corner of Fayetteville Street and Exchange Plaza.

Cost of the street's fine transition was $50,000 and though the work was a gift to Raleigh's people, its maintenance responsibilities were assumed by the City, about $1,000 a year.

Landscape Architect Richard C. Bell collaborated with the buildings' architects in this work.

Though the fountain has been removed, Exchange Plaza continues as a lovely breathing space that seems like a tributary of the Fayetteville Street Mall.

Moore Square

Moore and Nash Squares
Laid Out 1792 – Continuing 1992

Williams Christmas' "Plan for Raleigh" included four four-acre squares in the four quarters of the city for public use only. However, he noted that Burke Square would be a proper place for the "Governor's House" and so it is. Caswell Square was the site, as early as 1848, for the State's first School for the Blind and Deaf. Today the buildings on that square mainly house various State government offices. Only two squares remain as open space for public use; and through the last two hundred years, both have been the focus of lively goings-on, being located at the heart of the city.

Nash, named for Governor Abner Nash, who served between 1780 and 1781, has been at various times a rendezvous for law-breakers; the site of open-air, secondhand clothing exchanges and "tent" shows; and an untended tree, weed, and undergrowth spot where few but the most intrepid ventured at night. However, from the 1850s until after the Civil War, it was the site of the public school for the city's western district. In 1872, when the City of Raleigh, through an act of the General Assembly, acquired the management and maintenance of Nash and Moore squares, it ordered the school building, which was by then being used for housing, removed from Nash Square.

In 1879 Professor C.B. Fairchild signed a contract to lease Nash Square where he erected two greenhouses and agreed to proceed with the beautification and adornment of this area with shade trees, shrubs and flowers. Two years later, Henry Steinmetz had purchased these greenhouses and had laid walks and set out four rows of trees with a row on each side of the two main walks. In the center, he arranged both circular and square beds for ornamental plants, roses and shrubs. Then the city had him remove the greenhouses and since that time, no building has changed the park character of Nash Square.

At intervals, though, citizens urged the "clean up" of Nash Square. Then in 1934, ten feet were lopped off the square for the widening of McDowell Street to ease traffic congestion. The automobile was king even then in our society. Miss Isabel Busbee and Miss Elizabeth Thomas designed a new landscape plan to make Nash Square more inviting. The Public Works Administration thinned the trees and built impressive new entrances. And in 1976, the Wake County Historical Society, Inc., unveiled a plaque honoring the Revolutionary War governor for whom the park was named.

For more than thirty years, businesses located around this square have contributed funds to help with its beautification while the Raleigh Parks Department maintains it.

In 1812, Raleigh Baptists organized their first congregation and around 1814 built their church on South Person Street across from Moore Square. Soon this square became known as "Baptist Grove." In 1822, the little church was literally rolled across the street into the grove where it remained for over twenty years. Then in 1842 the square housed the Eastern Ward School which, after a time, was

209

moved to another location. During the War between the States, buildings were erected here where equipment was sold and mules traded. Wagon owners camped on it. Even the City Market, then located on Fayetteville Street, spilled over to this area by 1869. And it long served as a sales lot for Christmas trees.

Through the years, as with Nash Square, the City of Raleigh's need for widened streets and parking lots threatened, not only the size but the very existence of, Moore Square. While the square survived, it, too, has been made smaller to accommodate the growth of Raleigh and the increased use of automobiles by its citizens.

In 1913, the City Commissioners, responding to citizens' requests for a new and more sanitary market area, purchased land on Martin Street for construction of a new City Market. Designed by James Matthew Kennedy, a Wayne County native and graduate of what is now North Carolina State University, the Spanish Mission style building opened for business on September 30, 1914. The market flourished into the 'forties, but began to decline as Raleigh's population spread to the suburbs and supermarkets replaced the corner grocery. Market activity all but came to a standstill in 1955 with the construction of the Farmers Market on the north side of the city. The City Council formally closed it in 1957.

With the market closed, HANDS, Home and Neighborhood Development Services, worked with the Parks Department to upgrade Moore Square and improvements included the addition of a fountain. In 1976 the Wake County Historical Society, Inc., dedicated a plaque honoring Alfred E. Moore, Attorney General, 1782-90.

In the early 1980s the City of Raleigh received a matching grant from the National Park Service, through the Division of Archives and History, to study the Moore Square area. And in 1985 it was listed on the National Register of Historic Places. Armed with revitalization studies and opportunities for tax-credit investments, resulting from listing on the National Register, then Mayor Smedes York and the City Council spearheaded successful public/private partnerships for the redevelopment of the Moore Square area. North Carolina National Bank built Founder's Row, a well-designed condominium complex behind the old market. Artspace, a non-profit artists' studio and exhibition space, was established in a vacant building. The City Gallery of Contemporary Art was founded; and Moore Square Station, a transit point and parking lot, was built in the

center of an adjacent block. The collaboration of Federal, State and City governments with private enterprise and local citizens — all working side by side — began to bring many more people downtown and into the Moore Square area.

Gradually businesses began relocating in the neighborhood and today offices, restaurants and shops, one featuring market-fresh fruits and vegetables, are occupying space in and around the old market building and on adjacent streets. Also important to the rejuvenation of the area has been the opening of other non-profit and commercial gallery spaces. Numbering seven by 1990, the exhibition spaces are now known collectively as the Moore Square Art District. The galleries coordinate opening receptions with well-publicized gallery walks that draw 2,000 to 3,000 people downtown for each event. A broad spectrum of art is represented. Such a variety of galleries, concentrated in a small area, has made a great contribution to the revitalization of downtown Raleigh.

Now, two hundred years later, both Nash and Moore squares have attained their birthrights as splendid and beautiful downtown breathing spaces, but are no longer "four acres each."

Fayetteville Street, 1967

Fayetteville Street

1792-1992
Fayetteville Street Mall
Dedicated 1982

Seen in this photograph is the image of historical Fayetteville Street on its 175th anniversary. Modern banks built in 1965 and 1966 now dominate the Street's skyline.

Going backward in time, these buildings replaced earlier, smaller business establishments, some of which in turn had taken the land from existing residences. Before that, the dwellings themselves had displaced the deer runs within that original 1792 grove of hickory and oak.

During the time in between, parades heralding everything from circuses to returning armies left their prints on the old Street's history. Nineteenth-century fires took blocks of the buildings, only to be replaced by others; it was lighted by gas, then electricity. Its surface was variously mud, sand, cobblestones, and asphalt. Street car tracks bisecting it came and went; the great depression left it standing motionless.

Now, in 1967, it continues to change but—like all main streets from New York's Broadway to San Francisco's Market—it evolves with a certain stoicism, a basic unchangeability.

Twenty-five years later, on its 200th anniversary, Fayetteville Street is no longer a street but a pedestrian mall, with trees and fountains, outside eating and hot dog carts, and policemen in motorized Cushmans. Twenty-five years ago the skyline was dominated by buildings 14 and 15 stories tall; today there are buildings 29 stories tall.

Perhaps a Bicentennial year is a good time to value our historic scale while looking to the future. The challenge will be to complement the old with the new and to keep the pedestrian ambience of the small town with its small businesses and offices while reaching out to new development with its larger corporations. It will take planning and working together — the public, the private, and the non-profit sectors of the community. With that cooperation Fayetteville Street can evolve for yet another 200 years.

Fayetteville Street Mall, 1991

Winter on Capitol Square, 1967

Door on Old Stage Road

Illustration Credits

128. Ralph Mills
129. Ralph Mills
130. Ralph Mills
131. Lewis Downey
132. North Carolina Division of Archives and History
133. North Carolina Division of Archives and History
134. Ralph Mills
135. Courtesy of Charles G. Irving
136. Ralph Mills
137. Ralph Mills
138. Arthur Edwards
138b. Ralph Mills
139. Ralph Mills
140. North Carolina Division of Archives and History
141. Ralph Mills
142. Ralph Mills
143. Arthur Finn Bowen, Courtesy of Isabelle Bowen Henderson
144. Ralph Mills
145. North Carolina Division of Archives and History
146. North Carolina Division of Archives and History
147. Lewis Downey
148. Lewis Downey
149. Marshall De Lancey Haywood
150. Ralph Mills
151. North Carolina Division of Archives and History
152. Gordon Schenck, Courtesy of North Carolina Chapter of American Institute of Architects
153. North Carolina Division of Archives and History
154. Ralph Mills
155. Albert Barden
156. Ralph Mills
156b. Ralph Mills
157. Gus Martin
158. Leslie Wright Dow, Courtesy of The Executive Mansion Fine Arts Committee and The Executive Mansion Fund, Incorporated
159. Ralph Mills
160. North Carolina Division of Archives and History
161. Ralph Mills
162. Ralph Mills
163. Ralph Mills
164. Ralph Mills
165. Albert Barden

166. Collection of Marshall De Lancey Haywood, Jr., Photo copy by Lewis Downey
167. Ralph Mills
170. Ralph Mills
180. Ralph Mills
181. Ralph Mills
182. Ralph Mills
183. Ralph Mills
184. Ralph Mills
185. Albert Barden
186. Ralph Mills
187. Ralph Mills
188. Ralph Mills
189. Mitchell Studio, Courtesy of Raleigh Little Theatre
190. Ralph Mills
190b. Lewis Downey
191. Albert Barden
192. Colbert P. Howell
193. Courtesy of William Henley Deitrick
194. Ralph Mills
195. Ralph Mills
195b. Ralph Mills
196. Ralph Mills
197. Lewis Downey
198. Ralph Mills
199. Joseph W. Molitor, Courtesy of G. Milton Small
200. Lewis P. Watson
201. Lewis P. Watson
202. Ralph Mills
203. Lewis P. Watson
203b. Lewis P. Watson
204. Joseph W. Molitor, Courtesy of G. Milton Small
205. Ralph Mills
206. Courtesy of Synergetics, Incorporated
207. Lewis P. Watson
208. Ralph Mills
208b. North Carolina Division of Archives and History
209. Lewis Downey
210. Ralph Mills
210b. Ralph Mills
211. Ralph Mills
212. Lewis Downey
213. Ralph Mills
214. Ralph Mills

Bibliography

Abernathy, Elizabeth Hill, *Historical Facts of Raleigh and Wake County.* Raleigh, N. C.: Caswell-Nash Chapter of the N. C. Daughters of the American Revolution, March, 1938

Acquisitions from North Carolina Annuals, 1946-1966. Raleigh, N. C.: North Carolina Museum of Art, 1967

Addresses and Papers in Connection with Unveiling of a Monument to the Three Presidents North Carolina Gave the Nation. Raleigh, N. C.: The Graphic Press, Inc., 1949

Amis, Moses N., *Historical Raleigh From Its Foundation in 1792.* Raleigh, N. C.: Edwards and Broughton, Printers and Binders, 1902

Amis, Moses N., *Historical Raleigh.* Raleigh, N. C.: Commercial Printing Company, 1913

Ashe, Samuel A'Court, *Biographical History of North Carolina* (eight volumes). Greensboro, N. C.: Charles L. Van Noppen, 1905-1917

Barbee, Mrs. James M., *Raleigh Public Schools, 1876-1914-1942.* Raleigh, N. C.: Mitchell Printing Company, 1943

Battle, Kemp P., *Sketches of the Early History of the City of Raleigh, Centennial Address, July 4, 1876.* Raleigh, N. C.: Raleigh Job Printers, 1877

Battle, Kemp P., *Early History of Raleigh, The Capital City of N. C., A Centennial Address, October 18, 1892.* Raleigh, N. C.: Edwards and Broughton, Printers and Binders, 1893

Board of Aldermen, *Indebtedness of Raleigh.* City of Raleigh, N. C.: 1875

Boyd, William K., *History of North Carolina, Vol. II (The Federal Period).* Chicago and New York: Lewis Publishing Company, 1919

Briggs, James E., Hundredth Anniversary Booklet, T. H. Briggs and Sons, 1865. Raleigh, N. C.: An unpublished manuscript, 1965

Briggs, Willis G., "Hunters of Wake County." Raleigh, N. C.: An unpublished manuscript, 1940

Burchard, John and Albert Bush-Brown, *The Architecture of America (A Social and Cultural History).* Boston, Mass.: Little, Brown and Co., 1961

Byrnes, James B., "Sully's Copy of the 'Landsdowne' Washington," *North Carolina Museum of Art Bulletin,* Vol. 1, No. 3. Raleigh, N. C.: Autumn 1957

Cash, W. J., *Mind of the South.* New York City: Alfred A. Knoff, Inc., 1941

Carolina Charter, Tercentenary Exhibition. Raleigh, N. C.: North Carolina Museum of Art, 1963

Chamberlain, Hope Summerell, *This Was Home.* Chapel Hill, N. C.: University of North Carolina Press, 1938

Chamberlain, Hope Summerell, *History of Wake County.* Raleigh, N. C.: Edwards and Broughton, 1922

Chitty, Arthur Ben, "St. Augustine's College," *The Historical Magazine of the Protestant Episcopal Church.* Raleigh, N. C.: Episcopal Church, September, 1966

Christ Church, *Service Commemorating 100th Anniversary of Christ Church.* Raleigh, N. C.: Privately published, 1954

City of Raleigh, "Early Raleigh Neighborhoods," Linda L. Harris, Editor (pamphlets). Raleigh, N. C.: Published by the Raleigh Historic Properties Commission, Inc., 1983 (Boylan Heights, Cameron Park, Glenwood, and Downtown)

City of Raleigh, Historic Properties Commission Files. 1991

Colonial Dames of America in the State of North Carolina (Wake County Committee), Unpublished Papers, 1920

Connor, R. D. W., *Canova's Statue of Washington.* Raleigh, N. C.: N. C. Historical Commission, 1910

Coon, Charles L., *North Carolina Schools and Academies and The Beginnings of Public Education in N. C., A Documentary History, 1790-1840.* Raleigh, N. C.: Edwards and Broughton, 1908

Covington, Nina Holland, *Guide Book of Raleigh, N. C., Historical and Descriptive.* Raleigh, N. C.: Capital Printing Company, 1924

Creecy, Richard Benbury, *Grandfather's Tales.* Raleigh, N. C.: Edwards and Broughton, 1901

Dailey, Douglas C., "The Elections of 1872," *The North Carolina Historical Review.* Vol. XL, No. 3. Raleigh, N. C.: N. C. State Department of Archives and History, July, 1963

Daniels, Jonathan, *Tar Heels, A Portrait of North Carolina.* New York: Dodd, Mead and Co., 1941

Daniels, Josephus, *Tar Heel Editor.* Chapel Hill, N. C.: University of North Carolina Press, 1939

Dixon, Fred, "Raleigh, An Educational Center," *The Tar Heel Woman.* Vol. VIII. Raleigh, N. C.: N. C. Federation of Business and Professional Women's Clubs, Inc., February, 1938

Dow, Joy S., *American Renaissance (A Review of Domestic Architecture).* New York, New York: William T. Comstock, 1904

Edmisten, Linda H., Editor, "The 1914 City Market at Moore Square in Raleigh, N. C.," 1990

Edmundson, William, *A Journal of the Life, Travels and Sufferings of William Edmundson.* (second edition) London, England: Mary Hinde, No. 2 George-Yard, 1774

Elliott, Robert N., *The James Sprunt Studies in History and Political Science, Vol. 36, (History of the Raleigh Register).* Chapel Hill, N. C.: University of North Carolina Press, 1934

Fletcher, Sir Banister, *A History of Architecture.* New York: Charles Scribner and Sons, 1948

Goerch, Carl, "The Helpers," *The American Magazine.* Springfield, Ohio: Crowell-Collier, January, 1944

Goerch, Carl, *Carolina Chats.* Raleigh, N.C.:Edwards and Broughton, 1944

Gover, James Lee, "The Impact of Close-in Regional Shopping Centers on Urban Development" (Cameron Village). Chapel Hill, N. C.: A mimeographed thesis, 1962

Hamilton, J. G. D., *Reconstruction in North Carolina.* New York: Columbia University Press, 1914

Hamlin, Talbot, *Greek Revival Architecture in America.* New York: Oxford University Press, 1944

Harris, Linda L., Editor, *An Architectural and Historical Inventory of Raleigh, North Carolina.* Raleigh, N. C.: Published by the City of Raleigh and The Raleigh Historic Properties Commission, 1978

Harris, Linda L., Preservation Planner, City of Raleigh, *Early Raleigh Neighborhoods and Buildings.* Raleigh, N. C., 1983

Haywood, Marshall D., *Joel Lane, Pioneer and Patriot.* Raleigh, N. C.: The Wake County Committee of the Colonial Dames of America, 1900

Hill, Sallie F., "*Crabtree" The Old Home On Our Cover.* Birmingham, Alabama: Progressive Farmer-Ruralist Company, November, 1934

Hinton, Mary Hilliard, "Clay Hill-on-the-Neuse," *N. C. Booklet.* Vol. III, No. 6 Raleigh, N. C.: N. C. Society of the Daughters of the Revolution, 1903

Hinton, Mary Hilliard, "Colonel John Hinton," *N. C. Booklet.* Vol. XIV, No. 4 Raleigh, N. C.: N. C. Society of the Daughters of the Revolution, April, 1915

History of the Wake County Ladies Memorial Association (Confederate Memorials in Capitol Square). Raleigh, N. C.: Privately Published, 1938

Hobbs, S. Huntington, Jr., *North Carolina, An Economic and Social Profile.* Chapel Hill, N. C.: University of North Carolina Press, 1958

House, Robert, B., *Letters and Papers of Governor T. W. Bickett, 1917-1921.* Raleigh, N. C.: Edwards and Broughton, 1923

Housing Authority Annual Report, "Good Homes for Raleigh." Raleigh, N. C.: December, 1945

Iden, Susan, Scrapbooks and Clipping Books. Raleigh, N. C.: 1928

Illustrated, Raleigh, 1904. Raleigh, N. C.: Chamber of Commerce, 1904

James, Mrs. W. C., *Fannie E. S. Heck.* Nashville, Tenn.: Broadman Press, 1939

Johnson, Guion Griffis, *Ante-Bellum North Carolina.* Chapel Hill, N. C.: University of North Carolina Press, 1937

Johnson, Mary Lynch, *A History of Meredith College.* Raleigh, N. C.: Edwards and Broughton, 1956

Jones, H. G., *For History's Sake.* Chapel Hill, N. C.: University of North Carolina Press, 1966

Lassiter, Mary, Family Memoirs of Cornelius Jesse Lassiter. Raleigh, N. C.: Unpublished, 1875-1967

Raleigh City Government. Raleigh, N. C.: Prepared by The League of Women Voters of Raleigh, N. C., 1952

Handbook for Citizens of Raleigh, N. C. Raleigh, N. C.: Prepared by The League of Women Voters of Raleigh, N. C., 1963

Lefler, Hugh T., *North Carolina History Told by Contemporaries.*Chapel Hill, N. C.: University of North Carolina Press, 1934

Lefler, Hugh T. and Albert R. Newsome, *History of a Southern State*. Chapel Hill, N. C.: University of North Carolina Press, 1954

Lefler, Hugh T., *History of North Carolina* (4 Vols). New York: Lewis Historical Publishing Co., 1956

Lemmon, Sarah M., "Entertainment in Raleigh in 1890," *The North Carolina Historical Review*. Vol. XL, No. 3. Raleigh, N. C.: N. C. State Department of Archives and History, July, 1963

Lemmon, Sarah M., "Raleigh, An Example of the New South" *The North Carolina Historical Review*. Vol. 43, No. 3. Raleigh, N.C.: N.C. State Department of Archives and History, July, 1966

Lockmiller, David A., *History of N. C. State College of the University of N. C.* Raleigh, N. C.: Edwards and Broughton, 1939

Maps: William Christmas, 1792. Plan of the City of Raleigh (The Seat of Government of the State of North Carolina, 1792). A Plan of the City of Raleigh, 1834. Plan of the City of Raleigh from Johnson's Map of 1847. C. Drie's Bird's-Eye View of Raleigh, 1872. July 1, 1797, map of Raleigh. Current maps from the Raleigh City Planning Office.

Mial-Williamson Family Accounts. Raleigh, N. C.: Unpublished, 1775-1967

Minerva and Advertiser, 1799-1803, Raleigh, N. C.: N. C. State Library

Mordecai, Ellen, *Gleanings From Long Ago*. Savannah, Ga.: Braid and Hutton, Inc., (Limited edition), 1933

Mumford, Lewis, *Technics and Civilization*. New York: Harcourt, Brace and Co., 1934

Mumford, Lewis, *The Condition of Man*. London, England: Martin Secker and Warburg Ltd., 1944

Murray, Elizabeth Reid, *WAKE, Capital County of North Carolina*. Raleigh, N. C.: Capital County Publishing Company, 1983

News and Observer (Raleigh) 1890-1967

Noblin, Stuart, *Leonidas Lafayette Polk*. Chapel Hill, N. C.: University of North Carolina Press, 1949

Olds, Fred A., "Story of the Surrender of Raleigh," *Orphans' Friend and Masonic Journal*. Vol. 50, No. 28. Raleigh, N. C.: (No date) N. C. State Library

Ordinances of the City of Raleigh Regulating Horses and Cow Stables in the City of Raleigh. Adopted by the Board of Aldermen October 6, 1905. Raleigh, N. C.: Edwards and Broughton, 1905

Parramore, T. C., F. R. Johnson, and E. F. Stephenson, Jr., *Before the Rebel Flag Fell*. Murfreesboro, N. C.: Johnson Publishing Co., 1965

Peace College Bulletin, Series 4, Volume 95, Number 3. Raleigh, N. C.: Peace College, March, 1967

Plans, Minutes and Files from the Office of Raleigh City Planner, A. C. Hall. Raleigh, N. C.: Unpublished, June, 1967

Poe, Clarence, *True Tales of the South at War*. Chapel Hill, N. C.: University of North Carolina Press, 1961

Powell, William S., Editor, *Dictionary of North Carolina Biography*. Volumes A–C, D–G, H–K. Chapel Hill, N.C.: University of North Carolina Press, ©1971

Procter, Dr. Ivan Marriott, *The Life of Ivan Marriott Procter, M. D., F. A. C. S.* Raleigh, N. C.: Privately published by Edwards and Broughton, 1964

Raleigh Chamber of Commerce, "Industrial Survey of Raleigh, N. C." (Revised Edition). Raleigh, N. C.: Unpublished Report, 1960

Raleigh Historic Properties Commission, "Raleigh Historic Properties." Raleigh, N. C., 1988

Raleigh Illustrated, The Capital City of North Carolina. Special Souvenir Number. Raleigh, N. C.: The Merchants Association and the Chamber of Commerce, 1910

Raleigh Register, The, 1799-1863

Raleigh Times, The, 1950-1967

Reeves, Ralph Bernard, Jr., Editor, *The Dedication of THE STATE LEGISLATIVE BUILDING Raleigh, North Carolina*. Raleigh, N. C., 1966

Reid, Elizabeth, *From Raleigh's Past*. Raleigh, N. C.: Branch Banking and Trust Company, May 10, 1965

Report of Raleigh Housing Authority. Raleigh, N. C.: Unpublished, 1940

Report of Real Property Survey. Raleigh, N. C.: Work Projects Administration (Sponsored by N. C. Planning Board and Raleigh Housing Authority) 1939-1940

Report of Your City Government for the Fiscal Year 1947-1948. Raleigh, N. C.: Official publication of Raleigh, N. C. in the first year of council-manager government, July 1, 1947

Salley, Katherine Batts, *Life At Saint Mary's*. Chapel Hill, N. C.: University of North Carolina Press, 1942

Sanders, John L., "Housing State Government: A Review, 1792-1957." Chapel Hill, N. C.: Special Study Mimeographed for the Institute of Government, University of North Carolina and for The Commission on Reorganization of State Government, January, 1958

Seawell, Edward C., "The McPheeters House and Family" and the "Colburn-Seawell House." Raleigh, N. C.: Wake County Committee of the Colonial Dames of America in the State of North Carolina, 1965

Seawell, Edward C., Unpublished Family Papers. Raleigh, N. C.: November, 1966

Sharpe, Bill, *A New Geography of North Carolina* (Vol. IV). Raleigh, N. C.: Edwards and Broughton, 1965

Shenton, James P., *The Reconstruction, A Documentary History of the South After the War 1865-1877*. New York, New York: G. P. Putnam's Sons, 1963

Smith, Mrs. John Clayton, "Raleigh Historic Sites." Raleigh, N. C.: The Wake County Committee of the Colonial Dames of America in the State of North Carolina (unpublished), 1965

Spencer, Cornelia Phillips, *The Last Ninety Days of the War in North Carolina*. New York City: Watchman Publishing Company, 1866

Sprunt, James, D. D., "Windows on the Word" (History of the First Presbyterian Church). Raleigh, N. C.: mimeographed, March, 1958

Stanford, Charles W., Jr., *Masterpieces in the North Carolina Museum of Art*. Raleigh, N. C.: The N. C. Museum of Art, 1966

State of North Carolina, National Register Files. Survey and Planning Branch of the Division of Archives and History, Raleigh, N. C., 1991

Swain, David L., *Early Times in Raleigh*. Raleigh, N. C.: Walters, Hughes and Co., 1867

Sykes, Adelaide, Boylan Family Papers. Raleigh, N. C.: Unpublished, 1854-1954

"The Luminary," Newsletter of MESDA. Winston-Salem, N. C., Summer, 1988

The 175th Anniversary Committee, Compiler, *The History of First Presbyterian Church, Raleigh, North Carolina 1816-1991*. Raleigh, N. C., 1991

The Society for the Preservation of Historic Oakwood, Sponsor, "A Walking Tour of Historic Oakwood." Raleigh, N. C., 1982

The Woman's Club of Raleigh, Inc., Sponsor, "Capital City Trail." Raleigh, N. C., 1983

von Oesen, Elaine, "Public Library Extension in N. C. and the W. P. A.," *North Carolina Historical Review*. Vol. 29, No. 3. Raleigh, N. C.: N. C. State Department of Archives and History, July, 1952

Waterman, Thomas T. and Frances B. Johnston, *Early Architecture of North Carolina*. Chapel Hill, N. C.: University of North Carolina Press, 1941

Waugh, Edward W. and Elizabeth C., *The South Builds, New Architecture in the Old South*. Chapel Hill, N. C.: University of North Carolina Press, 1960

Waugh, Elizabeth C., "A Victorian Classic" and "Boylan's Imprint." Raleigh, N. C.: The *News and Observer* (Raleigh), March 15, 1953, and November 14, 1954

Watercolor Drawings of John White from the British Museum. Raleigh, N. C.: N. C. Museum of Art, 1965

Williams, Ben F., "The Birth and Growth of an American Museum," *L'Oeil*. Paris: November, 1967

Williams, Ben F., "A Visit to Passagno," *North Carolina Museum of Art Bulletin*. Vol. 1, Nos. 4 and 5. Raleigh, N. C.: Winter, 1957-Spring, 1958

Williams, Ben F., "Jacob Marling," *Retrospective Exhibition*. Raleigh, N. C.: North Carolina Museum of Art, March, 1964

Williams, Ben F., "Jacob Marling, Early Raleigh Painter," *North Carolina Museum of Art Bulletin*, Vol. 1, No. 3. Raleigh, N. C.: Autumn, 1957

W. P. A. State Series, *A Guide to the Old North State*. Chapel Hill, N. C.: University of North Carolina Press, 1939

W. P. A. (Writers' Program), *How North Carolina Grew*. Raleigh, N. C.: News and Observer, 1941

W. P. A. (Writers' Program), *Raleigh, Capital of North Carolina*. Raleigh, N. C.: Work Projects Administration, 1942

Index